DARKNESS YIELDING

DARKNESS YIELDING

Liturgies, Prayers and Reflections
for Christmas, Holy Week and Easter

Rowan Williams
W.H. Vanstone
Sylvia Sands
Martyn Percy
Jim Cotter

CANTERBURY
PRESS
Norwich

CAIRNS PUBLICATIONS

British Library Cataloguing in Publication data

A catalogue record for this book is available
from the British Library

978 1 85311 844 9

First published in 2001 by Cairns Publications,
Dwylan, Stryd Fawr, Harlech, Gwynedd LL46 2YA

This edition published jointly by Canterbury Press
and Cairns Publications

www.cottercairns.co.uk
www.canterburypress.co.uk

Printed in Great Britain by
William Clowes Ltd, Beccles, Suffolk

Contents

An Introduction
by Jim Cotter

Many of the inherited forms of Christian faith no longer connect with the lives of the majority of our fellow-citizens. In response, here and there, within and on the fringes of the Christian Church, there are movements of thought and reflection that reach back, reach in, reach among, reach out. In reaching back, some ask questions about the past: what really happened in Galilee and Judea two thousand years ago, and what are the implications of historical research for faith now? Some look within, listening to the creative Spirit to express in new images and language the heart of what they have inherited from their ancestors. Some seek to shape prayers, hymns, prose, and poetry that can be shared with others at gatherings for worship. Others seek to engage thoughtfully with the people of their own city or with those who may, almost casually, read a column in a newspaper. You will find all these 'angles' in this book, focusing on those moments of the year which mean most to Christian people and which for others may still carry rumours of God.

Rowan Williams, in the second of these introductions, speaks of his and Martyn Percy's attempts to reach out to readers of the *Guardian* and the *Independent*. Sylvia Sands, who has lived on the Shankill Road in Belfast for a number of years, brings the events of the last week of Jesus's life to bear upon the searing troubles of Northern Ireland. W. H. Vanstone, who died a couple of years ago, helped many of his generation to look more deeply into the suffering of God in solidarity with humankind, a suffering which came to full revelation on the Cross of Jesus. His measured voice still speaks, in this book through Good Friday addresses which he gave in 1987. Jim Cotter has worked for a number of years on ways of commemorating and celebrating Christmas Night, Maundy Thursday, Good Friday, and Easter Dawn, ways that combine material old and new, some meditative, some liturgical, four leisurely sequences of 'three hours', time out of time.

It is the hope of the authors of this book that readers will be able to use some of what they offer (none of them expects to appeal to everyone!) as ways of entering that 'time out of time', either alone or with others, when clock time fades into the back-ground, and significant, pondering, sometimes life-changing, sometimes celebratory time takes over. Whilst we hope you will not miss an important appointment, we do hope that you will say, Is that the time? I'd forgotten all about the clock.

JIM COTTER
Sheffield, July 2001

An Introduction
by Rowan Williams

On the whole, ours is a society without much in the way of rhythm or pattern in the passage of time. Seasonal change isn't felt by many beyond the countryside except as variation in the climate. Sunday is increasingly another and more convenient shopping day. Yet it's remarkable how the vestiges are still there of a more clearly marked rhythm: although Christmas and Easter have largely lost their religious associations (every year there seems to be a survey telling us that such and such a percentage of the population think that Christmas is Santa Claus' birthday and that Easter celebrates the invention of chocolate), there is still some sense of our undifferentiated passing of time being punctuated.

That sense is often honoured, rather awkwardly, by the media in the provision of items vaguely to do with religion. The major national broadsheets usually devote a feature or two to issues around the Church at the time of the major festivals and their weekly columns of religious comment attempt to say something appropriate to the season.

That is where the articles by Martyn Percy and myself come in. Writing in the press for a general audience forces you to think again and again of how to say Christian things in other than just tribal language. You hardly ever know, of course, if anyone outside the Christian framework ever reads them and thinks there may be something in this religious stuff after all. But it's worth it – even if it is mostly about encouraging Christian or semi-Christian readers to think around and behind the easy or obvious words.

It's also worth it if it continues to suggest to a wider public that time is indeed 'framed' by something, that the passing of days and years isn't ultimately through a featureless landscape. We believe that time is given us for growth into a maturity shaped by certain events in the world's history. Christmas and Easter are at least distant reminders of that idea of a human life set free for a deeper truthfulness, exposed to a deeper generosity because of what happens in Jesus of Nazareth. All the reflections, thoughts and prayers in this book are attempts to open doors into that truthfulness, that generosity, by looking for the words and the pictures that keep open the doors in our own imagination as writers, hoping that others may want to look in as well and find a vision that 'redeems the time' and restores some hope and some form to the history of ourselves and our social world.

ROWAN WILLIAMS
Newport, May 2001

Advent Absentee

Sylvia Sands

Here I go again,
carefully unpacking the figures of the crib,
tenderly wiping dust from Mary's eyes
and Joseph's beard,
all the while practising my contemplative skills.

Here I am,
duster in hand,
seeking to emulate
the shepherds' enthusiasm and openness,
(wipe, wipe)
the wise men's courage and generosity,
(dust, dust)
Mary's mysticism,
Joseph's humility,
the Christ Child's vulnerability.

Who am I kidding?

It is the absent figure that haunts me.
I stand shoulder to shoulder
in grim, callous, irritable solidarity
with that wretched innkeeper.
No room, no time, no way.

Nobody has ever dared carve him in wood
and include him in the Christmas crib,
Have they?

The Word became Flesh – But how?

Martyn Percy

Theologians do not usually think of the doctrine of the Virgin Birth as referring to an act that involves a sexual commitment on anyone's part. In two of the Gospels, all Mary has to do is give her consent: the Magnificat, her resounding 'Yes' to God. The finer details of how Jesus came to be flesh are lost to the more interesting stories about the nasty Herod, enthusiastic shepherds, wise men, and crowds of angels. In the tradition of Christian ikons Mary is portrayed as conceiving Jesus through her ear. She heard the word, and so Christ was formed.

Yet there are problems with trying to imagine what it is like to be incarnate through a non-sexual act. Christian doctrine affirms, through the Chalcedonian Definition of AD 451, that Jesus is both "truly God and truly man...two natures, without confusion, change or division, preserved and combined in one person." This definition, like so much early Christian doctrine, was an attempt to express the mature mind of the Church, to make sense of the mystery of revelation and salvation, to define but not to confine God. It was also a way of keeping heretics at bay, those who wanted a fully divine Jesus who only looked like a human (the Docetists), and those who wanted a basically human Jesus who became godly (the Adoptionists). The Church fought vigorously to keep the divinity and humanity of Jesus together, but these were discussions about doctrine and church order, not about biology or genetics.

If we ask questions about the conception of Jesus that are informed by science, we have to admit we have no surviving bio-logical evidence. There are no bones or tissue to analyze, and, depending on your point of view, the flesh-and-blood Jesus has either been resurrected into heaven or buried in a long forgotten grave. We have no hope of knowing the genetic identity of Jesus's father.

Genetically and biologically, the problem can be put like this. Women possess only X chromosomes, and so conception without a father (possible for some animals, and called haploid), could lead only to a female child with two XX chromosomes. There could be no virginal conception of a male Jesus unless there was some kind of divine creation of a Y chromosome in the ovum entering Mary's uterus. If there was such a divine intervention, what genes did Jesus possess? Did he have his mother's eyes and his father's laugh? Or did Joseph ever sit down with Jesus and say, "Now listen, son, about calling me 'Dad', you see it's not quite so simple…"?

Theologically, this presents something of a challenge to the idea that Jesus was fully human and fully divine. How can you be a human person without having a human father? Is not flesh of our flesh, bone of our bone, also DNA of our DNA? If Jesus does not have these human qualities, how is salvation to be thought of? Gregory of Nazianzus (in AD 360) said that "what was not assumed was not redeemed", arguing that if Jesus wasn't really human, we were not really saved.

Some modern theologians have attempted to side-step the issue, by resorting to an assortment of statements that keep the questions in the air, but the eyes firmly fixed on faith. John Robinson claimed that because God was invisible, "we see God with the face of Jesus…God stands behind Jesus, and it is Jesus who gives light, colour, and form to God." David Jenkins describes Jesus as "the man God chose to be": neatly ambiguous, as always. British theologians have made something of a speciality out of the doctrine of the Incarnation over the last hundred years or so, and even the most radical can usually assent to a statement like, "God was in Christ." The problem is this: how much of him? Are we talking about a person uniquely imbued with divinity, infused with God as it were, a bit like a spice with a meal? Or another person who was a pre-existent being in the perfect communion of the Trinity, but who once learned carpentry skills?

British theologians are divided. Some are really 'Christocentric monotheists' who like the ideology of the Trinity: it affirms plurality and unity, and they are attracted to the idea of God being in flesh to redeem us. In this scheme, God is one being, but Jesus is the best reflection of what he is like. The Incarnation and Trinity become socially significant ideas that help us live openly for others. But for all sorts of reasons they can't cope with the Virgin Birth. It seems, well, too interventionist – more magic than miracle.

Others see the Trinity as a starting point, and the Christ-event as a mysterious but saving episode in human history. So Jesus is human, but also divine. The Bible, as the early Church knew, was not sufficiently refined or comprehensive to come down on either side of the debate. Some passages speak of the Son being 'begotten'; others subscribe to the notion that there was no beginning for the 'Word that became flesh'.

There never was a time when the Word was not. Jesus has no 'career' as such, not even in Jesus – just eternal continuity. When the Church looks at Jesus it sees one person, but two natures. One is wonderful, human, yet at times weak. The other is almost crafty in its divinity. (Perhaps Jesus, rather like atoms, isn't at his best when he is being split?)

None of these musings helps the biological and genetic questions posed. But why should they? The early Church didn't know anything about genes. It sought through its creeds, councils, and controversies, to safeguard unity, promote peace, and snuff out heresy. It then tried to capture the mystery of the salvation wrought through the Incarnation, in forms of words that did justice to a God who was sufficiently committed to humanity to become one of us: to live as a human being, to love like one, to die as one, but not let that be the end of the story.

Oddly, heresy often makes sense to people: it is usually a reductive, comprehensible account of a mystery. Orthodoxy knows that it cannot afford too much rationalism when faced with mystery – which is why it is so difficult to believe. But the struggle to think is always worth it, for without that struggle there can be no real living of the mystery. To follow Christ is to be caught up in ambiguity, to lose your certainty, to watch the light, but often in the dark.

So there is no theological solution to the biological questions. We cannot know exactly what went on between God, Mary, and Joseph. All there can be is poetry, faith, hope, and love – and the inadequate theological formulas that try to give shape to the amazing reality within the Christmas story, that Jesus is, somehow, 'Emmanuel', God, with us.

3

Inhabiting the Ruins

Rowan Williams

Russell Hoban's novel *Riddley Walker* depicts a barbaric and cha-
otic England some generations after a nuclear holocaust; the
whole book is written in the distorted and jumbled dialect of this
imaginary future. This makes it hard reading, but often, as the
meaning slowly emerges, astonishingly moving. Not much sur-
vives of the old landscape, but, in this apocalyptic and devastated
scene, the ruins of Canterbury Cathedral still stand. At one of the
crucial moments in the book, the main character finds himself in
the ruins, overwhelmed by emotions he cannot express or make
sense of. "I opent my mouf and mummering…Jus only letting my
froat make a soun." Who made this? Why? They must have
known something we do not; yet they must have lost it somewhere. Things are got right for a fraction of a time: then they fall.
The vision is as fragile as the moment in the legend of St Eustace
when he sees the figure of the crucified between the antlers of a
stag – the legend shown on the walls of Canterbury, the 'Eusa
story' told in garbled form by these post-holocaust savages. Here
is a hunter chasing animals and suddenly there is 'a littel shining
man' on an animal's head.

You often see, in paintings of the Nativity by the masters of
the sixteenth and seventeenth centuries, a background of over-
grown ruins, a world fallen apart. Christ's birth takes place in the
context of a landscape of loss, destruction, haunted and half-
forgotten stones. And as Christmas approaches that image may
resonate a bit for some of us. There, still, is the Holy Family, the
figures of the story. Behind them lies the shadowy ruin of the
doctrinal vision that once 'housed' this story, the vision still
referred to in hymns and carols whose words get more and more
incomprehensible. "Veiled in flesh the Godhead see", "God of

6

God, Light of Light", "Of the Father's heart begotten", "A great
and mighty wonder, A full and holy cure". Even for Christians,
the foreground is what seems to make sense, the human story of
a birth. The old Christmas Gospel reading, the massive austerity
of John's prologue, has been replaced by the more accessible
human story in Luke.

It is fatally easy for sentiment to replace awe in religious language, especially in an age as sentimental as our own. We have to
tear our gaze from the accessible foreground from time to time
and walk about the ruins. "I put my han on a stoan tree trunk,"
says Riddley Walker, wandering in the petrified forest of Canterbury's ruins. And this means putting in question some of our
confidence that the ruins represent no more than the deposit of
lost and superseded beliefs, mythological curlicues obscuring the
robust shape of the human story. It means asking the sobering
question, What was it like to see these ruins as home? What might
it be to see them now as a potential home?

There is a passage from the early-twentieth-century Anglican
theologian J. N. Figgis on the virginal conception, a passage describing, very movingly, his own journey towards belief in this
mystery. He is quite clear that he speaks for no-one but himself,
and that he is not advancing a rational apologetic for the belief.
But he insists, with passion, that the appeal to the authority of religious experience does not run only in the direction of modernist
scepticism. For him, the rediscovery of this belief is simply part of
a discovery of a new universe: as he says, with tantalising brevity,
"Freedom...was seen to involve far more than had been
thought." And that discovery of freedom, God's freedom, is
directly connected with the experience of penitence and of the
sacramental life of the church. "The world grew younger every
day." (J. N. Figgis, 'Modernism versus Modernity', in *The Fellowship of the Mystery*, London, 1914.)

It is a passage that deeply annoys some, I realize. You might
take it to be saying that if you obediently go to confession and ask
no questions, everything will be all right and all your doubts will
vanish. But this would be to trivialize both what is said in this

particular passage and Figgis's own sceptical and tormented intelligence. A formidable historian of political theory, a reluctant ordinand and still more reluctant and bewildered recruit to the Community of the Resurrection at Mirfield in West Yorkshire in its early days, and perhaps the major Christian Socialist theoretician of his age, he is not easily written off as a sentimental reactionary. He is trying to do something rather difficult and even a bit costly – to describe the process by which the ruins become a place to live in. It is not just that he is persuaded that a particular miracle is functionally necessary or that the biblical text is after all reliable; it is more that, as time goes by, you begin to sense, if only faintly, how the architecture might work, what the 'world' of this ruinous structure might look like.

If this is going to be possible, we have to try and recognize that we do not necessarily understand in any very clear or immediate way how the structure got to be the way it is. One of the weaknesses of the impressive and sophisticated techniques of historical and textual scholarship is that they sorely tempt us to conclude that we can say pretty decisively why this is said in this way, why that detail is emphasized, rather as though we and the original constructors of the narrative and doctrinal structure stood alongside each other, offering variant accounts of what we can see, a sensible modern one and an unnecessarily complicated ancient one. The truth is more that we can glimpse what the original constructors saw only through what they said; how their vision shaped the way they said it is not something we can conclusively get hold of. Only by trying to *inhabit* what they actually said are we likely to see anything of what they saw. So the reductionist accounts of something like the virginal conception story will always run the risk of presupposing that we already know why the first Christian storytellers found this the best or the only way of witnessing to what had arrested and changed them. And that is an enormous and perilous assumption.

Let us go and see, say Luke's shepherds: a good Christmas maxim. First I must admit that I do not yet know and may never know what the Evangelists 'saw'. My only hope is to try and find a way into the place where they stand, simply by absorbing and turning over what they actually say. And that 'finding a way' is bound up with the whole painful and long process of exploring the new world defined by Christ, by the action of God in this life and death in Palestine. What did they know? I shall find out only by keeping my hands on the stone tree trunks, letting the ruinous and difficult words and images come to life at the end of my fingers, at the end of my gaze. If I do not instantly grasp how the story comes to be told in this way, that is no reason for constructing an explanation that simply assumes that I know what is being said in the first place. The landscape is strange and I am not yet a native. But if I am prepared to spend time letting the freedom of God sink in, absorbing the immense, uncouth, and at first alien scale of the narrative and of that freedom in action, there is no telling what I may learn, what I may see. Ruins built up; the raw and unexpected sight of the 'littel shining man'.

4

Midwifery as much as Theology

Martyn Percy

My two sons are both products of classes run by the National Childbirth Trust, which schools couples in how a woman can give birth 'naturally', with as little medical intervention as possible. The classes were good, but when it comes to the hour of reckoning, you still need support. We had some help, especially from the midwives, who were excellent.

Have you ever wondered who Mary did her breathing exercises with two thousand years ago? Whose hands did she squeeze as she pushed her pelvic muscles? Who fetched the water, the towels, the swaddling clothes? Christian tradition was divided on the issue from the earliest times. Early church theologians were quick to defend the virgin birth (as well as conception), but were less sure about Mary (or Jesus) really needing any help.

Yet the second-century *Protoevangelium of James* contains a remarkable story about the actual birth. Zeloni, a midwife recruited by Joseph, witnesses the virgin birth, after which it is claimed that Mary's hymen still remains intact. Zeloni tells another woman, Salome, who has a walk-on part rather like the proverbial doubting Thomas. Salome attempts her own medical examination of Mary to establish the facts, but as soon as her obstetric enquiry is finished, her hand withers as a punishment. It is healed only when it is placed on the new-born infant. Jesus is working miracles from day one.

In classic Christian thinking, iconography, and paintings, it is usual to see the infant Jesus as the saviour-in-waiting, and to portray the Madonna as a worshipping witness, not as a woman who has just given birth. No-one is there to give any *realistic* help to the mother and child. Apart from the complicated business of growing up, Jesus's path and destiny is already marked out. The more spiritually alert people – his mother, the wise men, Simeon, the shepherds – all seem to know what is happening. Salvation is coming through this one child: adore-while-you-wait. It will cost God everything, and you nothing. You cannot help God: but he has come to help you.

Yet the Gospels hold up for our attention a much more subtle picture. The bringing of salvation to the world turns out to be a task the cost of which is surprisingly shared out amongst many people, not left on the shoulders of one tiny infant. Mary must say Yes: her sacrifice begins at the Annunciation. Jesus escapes the wrath of Herod: hundreds of infants do not. They and their parents pay a heavy price for the coming of the Christ child. Others, such as John the Baptist, lose their lives before Jesus can sacrifice his. God's salvation incurs debts.

So the bearing of grace as 'God's Riches At Christ's Expense', as an old Sunday School mnemonic has it, is not quite accurate. Salvation, even when wholly initiated by God in Christ, is costly for other people too. In bringing heaven to earth, Jesus's sacrifice is not the only one. God cannot do it alone. Even the unknown helpers on the refugee trail to Egypt remind us that God is inviting our contribution from the very beginning.

Many of the characters in the Christmas stories are studies in Christian virtue, discipline, and generosity. The innkeeper offers hospitality when he is stretched for rooms. Yet he somehow manages to extend his boundaries to be inclusive: nobody is to be turned away. It is very like the ministry of Jesus, very like the mansions of God. There is room.

The wise men bring strange and extravagant gifts, speaking of a foolish generosity so rarely found in monarchical power, but especially bestowed in God's. The shepherds mirror the spontaneity and searching of Christ: you may find him, but he will come looking for you anyway. The people of Egypt, too often unsung, support and sustain the unlikely asylum seekers. The gospel may in the end cross all borders and boundaries, but Jesus the refugee is first received in a foreign land. Small wonder that as an adult, Christ will preach on the importance of welcoming the stranger.

These are the kinds of correction that can be brought to the notion of salvation as God solely bearing the cost and not in need of any help from human beings. The reason why the Sunday School *aide-memoire*, with its emphasis on 'expense', may be a distortion of the Christmas story is that it implies a penalty. Jesus pays the price which should have been ours. While that is one way of reading the tradition it is by no means the only way of interpreting the Gospel stories and the New Testament witness.

The Christmas salvation story itself is far richer in meaning. Grace is as expansive as it is expensive. God involves many people in the saving work of 'gathering up all things in Christ'. God invites human beings to share in the expenditure of salvation and in the distribution of its rewards. We are not only in debt, needing to be 'bought' out of bondage. We are also partners in this extraordinary business, in which everyone can receive a full and equal share in God's riches. This is generosity defined.

At the feast of the Passover, it is a Jewish custom to spill some of the wine as a reminder that the cup of joy is not filled to the brim, let alone overflowing. In order for the Israelites to go free, many Egyptians perished in the Red Sea, and they are God's children too. Similarly, the salvation that comes through Jesus can also require others to make sacrifices, even without their knowing the significance of what they are doing or of what is done to them. There are few who can passively receive the Christ-child. To accept him can often involve accepting a loss. God's riches may come at your expense too. Yet in saying that, one is whispering 'yes' to the invitation, making room for grace to grow, and making some space for the infant in your own stable.

God, even in coming to save us, reaches out to humanity to the extent of being partly dependent on us, so that we can begin to live the message even before we have fully heard and received it. This is God's true wisdom: coming to us not as someone who does not need our help, but as a helpless child who reaches out to us. The Christmas story is one of midwifery as much as it is one of theology.

5

A Lowly Cattle Shed?

Martyn Percy

Most of the portrayals of the birth of Jesus give a false impression. The stable looks clean and warm, the animals well-groomed, and the peasants recently showered. There is no sign or smell of the realities of a barn birth. The truth is probably more shocking: Jesus was surrounded by animals and filth, with nought for company but a few rough shepherds. He was, it appears, born poor – a working class lad from Bethlehem who made good.

Closer attention to the Gospels, however, reveals another side to Jesus which is much more comfortable – even middle class. The story is that Jesus was born in a stable only because the hotels were fully booked. Mary and Joseph could actually afford B & B: so they were clearly not *that* poor. They had their own transport – even if it was only 1 bhp. And when the wise men came to visit they brought quite expensive gifts: gold, frankincense, and myrrh have never been cheap. What do you suppose Jesus's parents did with these gifts? What would you have done? We can't believe our luck, let's hide them away for a rainy day. Or do we take them straight to the pawnbrokers? Or perhaps we put them on the mantelpiece next to the other ornaments.

It's arguable that portraits of Jesus have hidden his true class origins. Perhaps it is important that we see Jesus as being born into a relatively comfortable world. The stories show us a Mary and Joseph being resourceful enough to flee from Herod's wrath and live abroad for a few years in Egypt. The poor usually do not have such resources. Was Joseph the kind of carpenter who was highly skilled rather than turning out the basics? If the story in Luke is historical, the family could afford a pilgrimage to Jerusalem. As an adult Jesus was regarded as a rabbi: to be educated in those days you needed considerable means. Perhaps the stories of his death draw a veil over the horror, but they do portray him as wearing a seamless robe (and that wouldn't have been cheap) and as being buried 'decently' by a foreign merchant.

It is interesting that Eusebius, in his *Ecclesiastical History*, quotes a first-century source which claims that the descendants of Jesus's family were rounded up during a persecution with a view to their land being confiscated. Perhaps they had cashed in on the connection with their by now famous ancestor, but Eusebius tells us that "they had enough to be self-sufficient."

Well, we cannot know for sure what the circumstances of Jesus's early life were like. But if they were reasonably comfortable he certainly turned his back on them and embraced poverty. And that is as disturbing an implication for Christians as if he had been brought up poor. He proclaimed that the destitute were blessed. The poor were in God's Kingdom by right: the rich would have a struggle to get there. Jesus made friends from among the poor – sinners, prostitutes, the mentally ill, widows – and he invariably challenged the wealthy over their pride and complacency. The Christian paradigm, in Jesus, is "sell all you have," "take no gold and silver for the journey," and always bless the beggar, the homeless, and the hungry. It is radical stuff, and it's anti-bourgeois. No wonder he got on people's nerves.

The early Christian socialists – men like F. D. Maurice, Stewart Headlam, and John Ludlow – understood that God discriminated for the poor. They shared something of the radical nature of Jesus's chosen social incarnation. They worked with Chartists, radicals, and others to bring justice for the working class. They argued for universal suffrage, set up colleges and co-operatives, and laboured for the labourer. It was a costly agenda: Maurice lost his chair in Theology at King's College, London. But he never lost his imperative: the poor were God's cause, and a truly socialist society would never abandon them.

At Christmas we remember the wise men who came bearing gifts fit for a king. What they found was an ordinary family in temporary accommodation, struggling with a new baby. It must have been quite a shock. They had tried Herod's palace first but discovered it was the wrong address. Yet they gave their gifts, expensive as they were, and left them at the poor and lowly stable.

In their own way they were quite radical, and they throw a question to us. What gifts will we bring to the homeless, the displaced, the destitute, and the marginalized? And even if the question is not meant to be a tax bombshell, our response to the coming of Jesus must indeed "cost not less than everything."

6

God's Plain Style

Rowan Williams

Rhetoric is a word that has come down in the world. Once upon a time it was a necessary part of a serious person's study. How do you talk so as to persuade people? What is appropriate to this or that audience? Now we usually couple the word with an adjective like 'empty'. Rhetoric has become a designation for the ways in which the plain truth gets dressed up unnecessarily or even deceptively.

Well, in this as in other ways our ancestors were not as stupid as we often think. They knew quite well that there were ways of dressing up things to conceal poverty or confusion of thought; but they also knew that the truth was never plain – always something bound up with complex people engaging with one another in various and unpredictable ways. You could not, in other words, expect any language to be free from human relations, human desires, and the anxieties that go with them: better at least to have some skill in spotting how these work themselves out. And, not for the first time, postmodern theory has picked up the questions of premodern thought and dusted them off: scholars are more interested in rhetoric these days than for a long time.

Both in the early Church and in the Reformation period, Christians worried over how to speak honestly about God. They knew as well as anyone that you could talk about God in corrupt ways, ways that served the speaker's ego, ways that enshrined subtle patterns of oppressive power. Even in contexts where theoretical elaboration and artistic exuberance were in full flood, they wanted to write in some caveats that had to do with a proper rhetoric for this subject – not only through the tradition of negative theology (stressing the utter mysteriousness of God), but by insisting on the priority of 'plain style' in talking to God, what the Latin writers called *sermo humilis*, unadorned speech.

You find such an emphasis in St Augustine, St Francis, George Herbert, and, in our own age, in the wonderfully spare style of Dorothy Day and Pierre Maurin in the *Catholic Worker* journal. And it derives not from the conviction that the truth of the gospel is clear and obvious, and so needs expression in nice simple terms, but from a richer and, paradoxically, more complex recognition. Plain style draws attention to its lack of style; it is a way of saying, "I'm trying to avoid manipulating or showing my workings; I am trying to let something through that does not need the games of human power struggles to establish itself. That something is not necessarily simple, but it is both overwhelming and desirable to all who really begin to grasp it."

And, they would go on, we have to give priority to *sermo humilis* because, ultimately, that is how God speaks. God's 'rhetoric' is an anti-rhetoric, because God does not need anything to supplement, boost, or spin the truth of who and what he is. So God can afford, we might say, to communicate with us in embarrassingly unadorned terms, to remind us that he is not competing with us in a shouting match or an intellectual debate. God speaks in a human life, including that stage of human life that comes before ordinary speech (the cries of the baby) and in human death (the naked figure on the cross). And – so early Christian writers loved to remind their public – God speaks through a book that is full of grotesque oddities at first reading and is not written in acceptable literary language. It is all part of God saying to the world, "I do not need to play your games, to succeed in your terms; I am who I am."

Very unnerving; it can make us still more suspicious: what is the hidden agenda in this spurious simplicity? Or it can make Christians covertly protest: God may not need to play power games but we are dead if we do not. Of course there is a rather fishy way of appealing to simplicity, to avoid awkward and subversive questions; but the real *sermo humilis* is supposed to be wholly indifferent to any agenda of stopping anyone else talking: its only concern is to let something show through, never mind the consequence. But the nagging worry that God may not have got it quite right still makes Christians look longingly at forms of rhetoric that will give a bit more security than the manger or the cross seem to offer. Christmas begins to look less cosy if you take it seriously as the language of God.

There can easily be the sense that the weakening or cheapening of the traditional register and timbre of public Christian talk in English (new Bibles, new Prayer Books) means a retreat from some kind of cultural high ground, an admission of failure. Or there can be a burning impatience with a theology or spirituality that refuses to rethink itself in compellingly modern terms. Would it not be wonderful to *belong*, either as part of the precious cultural heritage of society, or as a perspective on things that would not offend the vaguely scientifically literate and socially emancipated public of the North Atlantic world?

To react to this with a bit of scepticism does not mean that the language of modern churchiness is anything but painfully banal (and pretty remote from a plain style of the sort George Herbert meant), or that ostrich-like fundamentalism is desirable. It is only to say that both cultural nostalgia and gung-ho modernism miss the point. To the extent that they are desperate bids to belong, to secure a place and reinforce certain sorts of power, they are attempts to avoid the challenge of God's plain style. In a world of competition, frenzied chatter, control obsession, there is a terrible aptness, a rhetorical rightness, in a God who speaks in a child's cry. And it is so cruelly hard – for believer and unbeliever alike – to face the possibility that silence, stumbling, apparent crudity tell you more about God than the languages of would-be adult sophistication. As if the best theology were the noise of someone falling over in the dark.

7

The Speechless Word

Martyn Percy

It is Christmas, that time when churches do their best to turn consumers into converts and say something meaningful about a season that seems to have lost its way. For several years the Christian Advertising Network has been doing its bit, running enjoyable and pithy campaigns designed to prod and to promote the 'reason for the season'.

Some of their more memorable posters have included, "Give Jesus your Christmas Presence – Deliver it Yourself" and "Make Room for God this Christmas", a skit on Joseph's failure to book ahead to get a room reservation. With the exception of the 'bad hair day' campaign – "You're a virgin, you've just given birth, and now three kings have shown up," the posters have all been rather safe, designed more to make a wet and wintry churchgoer chuckle than appeal to those beyond the frontiers of faith.

Last year's poster read, "Christmas – copyright: it's not a genuine Christmas without Church." Sympathetic as I am to the organization and its message, I beg to differ. Nobody 'owns' Christmas. The patent on a 'genuine' Christmas is not the property of the Church, and never has been. Christmas belongs to the people: the Church perhaps guards (not owns) most interpretations of its meaning, but not all of them.

Launcelot Andrewes, in his Christmas Day sermon of 1620, described the incarnation of Christ as 'the Word that cannot speak'. In using this phrase he meant to draw his listeners to the powerlessness of Christ as well as to the profundity of the revelation. There is irony here for religious advertising. The power of the image in contemporary life is undoubted; but religion, and particularly Christianity, is primarily a religion of words rather than of images. It is aural and oral rather than visual, cognitive rather than expressive. Apart from the cross or a crucifix, Christianity has no logo for its *Logos*. In today's world that implies that it has little with which to communicate effectively in the public domain.

Arguably, the most effective forms of Christian advertising are visual. Cathedrals are sermons in stone, paintings are homilies on canvas. And although there is some truth in the maxim that 'the camera is a blunt instrument compared to a pen and the imagination,' in contemporary culture it is the *image* that takes us to the text. The text seems not to stand on its own. The Bible itself functions as a rule book for fewer and fewer people. Its words are only a guide, in which the power of the story has superseded the didactic as a potential moral reference point. Thus the parable of the Good Samaritan is more important than the Ten Commandments, even the precise content of which has faded from most people's memories.

Ironically, it is 'secular' advertising that effectively adopts the religious imagery that could be said still to belong to the churches. Benetton, the clothes manufacturer, has run controversial advertisements that use no text but deliberately include religious themes to convey the 'United Colours of Benetton' global message. Recent work has included a grieving family gathering around an emaciated and dying man. A monk and a nun, both dressed in black and white habit or robes exchange a chaste kiss. A military cemetery of white crosses is pictured with a green grass background. A newly born child is still unwashed and attached to the umbilical cord which is held in adult hands. The use of skin colours carries an explicit message of racial unity and common human experience.

Such images are striking for their simplicity. They cover themes such as peace, reconciliation, life and death, as well as what all human beings have in common. The pictures speak, and the only words they relate to are 'united' and 'colours'. The images themselves convey a moral message, arresting the viewer and inviting reflection.

The question beckons: if a clothes manufacturer and its

advertising agency can achieve this, why can't the churches? One answer lies in the refusal of pictures that has bedevilled western Christian traditions for so long. As with 'story', an 'image' has no controllable meaning. People participate in them at their own level. They have multiple meanings inbuilt. Truth is plural. In their desire to define doctrine, to reform and rule, the Protestant and even the Catholic Churches have frequently sought the sanctuary of words at the expense of the image. Yet Christ is not a text.

Christmas celebrates 'the Word made flesh', a striking image indeed. The speechless Word who is God comes as a child.

So here is my suggestion for an advertisement for Christmas: a simple sepia photograph of a mother and child sitting in a hovel. The child sucks greedily at the breast, and in the background there is the shape of a figure trying to make a fire to keep them all warm. This image – of interdependence, warmth, vulnerability, poverty, and need – does not require any text. It tells the Christmas story in a simple still frame. I admit that it might not drive people to church. But it might at least make you stop and think, as you walk by with the shopping, hurrying home to your own Christmas.

8

In the Beginning, the Word

Martyn Percy

In the beginning was the Word, and the Word was with
God, and the Word was God. He was with God in the beginning. Through him all things were made; without him
nothing was made that has been made. In him was life,
and that life was the light of all creation. The light shines
in the darkness, but the darkness does not understand it.

…when he awoke from the dark he did not know where he was.
All was strange. He could barely see, barely sense, barely touch.
But he was conscious. Even if it was a dream, he was still there,
alive. He had being. He became aware of figures moving…of
noises, smells, and presence, all different from what he had
known. An oil lamp sat near his head. It was not the only light,
but it was the only one he noticed, and he instinctively turned his
head towards it. Even if he could not make it out or focus, it was
a kind of gentle warmth to him. He had little sense of what he
was wearing or what he was lying on. All he knew was that he
could not move: he was paralyzed – not because he was in fact
immobile but because he was bound in bandages from head to
foot. But he did not feel afraid. He felt safe, as he lay there in the
hinterland between dreams and the cold air that surrounded him.
Home had been warm and cosy, and although small he had had
the freedom to move. Now he was no longer there, but here; he
knew that, he thought. This place was so odd and unfamiliar.
For a start it smelled – lots of smells, mixed together and never
experienced before. And the noises! Moans, groans, rustling,
chattering, crunching, sucking, slurping, some very close and
threatening, others distant and calm. He tried to raise his hands
in defence or defiance, but being bound he could not. He began

to be afraid as he craved for the safe space that had once been all his, so dark yet so secure.

He could not speak. He tried to kick and punch, but it was impossible. So he began to open his mouth, and a scream came out. He did not know how. Was it loneliness? Anger? Fear? Hunger? Ah, yes, that was it: hunger. No sooner had he let out a cry than he felt his empty stomach for the first time that day. It ached for food. Hunger was a new pain for him, and how it hurt! Food came. It was a drink, warm and sweet. He drank greedily, barely pausing for breath as he gulped. Someone or something was feeding him. Even in this half light, there was now a familiar presence. Contentment spread through his body like the thawing of the frost on a sunny spring day. He fell into a state of peace, and into the land of sleep.

Then he dreamed. It would be his last dream for a long time. In his dream he danced. There were two others, a man and a woman, and they held hands lightly as they whirled around together on a huge lush grassy lawn. They were overlooked by a beautiful country house, a mansion indeed, with so many rooms, their windows smiling in the light. So much dancing, so many happy sounds came from that house as they danced together, whirling around and around, laughing into each other's eyes and enjoying the fulness of their love. They sang as they played together:

> We three, we three
> put the apple back
> onto the tree.
> You shall see through this dance
> All shall be free.

In that land, in that dream, everything was so big, so lovely, so overflowing. Nothing ever ended; the house seemed to go on for ever, the music never stopped, and the laughter seemed to expand and fill all space, and then go even beyond that. It was an endless place.

But the dream began to fade. The sights dimmed. The music faded to a distant echo and was lost. Loss indeed. Tiredness returned, the numbing feeling of displacement, the thought that all sensation is delusion. He was alone. He would never dream that dream again. It was lost for a lifetime.

When he awoke, it was with a start. He was still bound head to foot, there were still those unfamiliar smells and sounds.

Everything was so open, so exposed, so cold – and now so uncomfortable. He began to cry. He was lying in dirt and was wet. It was his wetness and his own filth. Once warm and pleasant to feel, it was now cold to the skin. Again he listened – he could see so little. Figures were shadows, the oil lamp a fuzzy glow. He began to cry again, this time for comfort. Deep coughing sobs welled up within him. He was so empty, so empty, like this place. In no time someone or something came. He was unbound, then washed, then held, then fed. Another drink, warm and sweet. Peace returned, and he fell back once again into semi-consciousness.

Where he now was could not have been more different from where he had come from. The place of freedom, the place of peace, the dark sea that had borne him and sustained him for what seemed like eternity was all to him. In it he had bathed and slept and known. Then, one day, there had been a cry, shrill and pained. The earth shook, the walls buckled, and the ground began to open up. Then the sea had gone, drained away and lost. A new journey had begun, a journey of panic, yet of hope. He had fallen: fallen through the ground and into an underground channel. He could see slippery crags, teeming with life and tears. Then he had been washed up on a beach. He was found by the Princess (not yet a queen) almost immediately. You see, she knew he was coming, from the dark sea. She had been waiting for months on the shore. When he had come, he was naked. But he held in his hand one thing, a hazelnut. Some said it was a lucky charm, others a message from a distant home as yet unknown. She did not know what it meant, and he just clutched it tightly, and that was that. Later, when he was older, he thought his father had given it to him, but he was not sure. When you are young you do not know what is true and false, for everything you imagine is real.

In the place where he now lay, spiders in rafters discerned a water-walker. Swallows in nests watched for a hatchling of their own kind. Sheep bleated that this lamb must be human, cows that this calf was the last sacrifice. The star that hung in the night pierced the darkness, and spoke of the day to come.

> He was in the world, and though the world was made through him, the world failed to recognize him. He came to that which was his own, but his own did not receive him. Yet to all who did receive him,

he made them children like himself, children of God.

> The Word became flesh and dwelt among us. We have see his glory, full of grace and truth,

and dreams, the glory of the child who came from above and was born below.

[The quotations are from the first chapter of the Gospel according to John. The image of the hazelnut comes from Julian of Norwich. And my imagination was stirred by Les Murray's poem 'Animal Nativity', from his collection, *Translations from the Natural World*, published by Carcanet.]

9

In Deepest Night

A Celebration of the Birth of Jesus Christ

From Christmas Eve into the early hours of Christmas Morning
10 pm – 1 am

Compiled by Jim Cotter

Part One

The first forty-five minutes is a short vigil which takes Advent towards Christ-mas. It could take place in a crypt or other quiet place. It maintains the theme of expectancy. The first two poems are but suggestions. A time of silence can be kept between the items. The Cries of Advent can also be reflected upon in a leisurely fashion. The point of a vigil is the waiting: its effect is destroyed by hurry.

Poem: 'The Coming of the Cold' by Theodore Roethke

> The ribs of leaves lie in the dust,
> The beak of frost has pecked the bough,
> The briar bears its thorn, and drought
> Has left its ravage on the field.
> The season's wreckage lies about,
> Late autumn fruit is rotted now.
> All shade is lean, the antic branch
> Jerks skyward at the touch of wind,
> Dense trees no longer hold the light,
> The hedge and orchard grove are thinned.
> The dank bark dries beneath the sun,
> The last of harvesting is done.

All things are brought to barn and fold.
The oak leaves strain to be unbound,
The sky turns dark, the year grows old,
The buds draw in before the cold.
The small brook dies within its bed;
The stem that holds the bee is prone;
Old hedgerows keep the leaves; the phlox,
That late autumnal bloom, is dead.

All summer green is now undone;
The hills are grey, the trees are bare,
The mould upon the branch is dry,
The fields are harsh and bare, the rocks
Gleam sharply on the narrow sight.
The land is desolate, the sun
No longer gilds the scene at noon;
Winds gather in the north and blow
Bleak clouds across the heavy sky,
And frost is marrow-cold, and soon
Winds bring a fine and bitter snow.

Silence

Poem: 'Advent 1955' by John Betjeman

The Advent wind begins to stir
With sea-like sounds in our Scotch fir,
It's dark at breakfast, dark at tea,
And in between we only see
Clouds hurrying across the sky
And rain-wet roads the wind blows dry
And branches bending to the gale
Against great skies all silver-pale.
The world seems travelling into space,
And travelling at a faster pace
Than in the leisured summer weather
When we and it sit out together,

For now we feel the world spin round
On some momentous journey bound –
Journey to what? to whom? to where?
The Advent bells call out "Prepare,
Your world is journeying to the birth
Of God made Man for us on earth."
        And how, in fact, do we prepare
For the great day that waits us there –
The twenty-fifth day of December,
The birth of Christ? For some it means
An interchange of hunting scenes
On coloured cards. And I remember
Last year I sent out twenty yards,
Laid end to end, of Christmas cards
To people that I scarcely know –
They'd sent a card to me, and so
I had to send one back. Oh dear!
Is this a form of Christmas cheer?
Or is it, which is less surprising,
My pride gone in for advertising?
The only cards that really count
Are that extremely small amount
From real friends who keep in touch
And are not rich but love us much.
Some ways indeed are very odd
By which we hail the birth of God.
We raise the price of things in shops,
We give plain boxes fancy tops
And lines which traders cannot sell
Thus parcell'd go extremely well.
We dole out bribes we call a present
To those to whom we must be pleasant
For business reasons. Our defence is
These bribes are charged against expenses
And bring relief in Income Tax.
Enough of these unworthy cracks!

"The time draws near the birth of Christ,"
A present that cannot be priced
Given two thousand years ago.
Yet if God had not given so
He still would be the distant stranger
And not the Baby in the manger.

Silence

Meditation: 'Cries of Advent'

Amen! Alleluia! Come, Jesus, Messiah!

**You are the Alpha and the Omega,
the first and the last,
the beginning and the end.**

Come! say the Spirit and the Bride.
Come! let each hearer reply.
Come forward, all who are thirsty!
Accept the water of life,
a free gift to all who desire it.

**You are the descendant of David,
the fulfilment of human hope,
the end of the darkest night,
the bright star of dawn.**

The giver of this testimony speaks:
Yes, I am coming soon!

Amen! Alleluia! Come, Jesus, Messiah!

Silence

O Living Word, proceeding from the mouth of God,
penetrating to the ends of the earth,
come and pierce us with the sword of truth.

Silence

O Wisdom,
dwelling in the womb of God,
generating and nurturing the earth
   through nights of darkness,
come and cherish in us the seed of wisdom.

Silence

O Adonai,
ruler of ancient Israel,
appearing to Moses in the flame of the burning bush,
carving in him on Sinai the words of living law,
come, etch your holy way even into the lines of our faces.

Silence

O Tree of Jesse,
O Flower of Jesse's Stem,
lifted high as a sign to all the peoples,
before whom even the powerful are struck dumb,
come and save us, and delay no more.

Silence

O Key of David,
O Sceptre of the House of Israel,
opening where none can shut
and closing what none can open,
come and free us, trapped in illusion and the lie.

Silence

O Bright Sun of Justice,
O Judge of all the world,
seeking to straighten what is crooked
and put right what is wrong,
come with dread power and stark mercy
   to our reluctant hearts.

Silence

O Lion,
regal in courage,
crushing our blighted bones and hardened hearts,
come with one bound and roar, awaken us,
    your stillborn whelps, to new and vigorous life.

Silence

O Swallow,
capering and darting through the heavens,
ending our winter when you build beneath our eaves,
come, bird from paradise, small and powerless,
    invincible as the phoenix.

Silence

O Cornerstone,
O Keystone of the Arch,
holding in your being the opposites of your creation,
come and give us courage in our bearing
    and our striving.

Silence

O Sovereign Stag, of Hind Embracing,
fresh and whole and eager,
carrying love's immortal wound,
come to us who are banished, barren, snared;
climb down to free us;
lead us home to headwaters, crags, and columbines.

Silence

O Salmon,
leaping like lightning from the womb,
bursting above cascades of chaos,
climbing love's deadly ladder,

come and sow your blood and burning water
    at the ancient source of all our sorrow:
drowning, you destroy our death;
leaping, you lead us to life:
O Ichthus, come in glory.

Silence

O Sovereign of all the Peoples,
uniting Jew and Gentile, white and black,
come and reconcile us
    whom you are shaping out of common clay.

Silence

O Divine Eagle,
soaring in the skies,
shadow gliding across the valley floor,
come and hover over us, your brood,
who pierced the only pinions
    that can bear us up from death and sin
    to sun and moon and eternal life.

Silence

O Voice of the Voiceless,
enabling to find words
    those whom others have made speechless,
come and lift the outcast
    from the dungeons of their silence.

Silence

O Wounded Healer,
enduring in the heart of God,
enfolding the universe in strong and gentle hands,
come and soothe our flesh with astringent balm.

Silence

O Morning Star,
Splendour of Light Eternal,
O Radiant Dawn,
O Dayspring from on high,
shining with the glory of the rainbow,
come and waken us from the greyness of our apathy,
and renew in us your gift of hope.

Silence

O Passionate Lover,
stirring in the loins of God,
yearning to create what is ever new,
come and open our flesh to love's fierce touch.

Silence

O Anointed One,
Long-awaited Messiah,
blessing, healing, and commissioning your people,
come and empower us to serve your purpose
of liberating love.

Silence

O Emmanuel, God-with-us,
at one with our humanity,
whose glory is our abundant life,
come and transform us who find our destiny in you.

Silence

O Music of the Spheres,
O Song of Silence,
echoing through ears that listen,
come with still small voice and heal.

Silence

O Midnight Star,
leading the way through the desert to the promised land,
come and carry the covenant in your flesh
and lead us through the thorns of love.

Silence

O Girl-Child, O Boy-Child,
free and unreserved,
laughing in play through the cosmos,
come and leap into our hearts in joy.

Silence

O Child of God,
calling together the creatures of the earth,
the vulnerable with the powerful,
come, gentle our strength,
coax our trembling into song.

Silence

O Unicorn,
creature of our dreams,
quivering, fierce, and tender,
come in the dead of night with new-born cry.

Silence

Maranatha!
Come, Lord Jesus, come soon!

Christ has come!
Christ comes now!
Christ will come!
Alleluia!

Part Two

This part of the Celebration works well outside, perhaps around a small fire. The invitation is to be 'the shepherds'. The passage from St Luke sounds more like 'the telling of a story round the fire' if it is read in a regional accent in the King James Version of the Bible. The angels' chorus can stream forth in the setting by Handel in his oratorio Messiah. *The hymn that follows, 'While Shepherds Watched their Flocks by Night' can be sung to a much livelier tune than the usual* Winchester Old. *In a* Second Collection of Sacred Music *published in York* c. *1820 can be found a tune by John Foster of High Green in South Yorkshire. It has been recorded on a CD issued by Hyperion (ref. CDA66924) with the overall title of* While shepherds watched: Christmas Music from English Parish Churches and Chapels, 1740–1830. *A hot drink could be served at the end of Part Two, and sipped during Part Three.*

A reading from the Gospel according to Luke, chapter 2, verses 1 to 16

Silence

Hymn: 'While Shepherds Watched their Flocks by Night'

Part Three

Part Three is a sequence of readings and carols, quiet and reflective. What follows are suggestions: the combination will vary according to resources and needs. It could take place informally, again around a fire, but this time indoors. Carols can be sung, by a choir or by everybody, or recordings of carols can be played.

Poem: 'The Innkeeper's Wife' by Clive Sansom

I love this byre. Shadows are kindly here.
The light is flecked with travelling stars of dust.
So quiet it seems after the inn-clamour,
Scraping of fiddles and the stamping feet.
Only the cows, each in her patient box,
Turn their slow eyes, as we and the sunlight enter,
Their slowly rhythmic mouths.
"That is the stall,
Carpenter. You see it's too far gone
For patching or repatching. My husband made it,
And he's been gone these dozen years and more…"
Strange how this lifeless thing, degraded wood
Split from the tree and nailed and crucified
To make a wall, outlives the mastering hand
That struck it down, the warm firm hand
That touched my body with its wandering love.
"No, let the fire take them. Strip every board
And make a new beginning. Too many memories lurk
Like worms in this old wood. That piece you're holding –
That patch of grain with the giant's thumbprint –
I stared at it a full hour when he died:
Its grooves are down my mind. And that board there
Baring its knot-hole like a missing jig-saw –
I remember another hand along its rim.

No, not my husband's, and why I should remember
I cannot say. It was a night in winter.
Our house was full, tight-packed as salted herrings,
So full, they said, we had to hold our breaths
To close the door and shut the night-air out!
And then two travellers came. They stood outside
Across the threshold, half in the ring of light
And half beyond it. I would have let them in
Despite the crowding – the woman was past her time –
But I'd no mind to argue with my husband,
The flagon in my hand and half the inn
Still clamouring for wine. But when trade slackened,
And all our guests had sung themselves to bed
Or told the floor their troubles, I came out here
Where he had lodged them. The man was standing
As you are now, his hand smoothing that board.
He was a carpenter, I heard them say.
She rested on the straw, and on her arm
A child was lying. None of your creased-faced brats
Squalling their lungs out. Just lying there
As calm as a new-dropped calf – his eyes wide open,
And gazing round as if the world he saw
In the chaff-strewn light of the stable lantern
Was something beautiful and new and strange.
Ah well, he'll have learnt different now, I reckon,
Wherever he is. And why I should recall
A scene like that, when times I would remember
Have passed beyond reliving, I cannot think.
It's a trick you're served by old possessions:
They have their memories too – too many memories.
Well, I must go in. There are meals to serve.
Join us there, Carpenter, when you've had enough
Of cattle-company. The world is a sad place,
But wine and music blunt the truth of it."

Carol: 'The Sheep Stood Stunned in Sudden Light' by Thomas Troeger

The sheep stood stunned in sudden light
The shepherds shared the creatures' fright,
While heaven's star-embroidered train
Swept over hills and down the plain.

They heard a rhythmic, rumbling roar,
Like breakers tumbling on the shore,
And running up the thirsty strand
To toss a treasure on the land.

And then the waves began to sing!
A sea of angels, wing on wing,
Was circling, chanting in the skies
The news of Christ before their eyes.

This night, O God, again we hear
Your hidden ocean drawing near,
Again we sense through Jesus' birth
The sea of grace that circles earth.

O when the voiceless night returns
And heaven's sea more softly churns,
May faith be like the shell that sends
The sound of ocean waves and winds.

Through faith we'll hear the angels' song,
And though the dark be deep and long,
We'll bravely live, for by our side
Is Christ who came on heaven's tide.

The painting: 'Adoration of the Shepherds' by Rembrandt

Hans-Ruedi Weber comments:
The shepherds have just rushed into the barn: a boy holding a dog, a woman with a child in her arms, a few men and two other women, with a girl struck with wonder in between them, all ordinary people. Some continue to talk, but those who have seen Jesus in the manger have suddenly become silent. Mary sits near her first-born, surrounding him with care, and Joseph stands behind them. The splendour of God shines no more from above around the shepherds. Only the new-born child is lit up by a lamp behind the kneeling man, and the human faces reflect the light of this and other oil-lamps. At first sight nothing extraordinary seems to happen in this scene from rural life. Yet as one meditates upon the predominantly dark and brown painting, one is overcome with the same awe which the persons around the infant Jesus express with different gestures.

Carol: 'On Rembrandt's Adoration of the Shepherds' by Kenneth Cragg

When muted heavens darken
And choirs celestial fade
The search of those who hearken
By lantern light is made.

Songs may celebrate on high
And angels sound their chord.
But lamps men tend their sheep by
Are lights that find the Lord.

Who vigil keep nocturnal
Where love and pity lie
The mystery eternal
Can best identify.

For those whose sight is heavenward
To read true glory's face
Are turned around to manward
A lowliness to trace.

When Rembrandt bathes in shadows
The birth where peasants gaze
God's artistry he hallows
In silhouettes of praise.

Reading: 'On the Incarnation' by Rubem Alves

What the doctrine of the incarnation whispers to us is that God, eternally, wants a body like ours. Have you ever thought about this? That at Christmas, what is celebrated is our body as something that God desires.

Carol: 'In the Bleak Midwinter' by Christina Rossetti perhaps to the setting by Harold Darke

Reading: 'On Christmas' by Thomas Merton

Into this world, this demented inn, in which there is absolutely no room for him at all, Christ has come uninvited. But because he cannot be at home in it, because he is out of place in it, his place is with those others for whom there is no room. His place is with those who do not belong, who are rejected by power because they are regarded as weak, those who are discredited, who are denied the status of persons, those unjustly accused and condemned. With those for whom there is no room, Christ is present in the world. He is mysteriously present in those for whom there seems to be nothing but the world at its worst...It is in these that he hides himself, for whom there is no room.

Carol: For an Up-Over Christmas

> In the hot midsummer
> Desert breezes sigh,
> Water trickles slowly,
> Earth is brown and dry.
> Shimmering blue of ocean –
> Sunlight aglow –
> In the hot midsummer
> Long ago.

Or, to match the 'bleak' midwinter and the relentless 'snow on snow':

> In the zeal of summer
> Scouring whirlwinds sear,
> Lips are scorched and barren,
> Earth is bleached with fear.
> Fevered brains bewildered,
> Lurching to and fro,
> Stumble through the mirage,
> Here and now.

From a Christmas sermon by Richard Holloway

...(Typical) of all these people (who are different from the norm, who do not possess characteristics that other people admire) has been a refusal to collude with the conspiracy of success that characterizes a moralistic Church. They have rejected the bright and shining lie of human perfectibility and learned to live with only two certainties – their own frailty, and the eternal forgiveness of Christ. Precariously, they live by grace and they minister it to others. By their wounds we are healed.

Increasingly, I understand the doctrine of the incarnation in this way. The Word becomes flesh in all its uncertainty and awkwardness. Grace comes to us through weakness. The traditional account of the nativity, purged of its Christmas-card glamour, captures the scandal of this paradox. There is the uncertainty that surrounds the conception. There is the confusion and incompetence that characterizes the birth. Yet somewhere an angel sings, because God's grace has found another of the despised to dwell with. Grace uses every available weakness to pull down our might. It undermines the cruelty of our strength by throwing us on the mercy of our weakness. This is why we should have a special regard for the despised, the little ones on the outside, the impure and the untogether. Not because they provide us with an opportunity for ministry, but because they afford us a means of grace.

Carol: William Blake's poem, 'Little Lamb, who Made Thee?', to the music of John Tavener

Poem: 'Christmas Venite' by John V. Taylor

Let not my humble presence affront and stumble
your hardened hearts that have not known my ways
nor seen my tracks converge on this uniqueness.
Mine is the strength of the hills that endure and crumble,
bleeding slow fertile dust to the valley floor.
I am the fire in the leaf that crisps and falls
and rots into the roots of the rioting trees.
I am the mystery, rising, surfacing
out of the seas into these infant eyes
that offer openness only and the unfocusing
search for an answering grace. O recognize,
I am the undefeated heart of weakness.
Kneel to adore, fall down to pour your praise:
you cannot lie so low as I have been always.

'Carol for the Last Christmas Eve' by Norman Nicholson

The first night, the first night,
    The night that Christ was born,
His mother looked in his eyes and saw
    Her maker in her son.

The twelfth night, the twelfth night,
    After Christ was born,
The Wise Men found the child and knew
    Their search had just begun.

Eleven thousand, two fifty nights,
    After Christ was born,
A dead man hung in the child's light
    And the sun went down at noon.

Six hundred thousand or thereabout nights,
    After Christ was born,
I look at you and you look at me
But the sky is too dark for us to see
    And the world waits for the sun.

But the last night, the last night,
    Since ever Christ was born,
What his mother knew will be known again,
And what was found by the Three Wise Men,
And the sun will rise and so may we,
    On the last morn, on Christmas morn,
Umpteen hundred and eternity.

Carol: 'John Bunyan at Christmas' by Kenneth Cragg
(adapted)

Who would God's poetry see
Though yet a stranger,
Let them expectantly
Come near this manger.
Let no disparagement
Deter thy firm intent
To read with glad consent
The Christmas wonder.

When merchandisers hire
Carols for trading
And pseudo-mirths require
Empty parading,
Take ye such baubles hence,
Come not with mocking pence,
Get ye the costly sense
Of the first Magi.

Those who but browse around
Christmas un-wondered,
Do but their loss compound,
Joy from truth sundered.
Though faith a hostage be
To bland festivity
Let nothing hinder thee
A pilgrim's finding.

And ye who merely tease
Deep winter's solstice,
Your weary boredoms ease
With gaudy poultice:
Love must your lack dispute
Have ye the more compute
The meanings we salute
Who reason season:

How in this mortal scene
God is credentialled,
Has graced in suffering been
All fleshly stencilled.
In Christ's conceiving see
How love and pity be,
Through crib and cross is He
The Master pilgrim.

This sacramental Lord,
Humanly being,
Doth His own self afford
To human seeing.
Learn ye the one Noel
In bread and wine we tell,
Know well Emmanuel
'With us' – nail-printed.

Who would perceptive be
Of womb and story
Must needs the logic see
Where hides the glory.
This Gospel of the face,
God's countenance of grace,
Take thou to love's embrace
And fellow-follow.

Part Four

By now it will be nearing the middle of the night, the time for the Midnight Communion, with as much colour and music and splendour as resources allow. What follows is a selection of material in approximately the traditional order.

Carol: 'Silent Night! Holy Night!'

Prayer

Blessed be God who alone works wonders!
Blessed for ever be God's glorious name!

Through the tender mercy of our God
the day has dawned upon us from on high
to give light to those who sit in darkness
  and in the shadow of death,
and to guide our feet in ways of peace.

Living Word of Light and Love,
you became a human being,
you pitched your tent among us,
and lived the fulness of our humanity,
full of grace and truth.

A Child is born to us, alleluia!
A Son is given to us, alleluia!
All the ends of the earth
have seen the salvation of our God.
Alleluia! Alleluia!

Recognition and Reconciliation

An alternative title to Confession and Absolution. *As befits a celebration, this is not a time for extended detailed personal or corporate confession, but simply to recognize our failings with the quiet dignity of those who have come to think of themselves as sons and daughters of God, and not as slaves. So the emphasis is on our freedom in Christ, not on our enslavement.*

From reconciliation to peace: the sharing of the Peace is described here as a ritual, not as a sign of personal affection (provoking bear hugs for some and an embarrassed retreat for others). The gesture here is the same for everybody, whether it be a hand clasp or palms enfolded round the palms of one's neighbour.

As the Peace is passed, let each person's eyes focus in turn on each person as he or she receives the greeting. And if the company is too large for each to see everybody else, the manner of the passing has to be different. For example, if there are children present, they can give the Peace to the people at the ends of rows, who then pass it along the row.

Let us reflect in silence
  on how we have failed to follow the way of Christ,
the way of Love Incarnate…

Silence

Kyrie eleison
Kyrie eleison
Christe eleison
Christe eleison
Kyrie eleison
Kyrie eleison

The Gospel of Love and Truth is lived out
    in deeds of compassion, justice, and forgiveness.
In Christ we see God revealed to us in a human being
    who lived and died in that very way,
a way that even death could not defeat,
a way that led men and women to rejoice
    in the wonder of his birth.

In the Spirit of Christ we are released
    from all that traps us,
    from our fear of love,
    from our refusal to believe in our own worth,
    from our desire for revenge against those who have hurt us,
    from our need to live a lie,
    from the ghetto in which we have locked our infant selves,
    from our anxiety,, and from the fear of death,
    from a brooding sense of guilt and failure.

Let us in the Spirit of Christ claim our freedom,
let us be assured that we are accepted for who we are
    and not for what we have achieved,
let us celebrate our release from all that would drag us down
    to destruction and disintegration,
let us remember that we are all enfolded
    in the love and peace of God.

Amen. Thanks be to God.
The Peace of the Angels and of the Child be with us.

Gloria

> **Worship give to God most glorious –**
> **Peace to those who love God well –**
> **Adoration from God's people –**
> **Thankfulness our voices tell.**

God we bless you for your glory,
Full of light and truth and grace,
Word made flesh in Christ incarnate,
Shining through a human face.

Born in cave and killed on gibbet,
Outcast dying in disgrace,
Burned by fires of human hatred,
Raised by love's fierce last embrace.

Jesus Christ our glorious Saviour,
Lamb who takes our sin away,
Lifted high in Love's enfolding,
For your mercy here we pray.

You alone are Love most holy,
You alone great deeds have done,
Intimate in God in glory,
In the Spirit, Three-in-One.

Prayer

Eternal and loving God,
wonderfully creating us in your own image,
becoming human in Jesus,
sharing the flesh and blood of our humanity,
so fill us with your Spirit
    that we may come to share in your divinity,
and that in the company of those
    who knew your birth among us
we may cry glory and know your peace.
This we pray in the name of Jesus of Bethlehem and Egypt,
    of Nazareth and Jerusalem.
Amen.

Words echoing the Prophet Isaiah

The people who walked in darkness
have seen a great light;
those who dwelt in a land of deep darkness
upon them has the light dawned.
As a child you have been born to us,
as a son you have been given to us:
Wonderful Counsellor, Creator God,
Beloved Abba, Harbinger of Peace.
From the days of our ancestors of faith
in fulfilment of the covenants of promise,
your Word of Love has struggled to be born,
and at last is made clear in the Word made flesh.

Psalm: adapted from Psalm 150

We praise you, O God, holy and beloved!
We praise you for your glory and wisdom!
We praise you for your marvellous deeds!
We praise you with the sound of the trumpet!
We praise you upon the flute and harp!
We praise you in the cymbals and dances!
We praise you on the strings and pipe!
We praise you on the deep resounding drums!
We praise you in the Infant Jesus!
We praise you, Emmanuel, God-with-us!
Let everything that breathes under the sun
and everything that rests through the winter,
on this glad night give you praise:
Alleluia! Alleluia!

A reading from the first letter of John, chapter 4,
verses 7 to 14

Beloved, let us love one another. For love is of God, and everyone who loves is born of God and knows God. If we do not love, we do not know God. For God is love.

The love of God was manifested towards us when God sent his only begotten Son into the world, that we might live through him. Here love finds its focus: it is not that we loved God but that God loved us, and sent his Son to be the means by which we have been set free.

Beloved, if God so loved us, we ought also to love one another. Not one of us has seen God at any time. But if we love one another, God dwells in us, and God's love is brought to perfection in us.

We know that we dwell in God and God dwells in us because he has given us of his Spirit. And we have seen, and we testify, that the Father sent the Son to be the Saviour of the world.

Carol: 'Along the Roads the People Throng'
by Kenneth Cragg (or another gentle carol)

> Along the roads the people throng:
> To Caesar's crowds the inns belong.
> O'er Bethlehem the sun goes down,
> Night envelopes a heedless town.
>
> And Mary's heart is sad with care,
> Unhoused the son that she must bear.
> Homelessly born is heaven's Child,
> Laid on the straw this Saviour mild.
>
> In lowly birth God's glory hides,
> Incarnate God in man confides,
> In open fields the shepherds kneel,
> While open'd skies earth's joy reveal.

The eastern star a summons brings.
'Cross desert sands ride seeking kings.
And down the years the lovers throng:
To Mary's child the worlds belong.

The Gospel for Christmas:
the Prologue to St John's Gospel

The Fourth Gospel is as much poem and prayer as it is prose. This paraphrase, cast in the form of a poetic prayer, turns a 'hearing' into an 'absorbing'.

Eternal Word,
with God from the beginning,
in whom and through whom
everything has come to be,
in you is life, the life that is our light,
the light that shines on in the darkness,
which the darkness has never overcome,
the true light, enlightening us all,
shining in the world.
Yet we did not recognize you.
You came to your own people –
and we knew you not.
**You came to your own home –
and we received you not.**
But to those who did receive you,
who believed in your name,
you gave power to become your children,
to be known as your servants and your friends,
born not of the will of flesh and blood,
but of the desire of your love.
**Living Word of Light and Love,
you were made flesh.
You came to dwell among us,
full of grace and truth.**

We saw your glory,
divine glory shining through a human face,
as a mother's eyes live through her daughter's,
as a son reflects his father's image,
your glory in a human being fully alive.

A Creed

Carol: 'O Little Town of Bethlehem'
(traditional verse 1 and Kenneth Cragg verse 2)

> O little town of Bethlehem,
> how still we see thee lie!
> Above thy deep and dreamless sleep
> the silent stars go by:
> yet in thy dark streets shineth
> the everlasting Light;
> the hopes and fears of all the years
> are met in thee tonight.
>
> O little town of Bethlehem,
> how still we see thee lie,
> whose hearts and halls as prison walls
> the fear of Herod cry,
> where in thy dark streets prowling
> go troops with torches bright,
> and scars and cares of ancient years
> are yet in thee tonight.

The Prayers

A time of prayer for particular people, either in silence or aloud, and then these prayers:

Let us rejoice in the Mystery of the Incarnation,
in the Humanity of God,
in the Wonder of the Word made Flesh.

Let us rejoice that God is with us,
a hidden silent presence,
transforming to gold the leaden rock of earth.

Let us rejoice that the best name of God is Love,
a Love that draws us like a magnet,
that nothing can defeat, neither evil nor pain nor death.

Let us rejoice in God revealed to us as a baby,
whose weakness is stronger than our brittle pride,
whose light shines clearer than our wilful blindness.

Let us rejoice that God has given us one another,
that we might learn to bear the beams of love.

Let us pray that we may not betray God's trust in us,
nor our own in one another.

Let us pray that we may have courage to change our lives,
as nations and as individuals,
that the hungry may be fed, the poor achieve dignity,
the oppressed go free, and the stranger be welcomed.

Let us pray for those in authority among us,
that they may respect the law and seek to reform it,
and work for justice and the common good.

Let us pray for the peacemakers of the world,
and all who through their vision and struggle
seek to make us citizens of one earth.

Let us remember the lonely and anxious among us,
the elderly, the homeless, and the starving,
the foolish and the despairing,
the sick at heart and those in pain,
the dying and those who mourn,
and those whose hearts are hardened against the love of God.

Let us remember those who rejoice with us,
but upon another shore and in a greater light,
that multitude that no-one can number,
whose hope was in the Word made flesh,
and with whom, in this, we for evermore are one.

Praying with Christ,
based on Louis Evely's meditative book, **Our Father**

Dear God, our Creator,
Beloved Companion and Guide upon the Way,
Eternal Spirit within us and beyond us:

let us honour your name
in lives of costly giving love;

let us show that we and all whom we meet
deserve dignity and respect,
for they are your dwelling place and your home;

let us share in action your deep desire
for justice and peace among the peoples of the world;

**let us share our bread with one another,
the bread that you have shared with us;**

**let us in the spirit of your forgiving us
make friends with those we've hurt
and failed to love;**

**let us overcome our trials and temptations,
our suffering and dying,
in the strength and courage
with which you overcame them too;**

**let us in your love free the world from evil,
transforming darkness into light.**

**For the whole world is yours,
and you invite us to be partners
in the work of your creating.**

**Amen.
So be it.
So will we do it.**

Hymn: 'Hark! The Herald Angels Sing'

The Offering

Blessed are you, eternal God,
Source of all creation:
through your goodness
we have this bread to offer,
which earth has given
and human hands have made:
it will become for us the Bread of Life.
Blessed be God for ever.

Blessed are you, eternal God,
Source of all creation:
through your goodness
we have this wine to offer,
fruit of the vine
and work of human hands:
it will become for us the Cup of Salvation.
Blessed be God for ever.

The Thanksgiving Prayer

Eternal Wisdom,
we praise you and give you thanks,
because you emptied yourself of power
and became foolishness for our sake;
for on this night you were delivered as one of us,
a baby needy and naked,
wrapped in a woman's blood;
born into poverty and exile,
to proclaim the good news to the poor,
and to let the broken victims go free.

Therefore, with the woman who gave you birth,
the women who befriended you and fed you,
who argued with you and touched you,
the woman who anointed you for death,
the women who met you, risen from the dead,
and with all your lovers throughout the ages,
we praise you, saying,

Holy, holy, holy, vulnerable God,
heaven and earth are full of your glory:
Hosanna in the highest.
Blessed is the One who comes in the name of God:
Hosanna in the highest.

Blessed is our brother Jesus,
bone of our bone and flesh of our flesh,
who on the night when he was delivered over to death,
took the bread that sustains us all,
gave thanks, and broke it,
and gave it to his disciples and said,
Take, eat,
this is my Body,
my Living Presence,
given for you:
do this to re-member me,
to bring us together in the world.

In the same way he took the cup of wine,
the wine of our sorrow and our solace,
gave thanks, and gave it to them and said,
Drink of this, all of you,
this is my Blood,
my Very Life,
spent for you;
do this to re-member me,
to bring us alive in the world.

Silence

Let us proclaim the mystery of faith:
Christ has died; Christ is risen;
Christ is here; Christ will come.

Come now, dearest Spirit of God,
embrace us with your gentle power.
Brood over these bodily things,
and make us one body in Christ.
As Mary's body was broken for him,
and her blood shed,
so may we show forth his brokenness

for the life of the world,
and may creation be made whole
through the new birth in his blood.

The Breaking of the Bread

The bread which we break
is a sharing in the Body of Christ.
The wine which we bless
is a sharing in the Blood of Christ.

Agnus Dei

Lamb of God, taking away the sin of the world,
Pour mercy upon us.
Child of God, affirming the worth of the world,
Whisper your love for us.
Healing God, bearing the pain of the world,
Make us whole.

The Invitation to Communion

Let us open our hands, open our hearts,
open the hidden places of our being,
and into our deep soul-self
let there enter the heartbeat of those we love,
the lifeblood of our villages, towns, and cities,
the lifestream of the tides and currents and seasons,
the pulsing of our planet and of the stars;
let there enter all the joys and pains our cup can bear;
let there enter the nourishment through the brokenness;
and in and through it all, to transform it to glory,
let us receive the Body, the Living Presence,
the Blood, the Very Self, of Jesus,
and let us feed and live and love, in faith, with gratitude.

Beloved, we draw near to be loved by you,
in deep yet trembling trust,
through this matter of your creation,
this material stuff of bread and body,
this fluid of wine and blood,
that your desire for us and ours for you
may be blended in deep joy and ecstasy,
that we may be enriched and doubly blessed.

**We draw near to receive this offering of yourself,
your intimate, vulnerable, and naked body,
imparted to us, incorporated in us,
that we may dwell and love and create,
you in us and we in you.**

The Communion

Hymn: 'O Come, all ye Faithful'

The Blessing

**The blessing of God be with us,
Father and Mother,
Sustainer of our earth,
Source of all that is and that shall be.**

**The blessing of God be with us,
our Messiah, our Christ,
our Risen and Glorious Loved One and our Friend.**

**The blessing of God be with us,
Spirit spreading love and joy in our hearts,
giving hope to the battered ones,
inspiring justice and peace for the little ones.**

May this rich blessing be with us,
with all humankind living and departed,
with all being born this night,
with all emerging into life and light,
and with all the creatures of land and sea and air.
May our days be long on this good earth.

For we have been nourished by the Bread of Life.
We have been quickened by the Lifeblood of the
   Universe.
With courage and in hope let us continue on the journey.
Amen. Thanks be to God.

If we are taking time out of time, in prayer and play, there shouldn't be (nor I guess is there likely to be!) anything in the diary immediately after the worship. Granted that we are unlikely to party through the night [who says? – ed.], mulled wine and gingerbread stars are suggestions to feed your imagination. They have worked even in a conventional parish, even if to the slight bemusement of the once-a-year visitors...

Let a Child be a Child

Rowan Williams

"O almighty God, who...madest infants to glorify thee by their deaths..." I cannot quite remember when I first realized that the *Book of Common Prayer* – which I love dearly – was capable of coming out with sonorous blasphemy. But I do not know what else you could call its Collect for the commemoration of the Holy Innocents, the children massacred by King Herod in his attempt to eliminate the child Jesus. It is not exactly that God is being accused of engineering the deaths of these infants, but that he is being represented as guilty of one of the most nauseating sins of our and other cultures. The sacrifice or suffering of children is colonized by some adult system of meaning, it is given a significance that makes it possible for us to contemplate it without horror.

In Central Africa, in the armies of Laurent Kabila, or in Iran or Iraq, with their revolutionary guards, it is the same phenomenon, children conscripted into a bloody adult conflict, their pain supposedly transfigured by an adult cause, glorifying something by their deaths. Any offence against the integrity of a child is a kind of murder, forcing the child to glorify an alien principle or agenda. The abuser destroys children to glorify a particular kind of adult desire. How is this basically different from God turning a sickening massacre to edifying religious ends? The *Book of Common Prayer* rapidly escapes to the remote territory of metaphor, talking broadly about how we must mortify our vices and recover our innocence. Worse and worse: the butchered child ends up as nothing more than a symbol for something else, for my moral problems.

A Christian at prayer ought to know better. One of the enormous and disturbing originalities of Jesus in the Gospels is his

insistent pointing to the child not as metaphor but as reality –
even as instructor. Better not to be born than to offend against
"one of these little ones". You want to know what it is like to live
in the Kingdom of God? Look at a child. Jesus is not sentimen-
talizing childhood innocence. He is saying something more like
this: the child is in the most serious and irreducible way an
'other' to any adult; the child does not share an agenda, perhaps
does not even share a language, with adults; the child is simply
there, a human reality that is not involved in adult rivalries and
negotiations. What matters about the child is his or her presence
and difference, all at once. The child should strip us of the
assumption that our agenda is the natural, the obvious, the
authoritative one. Only when this happens, says Jesus, do we get
any inkling of what the Kingdom of God might mean. To bring
the child into our framework and our priorities is to destroy that
otherness and so destroy something of our own possibilities of
new life.

And while it may be easy to shake our heads over Kabila or
the Ayatollahs, it is less easy to talk of the routine ways in which
we conscript children into adult fantasies and projects here in
Britain, either by exploiting the pre-teen market, making sure
that children are drawn into the consumerist addiction as soon as
possible, or by tolerating the social conditions that force the child
into struggle and violence, in some estates and streets familiar to
you and to me, or by the casual and knowing sexualizing of the
image of young girls – and boys – by the beauty and fashion
industry – or just by the barbarous functionalism of so much of
our educational rhetoric.

Jesus seems to say that the child must be left to be just that: an
'other', whose importance for us adults is that they are not like us.
And one consequence of this is that we have to resist the temptation to impose meanings on the sufferings of children; to let ourselves be nakedly shocked precisely because the pain that children
experience does not let itself be used and processed into any of
our systems.

No glorifying, then. I cannot say that Collect and I do not

think anyone should. Perhaps the only thing that we should hear or see in the pain of a child is: Look – shut up and look. Do not make it tidy. Remember Dennis Potter's haunting remark, "Religion is the wound, not the bandage."

The Powers at Christmas

Martyn Percy

Here is one of the better jokes pulled from a Christmas cracker. Good King Wenceslas rings up his local pizzeria. "I'd like a pizza delivered, please." "Will that be the usual order, sir?" asks the voice at the other end. "Yes," says Wenceslas, "deep pan, crisp, and even."

St Stephen's job in the early Church was to organize the giving of alms to the poor. In later Christian tradition St Stephen's Day became a festive occasion when the poor were particularly sought out. Gifts were given to them. Masters waited on servants. Boxing Day derives its name from the custom of apprentices and servants breaking open the boxes in which they had collected their tips and sharing the money out among themselves. The spirit of the day is captured in J. M. Neale's famous nineteenth-century carol, celebrating Wenceslas as he tracks down an unknown beggar in a snowstorm to give him a feast. The carol ends with a moral:

> Therefore, Christians all, be sure,
> Wealth or rank possessing,
> Ye who now will bless the poor,
> Shall yourselves find blessing.

It cannot be coincidence that nearly all the feast days following Christmas Day are concerned with the needs of the poor, with seismic clashes of power with the state, or with the serious defiance of authority. The feast of St Stephen celebrates the first martyrdom 'in the name of Christ'. Stephen is stoned to death by the authorities for blaspheming. His exalted claim for Christ is heard as heresy by the Jewish leaders in Jerusalem, and Stephen pays with his life. As Tertullian later proclaimed, "The blood of the martyrs is the seed of the Church."

More blood flows on 28 December. The coming of the Christ-child, 'a new king', prompted Herod to act on the threat to his kingdom posed by the infant that the not-so-very wise men confide they have come to honour. As any ancient ruler worth his salt would do, Herod organizes his own local holocaust, killing all the children under the age of two within his region of governance. The 'Holy Innocents', as the feast is now called, remembers state-organized infanticide. It is sobering to think that such acts do not belong only to ancient history, as a mere glance at what has happened in recent years in Europe reminds us.

Barely pausing for breath, the Church celebrates the feast day of St Thomas Becket on 29 December. He was the one who fell out with Henry II on the issue of state and church powers, prompting the irate king to issue the rash invitation within the hearing of fawning courtiers, "Will no one rid me of this turbulent priest?" Four knights duly despatch Becket at an altar in Canterbury Cathedral, thus assassinating an archbishop in the name of king and country.

And if you celebrate New Year's Eve, spare a thought for John Wyclif, whose day it is, burnt at the stake in 1384 for providing the English people with a New Testament they could read in their mother tongue. Wyclif fell foul of the church authorities of his day, who took the view that Latin obscurity served the interests of the Church better than common clarity. Latin was, after all, the language of the educated and powerful elites.

Given that Christmas celebrates the coming of a child who will, as the Magnificat, the Song of Mary, proclaims, "cast down the mighty from their thrones, lift up the lowly, fill the hungry with good things, and send the rich away empty," it is not surprising that those in authority felt – and can still feel – a little twitchy. It is therefore no less of a surprise to see that those in authority can often be seen spending time during the Christmas season consolidating their power.

For example, politicians often take advantage of the holiday from parliamentary activity to issue new policy initiatives, or simply attack their opponents. The leaders of political parties issue

New Year messages to the faithful. The Queen broadcasts to the nation. So does the Archbishop of Canterbury. No wonder those feast days appear in the Calendar when they do.

Yet in the midst of these seasonal displays of power comes the haunting cry of a new-born child, who threatens to turn the world turned upside down. The kingdom that comes is not like any state, nor like any church. Its very establishment threatens all existing forms of establishment. The old order will be swept away: the new is to come. There will not be a cosy relationship between the Christ child and the prevailing powers. From the moment of his birth the stories tell of conflict. The nineteenth-century poet, Mary Coleridge, expressed a true liberation theology long before the term itself was coined, in her ironically titled poem, 'Our Lady':

> Never a lady did he choose,
> Only a maid of low degree,
> So humble she might not refuse
> The Carpenter of Galilee.
> A daughter of the people, she...
> And still for men to come she sings
> Nor shall her singing pass away.
> *He hath filled the hungry with good things.* –
> Oh listen, lords and ladies gay! –
> *And the rich he hath sent empty away.*

It comes as a political and spiritual shock to discover that God *prefers* the company of the poor and the powerless. His love is biased – to the poor. The message of Christmas is not one in which the middle classes or the rich raise the status and prospects of those under them. The 'social inclusion' that Christ envisages is much more demanding than that. The world is turned upside down: rulers are toppled, the rich are actually *deprived* of what they have, the hungry are fed with good things, the lowly are raised up, and the powerful are *dispossessed*. How is one to respond to this? Surely this gospel is too demanding. Brother Roger of the Taizé community used to reply to just that question with these words, "*Il ne demande pas trop – mais il demande tout.*" ("He does not ask too much – but he asks for everything.")

So, is the message of Christmas profoundly anti-establishment? Not quite. By the time the season of Epiphany arrives, the mother and child receive some powerful and wealthy visitors with their symbolic gifts, tokens that today's presidents and prime ministers would doubtless have to register and declare.

But notice even here the direction of these gifts. Jesus is not pro-establishment either. Each of these late-December feast days picks up an easily forgotten dimension of Christmas that questions the prevailing powers of the day. The story promises a new order, in which the established political powers and regulating religious authorities will finally be pushed aside. As the seasonal scripture promises,

> The government will be upon *his* shoulders.

Rulers, beware.

12

Babe, the First Cut is Deepest

Martyn Percy

The Jewish feminist joke is well known. The patriarch Abraham is talking with God, who is promising to bless him, and make him the father of many nations. There is only one problem. As a sign of this covenant God requires all male children to be circumcised. "What is circumcision?" asks Abraham. God chuckles and says, "Why, Abraham, do you not know? It is snipping off your foreskin." Abraham sighs. "But I do not know what a foreskin is," he protests. "That useless bit of flesh on the end of your penis," retorts God. Abraham pauses, and then says, "But I thought that was called a man." "No," says God, "I mean the other end."

Circumcision is clearly an ancient Jewish tradition. But what is perhaps surprising is that it has its place in Christianity too. On New Year's Day the Church celebrates the feast day of the naming of Jesus, eight days after his birth, when he would have been circumcised. It is a reminder to Christians that the one whom they call the Son of God is also flesh and blood.

In medieval times people regarded with particular reverence and awe anything that could be construed as part of the actual historical flesh of Jesus. Although his body was believed to be in heaven, whole, what of his milk teeth, umbilical cord, blood, sweat, and tears? Or come to that, droplets of Mary's milk that might once have fed the babe? These things were not resurrected, and could be assumed to be collectable. It is hard for modern minds to understand this, but such holy relics were something powerful that underwrote devotion to the bread and wine in the Mass. Symbols and reality belonged together.

Several cathedrals in Europe in the Middle Ages competed with one another as to which had the genuine foreskin of Jesus. There was even devotion to these relics, and visions reported of its power. Catherine of Siena's wedding ring, with which she 'married Christ', is supposedly made of his circumcised flesh. Birgitta of Sweden received a revelation of where the real flesh was to be found. The Viennes Beguine Agnes Blannbekin received (in a vision) the foreskin in her mouth and it tasted as sweet as honey. Henry V's wife had one such relic as part of her dowry. But, alas, nothing has survived to the present day.

As Caroline Walker Bynum notes, in her exemplary work, *Fragmentation and Redemption* (1992), we should be wary of mocking these accounts. Renaissance theology lay strong emphasis on the 'humanation' of God. For those who experienced these visions, the circumcision of Christ was his first 'bleeding', a foretaste of Calvary, and also evidence that Jesus was 'real flesh' in a way that his miraculous birth only points to. Some recent scholars of medieval Christianity point out that what we have here is devotion to 'the body of Christ': a host-shaped piece of flesh that spoke of ritual, gift, suffering, and redemption.

To pursue this line of enquiry may seem a little odd. After all, what has a lost foreskin got to do with the Christian message, especially at the start of a new year? Well, quite a lot, actually. Three things come to mind. First, the Christmas message, that God has come amongst us as a human being, is a message about 'enfleshment'. God, in Jesus, takes on the constraints of humanity in order to redeem it. This includes ritual suffering, such as the circumcision of Jesus (even if we now call the feast, in a somewhat sanitised way, the Naming of Jesus). Jesus must bleed, even at the beginning of his life.

Second, and still with suffering, the feast days that follow Christmas are nearly all concerned with blood: the martyrdom of Stephen, the Holy Innocents, and the Circumcision. There is no gift without sacrifice, not even at Christmas. This child, born to die and redeem, enters the world in 'blood' that points to his later passion. Jean Malouel's portrait, 'The Lamentation of the Holy Trinity', painted in 1400, depicts the dead Christ being held by three witnesses. The wound in Christ's side, flowing with blood, defies gravity, and flows down into his crotch. It is an artistic device, linking the first wound of circumcision with the last wound of crucifixion.

Third, the Gospel according to John asks us to believe that this 'Word' existed from before the foundation of the world. Christ is something before and after flesh, a full revelation of God, but also of redeemed humanity. Here is the firstborn from the dead, the new Adam, created as we are, in the image of God, yet without sin. You can begin to understand why – even if you do not agree – Roman Catholics devised the doctrine of Mary's immaculate conception. The move does not so much divinize Mary as protect the humanity of Jesus.

So the first day of a new year commemorates a Jewish custom inflicted on the male line. The purpose of circumcision was ever thus: to remind people of God's eternal covenant with them. In Jesus, even as a babe, the first cut is as deep as those final wounds, reminding Christians that the suffering servant has come amongst us for all time. He is Emmanuel: God-with-us.

13

Epiphany

Martyn Percy

The feast of the Epiphany comes at that time of year when the magic of Christmas has finally worn off. The decorations are coming down, and you are left only with wondering how you will get the needles out of the carpet and the forlorn tree to the re-cycling dump. I always struggle with what to do with the cards. Most of them are ghastly, fictional portrayals of ye olde England, warming pictures of the carol singers and snow-covered thatched cottages of a bygone era that was never as cosy and rosy as the images make out. The religious cards are worse. Most of the portrayals of the Holy Family are sheer kitsch, to say the least. Jesus is born in a clean swept stable, the birth process sanitized and poverty romanticized, the stable straight from a Laura Ashley catalogue – Mary and the child – a home birth – *au naturelle*.

It is not much better with the 'wise men', often depicted as oriental kings or mysterious astronomers or astrologers, travellers from afar. As T. S. Eliot wrote in his poem, "they came late" for the birth, and their arrival, in folklore, extends a one-day birth announcement into a twelve-day religious festival.

Traditionally, the coming of the wise men marks the revelation of Christ to the Gentiles. The *word* Epiphany means 'manifesta-tion', declaring that it is now clear who Jesus is, for everyone. But the meaning of the *story*, told in a few verses in the Gospel according to Matthew, is far from clear. First, the 'wise men' are not called that: the Greek word describing them is 'magi', an ancient Persian priestly caste skilled in astrology and magic. Second, there is no mention of their number: 'three' is deduced from how many gifts they bring – gold, frankincense and myrrh – but there could have been two or considerably more than two. Third, these magi are on a quest, and the science of their craft is far from precise.

Following a star they have seen in the east (the geographical east or the eastern sky?) they stop at Herod's palace, the logical place to look for a new ruler. But Jesus is not there. The magi must continue their journey and search elsewhere. But what they lack in discernment they make up for in persistence, and they eventually come to the stable and present their gifts.

As with all the stories surrounding the first Christmas, it is important to ask why they were told. Myth is the poetry of truth, and the story of the magi gives us a wonderful insight into how the early Church understood the significance of the birth of Jesus.

For example, how does Jesus come to be recognized that people start to worship him? In his adult years friends and acquaintances look at him and ask, "Is not this the carpenter's son?" For them, there is nothing special about this young man. And in terms of the story of his birth, life goes on at the inn that was too full to accommodate a pregnant woman and her new husband. Did anyone even remember the incident? Recognition of Jesus is gradual. Not everyone sees at once, and by Matthew's time there were still many who did not. So the Gospel writer emphasizes that, if you persist like the magi, you will find him – and, of course, you may, like Herod, over-react and panic and seek to kill him. (And Luke points to shepherds who rejoiced to hear of his birth.)

In the prologue to the Gospel according to John we read that "he came to his own home, and his own people did not recognize him."

Again, consider the significance of the twelve days from birth to epiphany. The number twelve is more symbolic than literal: recall the twelve tribes of Israel and the twelve apostles. One tribe on its own cannot really know who Jesus is. One individual apostle cannot entirely comprehend him either. The number is a cipher for plurality. This is not a crude form of numerology, for it makes a real point. You cannot know Jesus on your own. The whole Epiphany of Christmas – with its characters of shepherds, wise men, even enemies – is testimony to a mosaic of perspectives, insights, encounters, revelations, and projections. Emily Dickinson put it like this in her poem, 'Tell all the Truth':

> Tell all the truth but tell it slant:
> Success in circuit lies,
> Too bright for our infirm delight
> The truth's superb surprise.
>
> As lightning to the children eased
> With explanation kind,
> The truth must dazzle gradually
> Or every man be blind.

The myth of the three wise men is also a reaching back to an ancient and enduring story, captured in the Book Genesis. It is a curious tale of how God appeared to Abraham in the form of three mysterious men. Abraham receives the strangers and gives them hospitality. They announce that Abraham's wife, the barren Sarah almost a hundred years old, will bear a son. Sarah laughs out loud at this, but the three visitors ask her if anything is too difficult for God. Nine months later Sarah gives birth to Isaac. Matthew may have had this story in mind when he wrote his nativity narrative. In any case, the fascination with the three strangers has continued in Christian iconography. Rubliev's icon of the Trinity is a portrayal of Abraham's hospitality: the two threes have been conflated in one presentation.

What brings these stories together? It is partly that the strangers are known by their gifts and their gifts point to the future. In the case of Abraham, it is the future of Israel. For Jesus, the gold, frankincense, and myrrh point forward to his adult ministry and his death. In both stories, the receiving of unlikely news is an important key: God is manifest in the surprise. And the bringers of the news are themselves received – by Abraham and Sarah, by Joseph and Mary. Even beyond this, the stories point to the paradox that God is hidden and yet revealed. God is mystery and yet manifest. We can see God on our own yet discover him only when we are together. God is elusive, yet also the child next door or the visitor who turns up unannounced. We do not know God at all, and yet we do. In God, say the mystics and the poets, there is "a deep yet dazzling darkness". That is a wonderful oxymoron that takes us to the heart of the Epiphany.

14

Sensing the Crowds

Martyn Percy

Crowds can be conservative, unpredictable, and fickle. Their mood can change, almost in an instant, from quiet to frenzy. They can be whipped up into a vicious mob or an adoring assembly. Or they can turn the tables, and be quite unmoved.

Jesus spent quite a bit of time with crowds. One senses that he knew how to work an audience. In his rhetoric he used humour, pathos, irony, and appeal. He was persuasive. His stories hushed people in their hundreds. His sayings hit home, striking at both head and heart. In Jesus we see wisdom, oratory, empathy, passion, and coolness all combined.

Traditionally, Palm Sunday marks the triumphal entry of Jesus into Jerusalem. He is feted and celebrated by the crowds, who cut down palm branches from the trees and lay their clothes on the road he rides along on a donkey. The Gospel story tells us that the crowds lining the streets to see the famous Galilean prophet and healer cried out, "Hosanna! Hosanna in the highest! Blessed is he who comes in the name of the Lord." The event must have made quite an impact, and it would hardly have gone unnoticed by the authorities. Yet the same people who have greeted Jesus as a king change their cry a few days later to "Crucify him." Fickle indeed.

Understanding the whys and wherefores of crowds gives us an important key to what is going on as Jesus enters Jerusalem. Serge Moscovici in his work *The Age of the Crowd* (1985) examines the social and psychological factors in crowd behaviour. He is alive to the issues of power, charisma, and suggestion, and writes of the balance between leaders of various types and those who are led, and of the paradoxes that crowds present us with.

They are not simply passive. They are also proactive. They do not simply watch. They also make their own action. Neatly subverting the Marxist slogan, 'religion is the opium of the people', Moscovici claims that 'communication is the Valium of the people.' He is using the word 'communication' in a particular way. He sees it as a social process in which dialogue has broken down, collapsing into monologue. It is communication to the crowd, *stimulation* in which the message is the medium.

At root 'religion' simply means 'to bind'. This binding comes about through the conflation of 'ordinary' and 'transcendent' qualities such as power, charisma, order, and hope. The process finds its strongest form in a celebration, whether of a specifically religious nature or a famous win in a local football derby. Followers become transformed into 'fans', a word which derived from 'fanatic'. There are similarities between football fans and religious enthusiasts.

This is the problem of Palm Sunday. It is the very behaviour of the crowd that is worrying. Jesus moves from a position of having gained little recognition to one in which he is being crowned as 'the people's king'. Holy Week begins here because it is obvious that those who set him up will do him down. That is how crowds work. Any politician, celebrity, or sports star will testify that crowds, bound together in adulation, can quickly turn nasty, especially if you do not meet their expectations.

There is something else about crowds that Jesus knew. In the midst of throngs, often pressing hard upon him, jostling him, he was always alert to other things. But to what, exactly? We know that he healed nobodies: the stories in the Gospels do not usually bother to name the afflicted ones. He reached out towards those who were excluded from the mainstream of society and the mainstream of religion. They were mostly outsiders, whose stories were 'unpublished' – which is the literal meaning of the word 'anecdote'. It is the small, unpublished people that Jesus constantly turns to – even when he might easily have been distracted by the crowds. The small man who cannot see, he sees. The small voice amongst all the noise, he hears. The untouched body in the pressing throng, he feels. The incarnate body is richly sensate to the 'unpublished'. As Mary Grey writes, the healings of Jesus are "characterized by a redemptive mutuality in which people come into their own."

So, in the Gospel according to Luke the triumphal entry into Jerusalem is preceded by Jesus's encounter with Zacchaeus, a collector of taxes. We are told he was rich but that he could not see Jesus on account of 'his small stature'. He climbs a tree for a better view. And it is from this position that Jesus calls to him, inviting himself to Zacchaeus's house. Perhaps Jesus noticed something about him that drew his attention in a way that the dozens of others who must have been up trees and on rooftops did not.

In Christian memory and tradition Zacchaeus is portrayed as either fraudulent or as a collaborator with the occupying Roman government. (I cannot recall hearing a sermon or reading a Bible commentary when this was not explicitly stated.) The reaction of the crowd bears this out. They all 'murmured' that Jesus had gone to be the guest of a 'sinner'. Zacchaeus, meanwhile, has responded to Jesus's visit by giving half his goods to the poor. Then comes the hidden sting in the story, for he adds that if he has defrauded anyone of anything he will restore it fourfold. If. That 'if' must be one of the most important two-letter words in the Gospels. That Zacchaeus is despised by the crowd is not in doubt. But nowhere in the story does it say that he was dishonest. He is simply hated for what he does, but he almost certainly acts with honesty and integrity.

What then does Jesus's action signify? Simply this: that in the midst of a crowd bestowing their adulation he refuses to side with their base prejudices. Zacchaeus is affirmed for who he is. He does not repent, contrary to how the story is usually read: he has no need to. Rather, a person who is despised is allowed to flourish, and he is now seen as a person of generosity. He has, after all, given away half of what he has. Consistently, Jesus sides with the ostracized, the rejected, the unclean, the impure, the (alleged) sinner, and the half-breeds. He is no crowd pleaser, he is their confounder. Even before the palm branches are stripped from the trees, and the cries of 'Blessed!' are heard, Jesus is a disturber of crowds. He does not want their praise: he wants their commitment. And they will make him pay for this, his failure to deliver what they promised themselves.

Palm Sunday prepares the ground for Holy Week. The hot passion of Peter's rhetoric, the bathetic sentiments of the crowd, the pledges of the disciples – they will all be for nothing. Words will fail. The thousands of followers will be reduced to a few, standing in silence, keeping their distance, on a cold dark Friday. How the mighty are fallen.

15

Jonah and the Journey

Martyn Percy

It is fifteen years ago, but I remember the day clearly. A colleague and I had to travel north on a business trip. Even before I got to the car I had a chill sense that I should not be making the journey. Even now, as I write, I can recall that feeling so vividly. Nonetheless, I drove: few of us would re-organize our travel plans around our vague-but-dark hunches or a general sense of foreboding. Almost an hour later, a cyclist ambled across the dual carriageway we were travelling along. He never saw our car, and though I braked hard and early, we collided. The impact killed him instantly.

Some years later, still haunted by the events of that cold spring morning, I asked my former colleague if there was any way I could have avoided the accident. Was it my fault? Perhaps if I had been driving slower, things might have been different? He replied that I had driven well, and if I had not, we might all have been killed. Then he added an absolution: "I'm just glad it wasn't me who was driving that day." But I still felt that I had been somehow warned before we had set off, that I had had an inkling about the future. And I had ignored that voice, deep inside.

Ah, the wisdom of hindsight. If only we knew how our journeys might end, how many of them would we actually begin? The start of Holy Week is arguably the archetype of bad journey decisions. True, Palm Sunday suggests that Jesus's entry into Jerusalem might trigger an unlikely coup. But wiser heads knew better. If Jesus had wanted to live, he should have turned back long ago. But his course had been set: as Luke tells the story, Jesus had for some time been drawn to Jerusalem to meet his final destiny. He had "set his face towards" the city. There was to be no turning back. Whatever doubts he may have harboured about his ultimate fate, he was not to be deflected. He was on his way.

By a happy coincidence, the Monday of Holy Week this year was also set aside to commemorate a modern saint of the Church who also made a bad journey decision. Dietrich Bonhoeffer was a Lutheran pastor and theologian who witnessed the rise of the Third Reich at first hand. He was fundamentally opposed to the philosophy of Nazism, and was one of the leaders of the break-away Confessing Church that refused to offer religious support to Hitler's State. He lost position and was frequently harassed by the Nazis.

When war broke out, Bonhoeffer was on a lecture tour of the United States. He could easily have stayed there: he was not short of offers of work. But he returned to Germany to carry on the fight against Nazism from within his own country. He was arrested in 1943 and executed at Flossenburg concentration camp on 9 April 1945. His ground-breaking book *The Cost of Discipleship*, in which he had reflected on the demands of Christian life in oppressive political circumstances, had already been published before the war, in 1937. But perhaps his most famous work is *Letters and Papers from Prison*, published only after his death.

It is impossible to gauge the impact Bonhoeffer might have had on theology and on the life of the Church had he lived. He was not yet forty when he died, and some say that to die young is the best career move of all. It is easier to venerate saints when their lives have been stopped well before retirement. They have not had time to grow old and make more mistakes. Does Princess Diana's memory and influence owe something to her early and tragic death – on another ill-advised journey?

It is hard to guess what was going on in Bonhoeffer's mind as he returned to Germany or in Jesus's as he approached Jerusalem. Common sense would have said, "Turn back and carry on the fight from a place of safety." But they didn't. What seems to us to be a bad decision about a journey was clearly different to Bonhoeffer and Jesus. They knew the dangers, but they nonetheless set out, with how much hope we do not know.

Hope? Yes, because, in a sense, both knew that they could not lose. Their confidence did not rest in their abilities, which were undoubted. It rested on a conviction that they were in that specific place for God, and that to be anywhere else would not be truly living. Survival was no longer the issue. God's voice was going to be heard without a word being spoken, simply by virtue of their making the journey.

The mere fact of their presence – in Germany or Jerusalem – questions (and it is God's questioning) the legitimacy of the prevailing powers. If the authorities are minded to silence Jesus or Bonhoeffer, they also silence God. And the powers know this. Nobody in high office gets directly involved in the crucifying of Jesus or the shooting of Bonhoeffer. It is left to the soldiers. The sentences were passed down the chain of command, until someone can finally say, "I was only obeying orders."

Our instinct for self-preservation is what separates our lives from those of the martyrs. The Bible is full of people making difficult and costly journeys to bring about redemption. Some of the characters are reluctant travellers. As a reluctant theologian and priest I identify strongly with Jonah. Zbigniew Herbert's poem, translated from the Polish by Czeslaw Milosz, speaks of a modern-day Jonah, and how he would deal with the call to Nineveh – by avoidance:

> The modern Jonah
> Goes down like a stone.
> If he comes across a whale
> He hasn't even time to gasp,
> Saved.
> He behaves more cleverly
> Than his biblical colleague.
> The second time he does not take on
> A dangerous mission.
> He grows a beard
> And far from the sea,
> Far from Nineveh,
> Under an assumed name
> Deals in cattle and antiques.

Agents of Leviathan
Can be bought:
They have no sense of fate;
They are functionaries of chance.

In a neat hospital
Jonah dies of cancer,
Himself not knowing very well
Who he really was.

The parable
Applied to his head
Expires,
And the balm of the legend
Does not take to his flesh.

Holy Week is, in one sense, about making costly journeys, including those that embrace death, in the hope that this may lead
to life for others. An old Christian legend tells of St Peter, fleeing
Rome for fear of his life, knowing that he will be executed if he
is caught by his Roman persecutors. As he hurries away from the
city he meets Jesus travelling in the opposite direction. Peter calls
to him, "Master, where are you going?" Jesus replies, "I am going
to Rome to take your place." Peter turns round, goes back to the
city, and goes on to meet his death and his maker.

We sometimes make journey decisions that we live to regret
(and some are tragic), but there is something different about the
Christian journey. The real possibility of death cannot be separ-
ated from the promise of vindication and the hope of resurrection. The wisdom of hindsight would not have made Jesus or
Peter, Jonah or Bonhoeffer, turn back or choose a different path.
They knew that it is precisely those journeys that help resist all
manner of evil that open up the possibility of new life for others.

16

The Curse of God

Martyn Percy

"Sticks and stones may break my bones, but words will never hurt me." A familiar proverb, but one that has never been true. Words can be demeaning, dangerous, damaging, and even damning. Libel trials and their vigilant lawyers deal only in words – and the reputations they defend or besmirch. The violence may not be a physical act, but a verbal violence does distort our perceptions, and how much in a court of law is its damage worth? Think of Archer, Fayed, Hamilton, or Branson.

In a recent survey conducted by various media regulators, swear words and other derogatory terms remain seriously offensive for many people, especially racist, religious, or sexual words that slander or malign. The truth is that words not only hurt: they maim, they condemn, they kill.

A curious feature of the stories about the last week in the life of Jesus – one usually ignored by preachers – is the amount of swearing and cursing that goes on. We do not accurately know the swear words that were used in Aramaic at the time of Jesus, but no doubt the language could have matched Anglo-Saxon four-lettered expletives word for word.

Holy Week begins, in Matthew's version, by Jesus cursing a barren fig tree: a cipher for the failure of Jesus's audience to realize and respond to the good news of the Kingdom of God. Peter, realizing that he has indeed denied Jesus, swears and invokes a curse upon himself. Jesus stands trial, accused of blasphemy. And he is himself insulted and mocked by the Roman guards. Judas knows he is cursed, and hangs himself. And resonating with all this is the 'curse of Adam' long before, countering the effect of which is what the events of this week are interpreted to be about.

To curse means 'to utter against' someone or something,

'using words which consign them to evil', in other words, to damn, denounce, or anathematize. It is never to be done lightly.

Now the Church has always had an ambivalent attitude towards cursing. On the one hand the Church of England dropped the practice of excommunication and disposed of the ancient services of Malediction or Clamour (meaning, 'appeal for justice'). On the other hand it allowed instead a public reading of Deuteronomy chapter 28, within the context of a Commination, the minister reciting a litany, a register of God's cursing certain types of sins and sinners.

In medieval times, and later, there are many curses uttered as part of an undercurrent of 'folk religion'. People prayed for the forces of evil or the vengeance of God to be visited upon their enemies – and sometimes on their neighbours.

The thinking behind these formal services and informal practices was simple enough. If God would bless those that a blessing was pronounced upon, would he not also curse those who had a curse pronounced upon them? Indeed, the form of words is frequently parallel. To bless people or things is to raise them to their proper status before God, enabling fuller praise to be returned through the very thing that is blessed. Cursing is the direct opposite of this, a spiral of denigration, denial, and finally the absence of hope that is despair.

Like a blessing a curse is what linguistic scholars call a 'speech-act', since it is simultaneously a verbal utterance and a deed performed. In the very act of speaking, there is action. In cursing himself for denying Jesus, Peter attempts to complete in action what he already perceives in his mind, his separation from God. Likewise, the accusations levelled at Jesus, namely blasphemy, actually consign him to isolation, and then to death.

In all the cursing and swearing of the Gospel finales, we are of course left with one victim – Jesus – who himself becomes 'cursed' by God, consigned to evil. But this is not done by words alone. It is the silence from heaven that is deafening and defining. Jesus becomes cursed not by what is said, but by what is left unsaid. And Jesus knows it too. Abandoned to his ignominious fate,

he cries, "My God, my God, why have you forsaken me?" As
Sydney Carter put it in his hymn 'The Carpenter', written from
the point of view of one of the thieves executed with Jesus, "God
is up in heaven, and he doesn't do a thing, with a million angels
watching, and they never move a wing."

It may seem strange that the 'word made flesh' is finally condemned by God's silence. But there is paradox here. It is the very
words of blessing that flow from the dying Jesus that give us a clue
to at least something of what is going on in the crucifixion. To
those who curse and mock Jesus, there are words of forgiveness.
For the dying thief, there is an invitation to paradise. It starts to
look as if the cross, the place of cursing, is turned into an instrument of blessing. Perhaps the close link between the two should
not surprise us. It is ironic. Jesus, who is the true praise of God,
is also on the cross the accursed of God. Sydney Carter's hymn
ends as a reminder of the foolishness of the cross: "It's God they
ought to crucify instead of you and me, I said to the carpenter
a-hanging on the tree."

Precisely. Here hangs one "who saved others but cannot
save himself." In choosing to be cursed with betrayal, torture,
abandonment, and death, the lamb of God becomes an appar-
ently ordinary scapegoat. Our swearing, cursing, and vilification
is finally directed against God. And God's response is one of
silence and then of blessing.

So the hope of Good Friday is that the cursing directed against
one another and against God is wasted, for it is all absorbed by
Jesus on the cross. The crucifixion itself is a speech-act: it is
eloquent in its silence, abundant in its proclamation of blessing,
and in its display of love and sacrifice an utterance and an
accomplishment.

A clue to this is discreetly hidden in a throwaway remark made
by Luke near the end of his Gospel. In the story of the Road to
Emmaus, after the mysterious appearance of Jesus, the witnesses
scurry back to Jerusalem to give the news of resurrection. But
Luke writes that Jesus had already "appeared to Peter". John tells
of that reunion in his own way, in a touching dialogue. Luke's

remark leaves us to ponder. Perhaps Peter, the man who cursed himself only a few days before for denying knowledge of Jesus, could begin to understand how this same Jesus – the accursed of God – had at the same time become the instrument of God's blessing to humanity.

17

Redeeming Judas

Martyn Percy

The Billy Connolly joke is well known. Thomas turns up late for supper and is met by a merry Peter. Peering round the door, he sees the disciples tucking in to take-away and lagers. "Thomas," says Peter, "I've got some bad news and some good news. The bad news is that Jesus has been arrested. The good news is that Judas has come in to some money."

I like the joke because it goes against the grain. Judas generally gets a bad press, both in the New Testament and afterwards. In Christian tradition his name is synonymous with betrayal and possession. In Dante's *Inferno* Judas belongs in the inner ring of hell along with Cassius and Brutus, the arch-traitors. Yet the Gospels tell us very little about him, who he was, why he betrayed Jesus, and what on earth possessed him.

There is a tradition that Judas was the nephew of Caiaphas the High Priest, he who was determined to get rid of Jesus. Judas was persuaded to become a secret agent in a plot to ensure the downfall of Jesus. In the Gospel according to John we are told that he betrayed Jesus for money and that he was a thief. In the other Gospels the name 'Iscariot' seems to be linked to a fanatical sect of Jewish nationalists who were professional revolutionaries determined to overthrow their Roman masters. According to this tradition of possession, Judas is gripped by the spirit of the Zealots, and when he realizes that Jesus is not going to be the new political Messiah he had hoped for, he hands him over to his enemies.

We also read in John chapter 13 and Luke chapter 22 that Judas was possessed by Satan. The words used are "Satan entered him," implying that he is somehow taken over by the Devil in order to carry out the most wicked of deeds. One modern writer suggests that Jesus was betrayed in the lost childhood of Judas. It wasn't his fault – blame his parents.

Poor old Judas. The writers of the Gospels agree that he was a bad man and give us at least three possible reasons why: he was in it for the money, he was politically disaffected, he was possessed by the Devil. Of course they may all be right: most of us have mixed motives for what we do. The point here is that when an evil act is committed, even the gospel writers are not above the language of blame and scapegoating. They shift the responsibility all too easily from a tragic and suicidal human being on to a cosmically evil figure in which Satan appears to triumph over God.

Judas is one of those figures who are vilified by the evangelists. Even gospels of salvation name their enemies, and this problem, ironically, reaches its peak in the commemorations of Holy Week. It begins in churches all over the land on Palm Sunday, with the dramatic readings of the Passion narratives. Congregations are reminded that it was the Jews who called for Jesus to be crucified. "Let his blood be upon us and upon our children." We are left in no doubt that the blame for Jesus's death belongs partly to a Jewish crowd, baying for blood. Judas comes at the end of this narrative, the arch-betrayer and instrument of Satan. The Romans are simply foreigners who go about their job: the execution of Jesus is not their fault.

This anti-Semitic tone makes many Christians squirm today. So does the treatment of Judas at the hands of the writers of the Gospels. Laying full blame at the feet of one man or one race seems crude, simplistic, even primitive. Is not running away just as much a betrayal? Alas, these crude instincts still flourish, as any failed sports hero or politician can bear witness. One person to blame is convenient and neat: we are let off the hook.

Look at Judas another way, as the shadow of Jesus. He too can cry for their forgiveness for they do not know what they do. He too is despised and rejected, acquainted with grief. He gets mixed up in the politics and the passion, and he kills himself in despair. He dies with nothing achieved and with no hope. Like Jesus, he has been misunderstood, his mission has failed. This sentiment is captured wonderfully by Peter de Rosa in his poem, 'Judas':

> Judas, if true love never ceases,
> How could you, my friend, have come to this:
> To sell me for thirty pieces of silver,
> Betray me with a kiss?
>
> Judas, remember what I taught you:
> Do not despair while dangling on that rope.
> It's because you sinned that I have sought you,
> I came to bring you hope.
>
> Judas, let's pray and hang together,
> You on your halter, I upon my hill.
> Dear friend, even if you loved me never,
> You know I love you still.

A few years ago the artist Laurence Whistler created a set of thirteen engraved windows for a church, one for each of the twelve disciples, and one for Christ. It was the twelfth of these windows, the one featuring Judas, that caused controversy. The parish rejected it, clearly feeling that Judas belonged in hell. But Whistler had drawn on other Christian traditions. Julian of Norwich in one of her 'shewings' went to hell and found no-one there. Catherine of Siena said she would not go to heaven if she thought there was anyone in hell.

Whistler's engraving was nicknamed the 'forgiveness window'. It showed Judas with a rope around his neck being pulled into heaven, the coins – blood money – falling from his hands and becoming petals and blossoming flowers on the ground. This is the very opposite of Dante's vision of what befell Judas. But it ties in well with another modern myth about him. Noting that on Good Friday, after the death of Jesus, all the disciples having fled and run away, Norma Farber in her poem 'Compassion' asks where we might have found Mary, the mother of Jesus, later that day:

In Mary's house the mourners gather.
Sorrow pierces them like a nail.
Where's Mary herself meanwhile?
Gone to comfort Judas's mother.

18

After Virtue

Martyn Percy

Maundy Thursday is probably the oddest day in the Christian calendar. Many clergy begin it in earnest by attending their cathedral and renewing their vows. They also participate in the blessing of oils by the bishop, oils which will be used in the parish churches during the coming year for anointing those who are ill, and at baptisms and confirmations. Later in the day, in a different cathedral each year, the Queen walks among a hand-picked group of pensioners and distributes alms, now called the Maundy money, one coin for each year of her reign.

In the evening Christians gather to commemorate the Last Supper of Jesus with his disciples. But there is no blessing at the end of the service. Altars are stripped, the desolate Psalm 22 is said or sung, the lights are gradually extinguished, and a vigil of prayer begins, recalling Jesus's agony in the Garden of Gethsemane, his betrayal there by Judas, and his arrest by the officers of the law.

In many churches on this night there is a further ritual, the priest washing the feet of members of the congregation. It follows closely the account of that last evening of Jesus's life, the version recorded in chapter 13 of the Gospel according to John. Like other ceremonies of the day, this ritual is about service: to the poor, to one another, to the sick and dying. Even before Jesus's death is remembered, and in some places dramatized, the first-fruits of the gospel message are in evidence.

The problem is that rituals can distance us from reality, practical reasons of time and safety robbing the commemoration of the power of the original event. At one time it was the monarchs who washed the feet of their subjects. The poor, the sick, the lepers would queue for 'the king's touch', and afterwards food and clothes would be distributed.

As Shakespeare puts it in *Macbeth*, a king "solicits heaven, himself best knows; but strangely-visited people, all swollen and ulcerous, pitiful to the eye...he cures, hanging a golden stamp around their necks, put on with holy prayers..."

Today the ceremony is carefully choreographed. The Queen wears gloves, and gives out those specially minted coins. It is not easy to picture her stooping low to wash the feet of any one of a number of our neighbours, bunions and all. Nor is it easy to get inside both the ordinariness and the originality of Jesus's action. Foot washing as a gesture of service is alien to our society. But there is a similar custom, now quite rare but still in the public memory. Shoe shiners on street corners in our cities would, for a few pence, stoop at your feet and buff up your brogues. There was often conversation and rapport, and, although paid for, it was an act of service. To clean shoes publicly on the streets required a certain humility and might on occasion be humiliating. It was to acknowledge that you had no power or position, and few possessions.

To look at Jesus's gesture at the Last Supper in this light begins to get at what he was really doing. He washes his disciples' feet as a slave would do, and this mirrored what was happening to him. He was being stripped of his power and status as a teacher and healer. He is sinking low in the eyes of those around him, and here, at the table, his face is focused on feet, his eyes cast low. The darkness of Good Friday is already overshadowing him, stripped of clothes, shamed and outcast, dying on a cross.

At the same time, strangely, Jesus is also setting his followers an example. The foot washing is a symbol of deep and abiding friendship, even of citizenship in a new kind of society. They are bidden to wash one another's feet. Service is the hallmark of a genuine community and a profound expression of faith in Jesus himself. If the slaves and the destitute will be first in the Kingdom of God, the new community will be led by the servants of the servants of God.

We live in an age of 'service industries', costed, accounted for, sometimes questioned as to whether or not we can afford them.

But this ritual of Maundy Thursday brings such service to the centre of the wellbeing of any community. Nobody is so great that they have graduated to a status that is beyond the need to offer humble service. And because a mutuality is implied by Jesus's command, each of us should be willing to receive the service of others.

In churches riddled with hierarchies, it is no accident that we make Jesus in our own preferred image of King. The order of heaven supposedly is reflected in the order of earth, and vice versa. Servanthood is not valued for its own sake, but only as a condition of being given power. Christ is celebrated as ruler over all, and the Church governs and manages in that mode on his behalf. The foot-washing story challenges us to recognize that to picture an aloof Jesus reigning on high is to invert the Gospel. A Christ who is not a servant is not worthy of worship. The Scottish poet Maureen Sangster puts the challenge more sharply in this extract from 'Out of the Urn' (Scottish Cultural Press):

> Oh Christ, ye're just a meenister.
> Ye're nae bloody eese tae me.
> Ye winna come an mak
> Ma mither's tea.
>
> A stuck up little mannie,
> Bawkin oot yer words o Love,
> For God's sake, come down tae earth
> An wear the oven glove.
>
> Fit wye is this, Messiah,
> That I maun lose ma life
> Carin for ma mither
> Fan ma brither's got a wife?
>
> If ye'd come roon on Sunday,
> Gie a helpin hand,
> One shot o handlin the commode
> An you wid understand.

> Ma life is juist a constant roon
> O meals and bloody peels.
> If the hand of God is in this, Christ,
> It's a mystery nae revealed.

In our fragmented society we badly need a new ethic of service, in which all citizens participate. Service cannot just be something we sell, procure, or receive. To treat it like that is only to mirror the religious rituals that have evolved from the original action. What Jesus did shows us that we too must be willing to stoop low, humble ourselves, and take on the mantle of service.

In his seminal *After Virtue*, published in 1981, Alisdair MacIntyre tells us that our society no longer speaks a shared moral language, and it has no sense of what the 'common good' might be. When we speak of goodness or service today, all we are doing is handling the fragments of an old system of thought, but without understanding that they are only that – fragments: the vessel is broken. The Maundy Thursday rituals are echoes of the past which now lies in pieces in the present.

Yet those same rituals are pregnant with longing for a future. MacIntyre beckons us forward, to a Good Friday and beyond. What society now needs, he says, is not a programme or a prescription, but rather persons who will help us to recover new forms of community which will endure through the new Dark Ages "that are already upon us." He hopes for a new "and no doubt very different St Benedict" who will achieve this. But in actual fact, any true servant would do.

19

As Night Falls

The Commemoration of the Foot Washing, the Last Supper, and the Garden of Gethsemane

The evening of Maundy Thursday
8 pm – 11 pm

Compiled by Jim Cotter

This commemoration has three parts, each with its own mood. The Foot Washing needs space, the Last Supper needs a table, and the Vigil a place of quiet, perhaps a crypt, a chapel, or even a garden.

Of course, one place could be adapted for all three, with the simplest of equipment being moved in and out as appropriate.

The Foot Washing is leisurely and meditative. It involves everybody – hence the need for space. In groups of three, each person in turn is the one who washes feet, the one who receives, and the one who 'looks on' and absorbs the scene. The following equipment is needed for each group of three:

> *Sheet*
> *Large bowl – washing-up bowl or similar*
> *Salt*
> *Jug of hot water*
> *Soap*
> *Towel – one large and three hand towels*
> *Three saucers or small bowls for oil*
> *Olive oil*
> *Scented oil*
> *Hand towels*

First comes the washing of one another's hands. This is a simple act that can be a substitute for the washing of feet or, better, a short preliminary act which gets over any initial embarrassment. In practice, it is but a few minutes

before a quite profound silence descends upon the company. And of course no-
body need feel bullied into participating. Those who sit to one side and quietly
pray are involved as much as those who are more active.

For the foot washing itself, first salt is rubbed into hard skin, a symbol of
the necessary astringency we need in removing what has become deadly and
deadened in our lives. Then the feet are washed with warm water and dried
with a towel. Lastly, they are gently massaged and anointed with oil. A slight
variant is to go through the whole sequence with one foot and then repeat with
the other: the contrast between before and after is worth experiencing!

So we are reminded of a truth central to Christian life and characteristic
of Christian ministry. We are living sacraments of the presence of Christ to
one another. We become servants and friends, waiters and hosts.

In commenting on the story in St John's Gospel, Alan Ecclestone, in his
classic book on prayer, Yes to God, *was particularly interested in the ques-*
tion that is put by Jesus to his friends, "Do you understand what I have done
for you?" He thought that the answer has almost invariably been "No."

The language of Christian prayer has been dominated (and perhaps that
it indeed the right word) by an understanding of God as all-powerful King
and Lord, exercising ultimate power over human beings, with the consequence
that there has been too much fear and trembling in our approach, despite the
contrast illuminated by the last two lines of the third verse of Brian Wren's
hymn with which this commemoration begins:

> *We strain to glimpse your mercy seat*
> *And find you kneeling at our feet.*

This simple action of washing feet subverts the inherited understanding. Jesus
is portrayed as laying aside his outer garment, divesting himself of status,
authority, and power, becoming as one of the utterly powerless, as a 'slave
woman', the anonymous one who would usually perform this menial service,
whose face would not be looked at, whose name would not be mentioned, and
who had no contribution in any major decisions that affected her life.

We miss the irony in John's portrayal of Jesus. "If I your lord and
master have washed your feet..." He has done something utterly shocking,
unveiling a world different from the one they are familiar with, lampooning the
titles of respect and power and – do we have to take our understanding this
far? – rendering them meaningless.

Welcome

We meet in the communion of the Holy Spirit.
The grace of the Lord Jesus be with you:
The Love of God dwell in your heart.

Hymn: 'Great God your Love has Called us Here'
by Brian Wren

A reading from the Gospel according to John, chapter 13,
verses 1 to 15

Prayer by Janet Morley

Strange and disturbing Lord Jesus,
whose feet were caressed with perfume and a woman's hair,
you humbly took a basin and towel
and washed the feet of your friends.
Wash us also in your tenderness as we touch one another,
that, embracing your service freely,
we may accept no other slavery in your name.

The Foot Washing

For us, the welcome of hospitality is different from that of the
time of Jesus. For most of the year an outdoor coat is more likely
to be taken from our shoulders than sandals from our feet. We ask
our guests, somewhat euphemistically, if they would like to 'wash
their hands'. We rarely do it for them. But we do wash the hands
of the vulnerable in moments of intimate cherishing – those of a
child in a high chair, or of a paralyzed woman, or of a confused
old man waiting to die. And, as Jesus did, we lay aside any skill,

any authority of office, any temptation to dominate, and we simply serve.

Let us do this for one another now.

In groups of three, we wash one another's hands, each person giving once, receiving once, and watching once.

To bare our feet in public can be embarrassing. We may choose to do so on a beach or in the privacy of our own homes, but we do it now to remind ourselves that we are all vulnerable to public exposure and shame. We rub salt into one another's feet, symbol of the removal of any kind of 'dead skin'; we wash them and dry them on a towel, again a moment of simple service; and we massage them with oil, symbol of healing and care, and of anointing for a costly endeavour.

We rub salt into one another's feet, wash them, dry them, and massage them with oil, again in turn each person giving, receiving, and watching.

Hymn: 'When Love is Found' by Brian Wren

The prayers come from the collection Lent, Holy Week, and Easter

A reading from Paul's First Letter to the Corinthians, chapter 11, verses 23 to 26

A reading from The Shape of the Liturgy by Gregory Dix

The Peace

Now in union with Christ Jesus
we who were once far off have been brought near
through the shedding of the blood of Christ.
For Christ is our Peace.

The Peace of the Christ of the Upper Room be with you always.
The Peace of Christ be with you.

Hymn: 'Sing, my Tongue, the Saviour's Glory'
by Thomas Aquinas and others, to the plainsong tune,
Pange Lingua.

The Offering

Blessed are you, eternal God,
Source of all creation:
through your goodness
we have this bread to offer,
which earth has given
and human hands have made:
it will become for us
the Bread of Life.
Blessed be God for ever.

Blessed are you, eternal God,
Source of all creation:
through your goodness
we have this wine to offer,
fruit of the vine
and work of human hands:
it will become for us
the Lifeblood of the World.
Blessed be God for ever.

Blessed are you, eternal God,
Source of all creation:
through your goodness
we have ourselves to offer,
gift of the womb
and shaped by human hands.
We will become for you
a Living Body.
Blessed be God for ever.

The Thanksgiving Prayer, by Janet Morley

Holy Wisdom of God,
eternally offensive to our wisdom,
and compassionate towards our weakness,
we praise you and give you thanks,
because you emptied yourself of power
and entered our struggle,
taking upon you our unprotected flesh.

You opened wide your arms for us upon the cross,
becoming scandal for our sake,
that you might sanctify even a shallow grave
to be a bed of hope to your people.

Therefore, with those who are detained without trial,

with those imprisoned for conscience or for faith,

with those who are being tortured,

with children maimed by landmines,

with those who have 'disappeared',

with those who have been forced from their homes
by the so-called 'ethnically clean',

with the people of Africa and all others,
past and present, who have been enslaved,

with Jews who have been offended by Christians for so long,

with gypsies, with gay and lesbian people,
and all other minorities who have been imprisoned or outcast,

with writers whose words are censored
and who are threatened with violence,

with children who are abused and exploited,

with those abandoned or betrayed by their friends,

with those who have died alone,
without dignity, comfort, or hope,

and with all the company of saints
who have carried you in their wounds,

that all the pains of humankind may be fresh-embodied
with new life, we praise you, saying,

Holy, holy, holy,
vulnerable and compassionate God,
heaven and earth are full of your glory.
Hosanna in the highest.
Blessed is the One who comes in the name of our God:
Hosanna in the highest.

Blessed is our brother Jesus,
bone of our bone, flesh of our flesh,
from whom the cup of suffering did not pass,
who, on the night that he was betrayed,
took bread, gave thanks, broke it, and said,

Take, eat, this is my Body,
my Living Presence,
given for you.
Do this to re-member me,
to bring us together in the world.

In the same way he took the cup,
after supper, saying,

**Drink of this, all of you;
for this is my Blood,
my Very Self, spent for you.
Do this to re-member me,
to bring us alive in the world.**

The cup is the new covenant in the Blood of Christ.
For in the mystery of faith,

**Christ has died,
Christ is risen,
Christ is here,
Christ will come.**

Therefore, as we eat this bread and drink this cup,
we are proclaiming Christ's death until he comes.
In the body broken and the blood poured out,
we restore to memory and hope
the broken and unremembered victims of tyranny and sin;
and we long for the bread of tomorrow
and the wine of the age to come.

Come then, life-giving Spirit of God,
brood over these bodily things,
and make us one body in Christ,
that we, who are baptized into his death
may walk in newness of life;
that what is sown in dishonour
may be raised in glory;
and what is sown in weakness
may be raised in power. **Amen.**

Praying in Christ

Abba, Amma, Beloved,
your name be hallowed,
your reign spread among us,
your will be well done,
at all times, in all places.
Give us the bread
we need for today.
Forgive us our trespass
as we forgive those
who trespass against us.
Let us not fail
in time of our testing.
Spare us from trials
too sharp to endure.
Free us from the grip
of all evil powers.
For yours is the reign,
the power and the glory,
the victory of love,
for now and eternity,
world without end.
Amen and Amen.

Hymn, Bread of Heaven *by Josiah Conder, 1789–1855,
to the tune* Bread of Heaven *by William Maclagan,
1826–1910*

Bread of heaven, on thee we feed,
For thy flesh is meat indeed;
Ever may our souls be fed
With this true and living bread,
Day by day with strength supplied,
Through the life of him who died.

Vine of heaven, thy blood supplies
This blest cup of sacrifice;
'Tis thy wounds our healing give;
To thy cross we look and live;
Thou our life! O let us be
Rooted, grafted, built on thee.

The Breaking of the Bread

Jesus of courage and justice,
because you broke bread with the poor,
you were looked on with contempt.

Because you broke bread
with the sinful and outcast,
you were looked on as ungodly.

Because you broke bread with the joyful,
you were called a winebibber and a glutton.

Because you broke bread in the upper room,
you sealed your acceptance of the way of the cross.

Because you broke bread on the road to Emmaus,
you made scales fall from the disciples' eyes.

Because you broke bread and shared it,
we will do so too, and ask your blessing.

The bread which we break
is a sharing in the Body of Christ.

The wine which we bless
is a sharing in the Blood of Christ.

Body and blood of a new humanity,
we shall be transfigured to glory.

Agnus Dei

Lamb of God,
taking away the sin of the world,
having compassion upon us –

Beloved of God,
affirming the worth of the world,
accepting us in love for ever –

Healing God,
bearing the pain of the world,
giving us and all creation your peace –

Pour mercy upon us,
whisper your love for us,
give us your peace.

Invitation to Communion

Come to this table to meet the living God,
love indescribable and beyond our imagining,
yet closer to us than our own breathing.

Come to this table to meet the living Christ,
flesh of our flesh, bone of our bone,
God-with-us, embodied in our living.

Come to this table to meet the living Spirit,
interpreting our search for truth and justice,
breathing into us renewing power.

Come to find, to meet, to hold the living God,
whose love is ever renewed in bread and wine.

We pass the bread and wine from one person to the next around the company,
using these words and responses:
    The Body of Christ: I am.
    The Blood of Christ: Amen.

After Communion

Every time we eat this bread and drink this cup we proclaim the
death of Jesus Christ, even to the day of the fulfilment of his
coming.

Eternal and ever-loving God,
we thank you that in this wonderful sacrament
    you have given us the memorial
    of the passion and resurrection
    of your Dearly Beloved, Jesus, Messiah,
    our Servant-Lord:
may we so reverence these sacred mysteries
    of the Body and the Blood
that we may know within our deep soul-selves,
    and show forth in our embodied lives,
    the fruits of your redeeming love.
We ask this in the name of the Christ
    who in the Upper Room
    stamped this eucharistic image
    on the Body of Humankind. Amen.

Invitation to keep watch

When the disciples had sung a hymn,
they went out to the Mount of Olives.

Jesus prayed, "Abba, if it be possible,
take this cup of suffering from me."

Jesus grieved that his disciples
were not able to keep watch with him one hour.

Jesus was there betrayed by the kiss of a friend and handed over to the powers that be.

Jesus was obedient even to death.

We walk in silence to the place of vigil.

The Vigil

The Vigil consists of readings from the Gospel according to John, chapters 13–17, interspersed with psalms and silence. Each reading and each psalm needs a reader with a small torch to see by: all can join in the refrain to the verses of the psalms if it is read out first by the reader and everyone immediately repeats it. It is helpful to have one person with a torch whose task it is to lead the refrain each time with confidence. The same person can time the silences so as to relieve the anxiety of the next reader. A discreet knock on the side of a chair can be the cue.

The version of the Psalms is from Jim Cotter, By Stony Paths *and* Towards the City, *new unfoldings of Psalms 51–100 and 101–150 respectively, Cairns Publications, 1989 and 1991.*

In imagination we can go back to the later years of the first century when the writer of the Gospel according to John was meditating long and deep on the significance of Jesus for himself and his community. He was a great poet, and, not least in the five chapters read at this Vigil, we can see how inspiration works: the human mind and heart open to the Spirit of God listening and waiting upon events and memories and images for a word to come, in this instance delving into the relationship between Jesus and his followers, in the days of his ministry, in the days of the early Church, and, through our own pondering, in our own day.

Night lights marking the way in and the way out can help avoid accidents, and candles in front of ikons or pictures can give a focus. If there are a number of these, each with a chair or stool in front, people can be invited to spend one or more sections of the Vigil concentrating on one or more of such aids to prayer.

One

A reading from the Gospel according to John, chapter 13, verses 16 to 30

Psalm 55

Renew the covenant of your love, O God:
may we in truth be your friends.
Renew the covenant of your love, O God:
may we in truth be your friends.

In these days of turmoil.
of restlessness and complaint,
we accuse and betray one another,
lashing out in the fury of pain.
We set on one another with greed,
we persecute with baying and clamour.
We see slaughter, and our hearts writhe,
the horrors of dying overwhelm us.
Violence reigns in the streets of the city,
vicious dogs snarl at the stranger.
Fraud flits through the market place,
greed wins softly behind baize doors.

Renew the covenant of your love, O God:
may we in truth be your friends.

My eyes flash wild with horror,
my limbs quake and I cannot still them.
My heart grows cold through fear,
the ice of death grips me.
I said, O for the wings of a dove,
that I might fly away and be at rest.
I yearn to flee to the mountains,
to make my dwelling in the wilderness.

O for a refuge of peace,
out of the blast of slander,
far from the tempest of calumny,
from the harsh wind of the double-tongued.

Renew the covenant of your love, O God:
may we in truth be your friends.

For it was not an enemy who taunted me,
or I might have been able to bear it.
It was not a foe who was so insolent,
or I might have hidden myself away.
But it was you, my equal,
my companion, my familiar friend.
Ours was a pleasant harmony
as we walked side by side to the house of our God.

Renew the covenant of your love, O God:
may we in truth be your friends.

You have not kept your word,
you have no love of God in your heart,
and have broken the covenant you have sworn,
deserting those who were at peace with you.
Your mouth is smooth as butter,
yet war is in your heart.
Your words are softer than oil,
yet your sword flashes in the dark.

Renew the covenant of your love, O God:
may we in truth be your friends.

My heart cries out in anguish and grief,
Get out of my sight, you hypocrite!
Go down in terror to your grave, you betrayer,
for you have worked treachery among us.

Yet how I yearn for the healing of pain,
for a love grown cold to kindle again.
I pray to you, God, that we may be reconciled,
drawn again to the way of your justice.
Humble the pride in us all,
your love and your power consistent forever.
May we lift the weight of oppression,
may our enemies release the spring of their traps.

Renew the covenant of your love, O God:
may we in truth be your friends.

I cast my burden on you, O God,
and you will sustain and encourage me.
I will call from the midst of my groaning,
you will redeem me to healing and peace.
My heart has been so constricted,
my affections so easily hurt.
Yet your arms are wide and welcoming,
in your presence we are relaxed,
and feel most strangely at home.

Renew the covenant of your love, O God:
may we in truth be your friends.

Silence

Prayer

O living God, whose love has been betrayed and denied over and
over again, whose covenants have been torn apart, forgive our
lack of trust and loyalty, and call us to yourself again, we who
bear the marks of Judas and of Cain.

Two

A reading from the Gospel according to John, chapter 13, verses 31 to 38

Psalm 61

In our despair give us hope;
in our death give us life.
In our despair give us hope;
in our death give us life.

I stand on a rock at the edge of the sea,
the wind hurls the spray at my face.
The depths of the ocean swell heavy with menace,
tides of despair drown my heart in the deep.
I collapse by a rock in the wastes of the desert,
the noonday sun scorches my skin.
Waves of heat beat upon my weary heart,
my eyes stare at the dry bones around me.
The spirit has gone out of me,
my self-centred desires are as nothing.
I have come to the brink of inner death,
I descend to the depths of my doom.

In our despair give us hope;
in our death give us life.

Rescue me, O God, pity the pitiful,
lend me the strength of your tower of rock.
Succour me under your hovering wings,
welcome me into your hospitable home.
My vows lie broken, yet would I serve you,
my heart's desire is to love your name.
May the angels of mercy and truth stand by me,
the hand of deliverance heal me.

In our despair give us hope;
in our death give us life.

With a glimmer of hope I remember your love
the love that finds me even as I search.
You have entered the void of my despair,
meeting me in the very place of your absence.
The music of praise sounds again in my heart,
the words of rejoicing take shape on my lips.
You renew my strength to fulfil what I promise,
the name that you give me endures through the years.

In our despair give us hope;
in our death give us life.

Silence

Prayer

Implacable God, face us with the truth that we have no power of
ourselves to help ourselves. Raise us from the depths of exhaustion and despair, and renew in us the spirit of life and hope, in
Jesus Christ our Redeemer.

Three

A reading from the Gospel according to John, chapter 14, verses 1 to 14

Psalm 84

The end is known in the midst of the journey:
the fulfilment is beyond our imagining.
The end is known in the midst of the journey:
the fulfilment is beyond our imagining.

How lovely are your dwellings, O God,
how beautiful are the holy places.
In the days of my pilgrimage I yearn for them:
they are the temples of your living presence.
I have a desire and longing to enter my true home:
my heart and my flesh rejoice in the living God.

The end is known in the midst of the journey:
the fulfilment is beyond our imagining.

For the sparrow has found a house for herself,
and the swallow a nest to lay her young.
Even so are those who dwell in your house –
they will always be praising you.
And your Spirit makes a home deep within us:
let us welcome and delight in your Presence.

The end is known in the midst of the journey:
the fulfilment is beyond our imagining.

Blessed are those whose strength is in you,
in whose heart are your ways,
who trudging through the plains of misery
find in them an unexpected spring,
a well from deep below the barren ground,
and the pools are filled with water.
They become springs of healing for others,
reservoirs of compassion for those who are bruised.
Strengthened themselves they give courage to others,
and God will be there at the end of their journey.

The end is known in the midst of the journey:
the fulfilment is beyond our imagining.

O God of our ancestors, hear my prayer:
guide me as you did your servants of old.
Bless those who govern on the people's behalf,
keep us close to your will and your ways.
One day lived in your presence
is better than a thousand in my own dwelling.
I had rather beg in the burning sun
on the threshold of the house of my God
than sit in cool courtyards
of luxury and worldly success.

The end is known in the midst of the journey:
the fulfilment is beyond our imagining.

For you are my light and my shield,
you will give me your grace and your glory.
You are ready with bountiful gifts,
overflowing to those who follow you.
Living God of love,
blessed are those who put their trust in you.

The end is known in the midst of the journey:
the fulfilment is beyond our imagining.

Silence

Prayer

O God of the desert pilgrims, we who are wearied by monotonous days in the sun, who are battered by the monstrous whirling
winds, surprise us yet with a monstrance of wonder, a revelation
of love, an oasis of refreshment, a taste of the harvest, a moment
of grace.

As Night Falls 115

Four

A reading from the Gospel according to John, chapter 14, verses 15 to 21

Psalm 64

I reel from blows of the enemy:
where can my heart find ease?
I reel from blows of the enemy:
where can my heart find ease?

Hear me, O God, from the depths of my being,
fearful as I am of being destroyed.
Who are these enemies that swirl around me,
who conspire against me in a hostile world?
How have I released this torrent of abuse?
Whence come these arrows of bitter words?
Those whom I thought were my friends
pile all my faults on my tired spirit.

I reel from blows of the enemy:
where can my heart find ease?

No innocence, O God, would I pretend,
my failure and guilt are too real.
But it feels they were planning in secret,
ready to pounce from a place unseen.
Through the years they smiled and spoke tenderly:
now the lash of their tongues is unleashed.
They have laid their mines with such skill –
they have even forgotten they did so –
and they blame me for stepping upon them.
Perhaps they did not even know what they did,
so dark and deep is the human heart.
They dare not face the truth of their pain:
they seek revenge for hurts unremembered.

I reel from blows of the enemy:
where can my heart find ease?

Deliver me, O God, from the paralysis of fear,
from the confusions of my mind and the turmoil of my heart.
I am consumed with anxiety and dread,
the hovering unknown fills me with terror.
The sky seems full of probing eyes,
an unseen lens orbits the earth.
Ears hide in dim corners of the room,
the wavelengths carry out secret thoughts.

I reel from blows of the enemy:
where can my heart find ease?

Reveal them to themselves, O God,
bring them down for the evil they have spoken,
those who say they hate only my sin,
but who slay me in the name of your justice.
Let the devices of our hearts be made known,
your arrows of truth piercing our confusions.
Reveal us in scorching light to one another,
that we may lay down our weapons and forgive.

I reel from blows of the enemy:
where can my heart find ease?

Even now we rejoice and give thanks to your name,
the distortions of our being are eased gently through judgment,
the fierceness of your love is holding us upright,
the light of your eye shines with compassion and justice.

I reel from blows of the enemy:
where can my heart find ease?

Silence

Prayer

Dear God, we bring to you everything of which we are unaware, the unknown murky devices of our fearful hearts, the untapped sources of generosity and laughter, the forgotten confusions and hurts from which come our excessive anger, the unrealised capacity for truth and forbearance. Reveal us to ourselves and reassure us in the true humanity of Jesus Christ.

Five

A reading from the Gospel according to John, chapter 15, verses 1 to 17

Psalm 130

Costing not less than everything,
all manner of things shall be well.
Costing not less than everything,
all manner of things shall be well.

Empty, exhausted, and ravaged,
in the depths of despair I writhe.
Anguished and afflicted, terribly alone,
I trudge a bleak wasteland, devoid of all love.
In the echoing abyss I call out:
no God of Compassion hears my voice.
Yet still I pray, Open your heart,
for my tears well up within me.

Costing not less than everything,
all manner of things shall be well.

If you keep account of all that drags me down,
there is no way I can stand firm.
Paralyzed and powerless, I topple over,
bound by the evil I hate.
But with you is forgiveness and grace,
there is nothing I can give – it seems like a death.
The power of your love is so awesome:
I am terrified by your freeing embrace.

Costing not less than everything,
all manner of things shall be well.

Drawn from the murky depths by a fish hook,
I shout to the air that will kill me:
Must I leave behind all that I cherish
before I can truly breathe free?
Suspended between one world and the next,
I waited for you, my God.
Apprehension and hope struggled within me,
I waited, I longed for your word.

Costing not less than everything,
all manner of things shall be well.

As a watchman waits for the morning,
through the darkest and coldest of nights,
more even than the watchman who peers through the gloom,
I hope for the dawn, I yearn for the light.
You will fulfil your promise to bring me alive,
overflowing with generous love.
You will free me from the grip of evil,
O God of mercy and compassion.

Costing not less than everything,
all manner of things shall be well.

Touching and healing the whole of my being,
you are a God whose reach has no limit.
All that has been lost will one day be found:
the communion of the rescued will rejoice in your name.

Silence

Prayer

Through the dark despairing depths and the drought of the
desert, through the abyss opened up by our failings and folly, we
dare to risk our cry to the living God. For you will not let us
escape from our greatest good. In our struggle with you, fierce,
fiery Lover, let some new glory be wrought, and new and unexpected life come to birth.

Six

A reading from the Gospel according to John, chapter 15, verse 18 to chapter 16, verse 4a

Psalm 129

The litany of lament grows loud and long:
the pulse of faith grows weak.
The litany of lament grows loud and long:
the pulse of faith grows weak.

Does the power of the wicked have no limit?
Why do you not restrain them, O God?
Your people of old knew a measure of affliction,
but they praised you for deeds of deliverance.
Their enemies scored their backs with ploughshares,
opening long furrows of crimson.

But you would not let the adversary prevail,
you cut your people free from the chafing bonds.
Their anger welled up within them,
cursing the enemy with withering scorn:
"May they be as grass that shrivels in the heat,
may they never come to the ripeness of harvest."

The litany of lament grows loud and long:
the pulse of faith grows weak.

An easy exchange it seems to us now,
faced as we are with cruelty unleashed –
exquisite refinements of torture's black arts,
children knifed and dumped in the gutters.
Woe to us when to cleanse means to slaughter,
when genocide seems the simple solution,
when bullets explode into a thousand splinters,
when young and old are abused and discarded.

The litany of lament grows loud and long:
the pulse of faith grows weak.

Why do you not act, mute God, in your justice?
How dare we name you as good any more?
We have entered deep darkness in the midst of the journey,
and the pilgrims are paralyzed, unable to move.

The litany of lament grows loud and long:
the pulse of faith grows weak.

Silence

Prayer

We receive no answers to our prayers, Silent God, and yet still we pray to you lest we despair. Justify your ways to us, and do not silence us, like Job, with power and grandeur. Convince us again of the invincible strength of vulnerable and crucified love, even when Golgotha and genocide seem worlds apart. Do not fail us in our extremity.

Seven

A reading from the Gospel according to John, chapter 16, verses 4b to 15

Psalm 52

Keep our eyes fixed on the truth,
the truth that will set us free.
Keep our eyes fixed on the truth,
the truth that will set us free.

So often the powerful ones of the world
seem to boast of their mischief and pride.
They trust in the abundance of wealth,
they take perverse delight in their greed.
They contrive destroying slanders:
their tongues cut sharp like a razor.
In love with evil they refuse the good:
telling lies, the truth is far from them.
They love words that harm and devour,
and every deceit of the tongue.

Keep our eyes fixed on the truth,
the truth that will set us free.

They step on one another as they climb to power,
they thrust the weak to the gutter;
seducing the gullible in the magic of words,
they trample the truth in pursuit of ambition.
O God, break them down utterly,
uproot them from the land of the living,
topple them from their babel of lies,
throw them down to the dust.

Keep our eyes fixed on the truth,
the truth that will set us free.

Yet so often we are the powerful,
if only with family and friends.
We wound with whispers of gossip,
mockery and scorn in our hearts,
bitterness souring our lips.
We have not trusted your goodness, O God,
our hearts have not been grateful.
We have not glorified your name,
neither by word nor by deed.

Keep our eyes fixed on the truth,
the truth that will set us free.

Too easy to call on God to destroy,
hard to be humbled by words that are true.
Even as we cry for the righting of wrongs,
for the destruction of those who harm others,
those who crush the weak and defenceless,
so do we know that revenge solves nothing,
annihilation reaping more violence still.

Keep our eyes fixed on the truth,
the truth that will set us free.

May your Spirit go deeper within us,
purging our hearts, burning the impure.
Hold at bay our murderous words.
May we strive with the angel of justice,
living the way of your truth and your Word,
our faces etched in the fierceness of Love.

Keep our eyes fixed on the truth,
the truth that will set us free.

Keep before us the vision of a life that is whole:
may we no longer grasp at material things.
Like a green tree may we spread out our branches,
to shield the passer-by from the heat,
offering the traveller refreshment and rest,
in quietness and confidence living for others,
people of truth and compassion,
oases of God in the most barren of lands.

Keep our eyes fixed on the truth,
the truth that will set us free.

Silence

Prayer

May our eyes turn to look again on you, O Christ. For you are the
Way, the Truth, and the Life. Give us courage always to be loyal
to the Truth, to follow wherever the Way may lead, costly though
it be, trusting that the goal is none other than Life with you.

Eight

*A reading from the Gospel according to John, chapter 16,
verses 16 to 33*

Psalm 143

Dissolving into the void,
disintegrating to dust,
I cry out in desperate need,
Deliver me from the fear of death.

My heart is open, I come without guile,
I dare to pray to a God who is faithful.
I cannot justify myself in your Presence;
with trembling I bring my desperate need.
I make no plea for justice,
I depend on your mercy and grace.

Dissolving into the void,
disintegrating to dust,
I cry out in desperate need,
Deliver me from the fear of death.

The devourer is crushing my bones,
the ravenous hounds knock me to the ground,
the unconscious dark overshadows me;
dumped in the ditch I am given up for dead.
My will to live grows faint within me,
my heart is appalled and terrified.
No longer does the stream flow through me:
my taste is of death, acrid and dry.

Dissolving into the void,
disintegrating to dust,
I cry out in desperate need,
Deliver me from the fear of death.

I cling to the memories of faith,
my heart once lifted in gratitude.
When I least expected your presence,
with the deepest joy you surprised me.
Let me be calm and reflect on your goodness,
on the innumerable gifts you have given me.

Dissolving into the void,
disintegrating to dust,
I cry out in desperate need,
Deliver me from the fear of death.

Trembling I stretch out my hands,
hungry for the food that sustains.
Without you I cannot but perish,
starved in the depths of my being.
Long have I believed you are with me,
however unaware I become.
Do not sever the threads that connect us,
lest I drift into space for ever.

Dissolving into the void,
disintegrating to dust,
I cry out in desperate need,
Deliver me from the fear of death.

Let me hear of your compassion and mercy,
rising with the warmth of the sun.
Show me the way I should travel,
your kindly Spirit giving me courage.
Deliver me from the shades of death;
for the sake of your name calm me.
Release the grip of the power of death,
disarm all those who oppress me.
May death and death-dealers have no meaning,
shrivelled to dust and transfigured to glory.

Dissolving into the void,
disintegrating to dust,
I cry out in desperate need,
Deliver me from the fear of death.

Silence

Prayer

Like the disciples of old, we are afraid of the power of the storm
that destroys and terrified of the power of the love that trans-
figures. May we hear again the accents of encouragement: Do
not be afraid, be of good courage, I am with you.

Nine

**A reading from the Gospel according to John, chapter 17,
verses 1 to 19**

Psalm 70

Hold to the God who is absent,
trust in the God who withdraws.
Hold to the God who is absent,
trust in the God who withdraws.

The ruthless seek to destroy,
they hurt beyond repair.
Gaunt and hollow-eyed,
their victims limp to the grave.

Hold to the God who is absent,
trust in the God who withdraws.

Refused even their dignity,
they have no voice of their own.
Their faces press to the window,
they slink starving away.

Hold to the God who is absent,
trust in the God who withdraws.

The cruel are oblivious:
surely they would be appalled
by a conscience revived,
by eyes that were opened.

Hold to the God who is absent,
trust in the God who withdraws.

The cries of the needy are drowned
by their baying taunts of mockery.
Blind to the needs of the weak,
they dismiss them as merely a number.

Hold to the God who is absent,
trust in the God who withdraws.

The needy cry to the heavens,
to the Eagle with piercing eye.
But the skies are empty and cold,
no deliverer descends in our day.

Is there a God of compassion?
Is there a God of justice?
Is there One yearning in love?
Is there a God who can save?

Hold to the God who is absent,
trust in the God who withdraws.

Why do you delay your appearing?
Why do you keep us nailed to our pain?
Why do you harden the hearts of the cruel?
Why is our sense of you slipping away?

Hold to the God who is absent,
trust in the God who withdraws.

Silence

Prayer

God, hard to believe in, bring us through dark nights of doubt to
the joy in which our ancestors danced your praise.

Ten

A reading from the Gospel according to John, chapter 17, verses 20 to 26

Psalm 133

May we be one in the exchanges of love,
in the look of the eyes between lover and loved.
May we be one in the exchanges of love,
in the look of the eyes between lover and loved.

At oases on the pilgrim way we rest together,
sharing the stories and meals that refresh us.
We remember we are called to be holy, not good,
to do what God requires, to delight in God's blessing.

May we be one in the exchanges of love,
in the look of the eyes between lover and loved.

Brothers and sisters, friends of God,
how joyful and pleasant a thing it is –
like the gathering of a mountain range –
when we dwell together in unity.

May we be one in the exchanges of love,
in the look of the eyes between lover and loved.

It is like a precious and fragrant oil,
like the dew of early morning,
or the scent of summer in the forest –
gifts beyond all expectation.

May we be one in the exchanges of love,
in the look of the eyes between lover and loved.

It is like the very beauty of holiness itself,
a sense of Presence in the places of prayer,
the Godward eyes of faithful people,
the times we are surprised by new blessings.

May we be one in the exchanges of love,
in the look of the eyes between lover and loved.

So we give you heartfelt thanks, O God,
that we can glimpse the harmony of humanity,
that we can trust that all creation will be restored,
that all things will be suffused with the light of your glory.

May we be one in the exchanges of love,
in the look of the eyes between lover and loved.

Silence

Prayer

May we hear your gracious invitation, O Triune God, to share
the hospitality of your table and the Dance of your Love, and so
respond to all that you have created for us to enjoy.

Eleven

**A reading from the Gospel according to Mark, chapter 14,
verses 26 to 72**

Psalm 88

There is drought in the depths of my being,
no rain, no water, no life.
There is drought in the depths of my being,
no rain, no water, no life.

The praise of your salvation, O God,
has died on lips that are parched.
The story of your wonders towards us
has turned hollow, bitter, and sour.
I doubt any prayer can enter your heart,
your ear is deaf to my cry.

There is drought in the depths of my being,
no rain, no water, no life.

Soul-deep I am full of troubles,
and my life draws near to the grave.
I totter on the edge of the abyss,
ghostly, ghastly, shrivelled.
I am like the wounded in war that stagger,
like a corpse strewn out on the battlefield.

There is drought in the depths of my being,
no rain, no water, no life.

I belong no more to my people,
I am cut off from your presence, O God.
You have put me in the lowest of dungeons,
in a pit of scurrying rats.
To a wall that drips with water I am chained,
my feet sink into mud.

There is drought in the depths of my being,
no rain, no water, no life.

I feel nothing but your pounding in my head,
surges of pain overwhelm me.
I cannot endure this suffering,
this furious onslaught, so searing.
I can remember no time without terror,
without turmoil and trouble of mind.

There is drought in the depths of my being,
no rain, no water, no life.

I have been dying since the day of my birth:
O God, have I ever really existed?
I have never known who I am,
and even my friends who once loved me,
who gave me some sense of belonging,
have drawn back in horror and left me.

There is drought in the depths of my being,
no rain, no water, no life.

My sight fails me because of my trouble;
there is no light in the place of deep dark.
I am alone, bewildered, and lost;
yet I cannot abandon you, O God.

Day after day I cry out to you,
early in the morning I pray in your absence.

There is drought in the depths of my being,
no rain, no water, no life.

Do you work wonders among the tombs?
Shall the dead rise up and praise you?
Will your loving kindness reach to the grave,
your faithfulness to the place of destruction?
Are the stories of old an illusion?
Will you again do what is right in the land?

There is drought in the depths of my being,
no rain, no water, no life.

Silence

Prayer

In times of despair, O God, rain showers of gentleness upon us,
that we may be kindly to one another and also to ourselves.
Renew in us the spirit of hope. Even in the depths of the darkness, may we hear the approach of the One who harrows hell and
greets even Judas with a kiss.

20

The Stations of the Cross

Sylvia Sands

First Station
Jesus is condemned to death

When the chief priests and other Jewish leaders made
their many accusations against him, Jesus remained silent.
"Don't you hear what they are saying?" Pilate demanded.
But Jesus said nothing.

> Silent.
> You were silent.
> Why didn't you speak up then?
>
> After all, you had enough to say
> in synagogues,
> up mountains,
> in the desert,
> by the lakeside –
> oh, and clearing the temple.
> Listen to your voice bouncing off the walls.
>
> I know your hands were bound,
> but why your tongue?
> God knows you'd have made a great lawyer,
> with your eloquence,
> your gift for dramatization.
>
> But there you stand,
> infuriatingly,
> frustratingly,
> heartbreakingly,
> silent.

Maybe the sound of those other voices
clamouring for vengeance
called you to say nothing.
For bigotry shouts but never listens.
And any of us who has been oppressed
knows the feeling of not being heard.

Perhaps that's why,
in the face of prejudice,
dole queues,
prisoners,
refugees,
abused children,
the starving,
homosexuals,
most women,
and a beat-up, tied-up Christ
(in the face of prejudice)
are largely
silent.

So,
silence
is not always compromise.

Teach us to know when words are superfluous,
a sheer waste of time.

And help us to hold in our hearts
the dignity,
the courage,
the creative energy,
the wisdom,
of the silence falling across the world
at the first station of the cross.

Second Station
Jesus takes up his cross

Pilate gave Jesus to them to be crucified, and he was taken
out of the city carrying his cross to the place known as
Golgotha.

I can't help remembering
that you were a carpenter,
and that you had lived by wood and nails.
Now you were to die by them.

I live in Belfast,
where words, like nail bombs, fly about.
"You cannot avoid the bullet
with your name on it."
So they say.

Well, this was your cross,
soon to have your name on it,
hammered as firmly as your hands and feet.

You stooped and took it up willingly,
that familiar piece of wood,
and swinging it on to your carpenter's back
you began to climb that hill.

In Nazareth
perhaps you had made doors,
yokes for oxen,
farmers' ploughs,
bowls, beams, pegs,
legendary little toys
that flew out of just such a piece of wood.

But nothing you made then
could equal what you fashioned
out of wood and nails on Golgotha,
our artisan, our working man,
our brother, our carpenter,
our Christ.

Third Station
Jesus falls for the first time

On the road to Calvary, sometimes called the Via
Dolorosa, the Way of Sorrows, tradition tells us that Jesus
fell three times.

Eat dirt.

We all like to see the mighty fallen.
Here's God in the dust…

Except…
crumpled and tumbled beneath his cross
he resembles nothing so much as
a child.

Grown-ups don't fall down, do they?
Well, not often.
Not unless they're
drunk, crippled, down and out,
mugged, starved, queer-bashed,
frail, raped, stoned,
or plain suicidal.

He's there in all those of course.

Dear Jesus of the gutter,
Friend to all humankind,
I cannot forget it was Roman feet you saw,
ready to kick you onwards…

Just as later,
your sisters and brothers
would see jackboots in Auschwitz.

So it is hard to watch you squirm,
debased, degraded, filthy,
beneath your cross.

But where and how else could we understand
your solidarity with the dispossessed?

Fourth Station
Jesus meets his mother

One of the most poignant features of the story of Calvary is the presence of Mary the mother of Jesus, following her son to the very end.

Did he ever say,
"Oh mother, don't fuss!"?

I have two sons,
one of them into music and motorbikes,
the other an idealist,
into universal sister- and brotherhood,
like this young man.

When one of them goes for burnout,
and the other sleeps under bridges,
I'd rather not know until afterwards,
thank you.

I lose my breath looking at this mother,
walking in blue
to meet her son in crimson.

Mary of the Magnificat,
strong, political,
autonomous, independent
woman:
I'm glad that later,
at the dying,
you were still there
(still there!)...

so that all the world,
all the world
could hear your son saying,

She
is your mother.

Fifth Station
Simon helps to carry the cross

"They led Jesus away to crucify him, and they enlisted a
passer-by, Simon of Cyrene, who was coming in from the
country, to carry his cross."

This will sound like poetic licence,
but it's happened.

The boy – sixteen-ish – greeted me at the church door.
His limbs flailed and his head jerked;
on his face he wore the beatific smile
of someone sure of being loved.
"Hallo!" he said,
as if I were a familiar friend
instead of a stranger in the parish.

"Multiply handicapped"
I noted professionally,
but unprofessionally smiled and chatted.
It's hard to resist innocent love
in the Limestone Road, Belfast.

Later in the church, empty but for me,
he came in noisily joyful with his father,
who showed him, helped him, painstakingly,
to light a candle.

They passed,
brushed by me
as I meditated on the fifth station of the cross.
The boy, smiling yet, said,
"Still here?
Don't get tired, now; don't get tired."

His father, grey-haired, ashen-faced,
met my eyes solemnly, with a kind of gratitude,
and followed the boy, three paces behind,
with a terrible weariness,
out of the church into the world.

Sixth Station
Veronica wipes the face of Jesus

Tradition has it that as Jesus climbed towards Golgotha,
he was met by a woman named Veronica, who broke
through the crowd to wipe his ravaged face with a linen
cloth. Forever after, it is said, the face of Jesus remained
imprinted on her square of linen.

Who was she then, this Veronica?
People get uptight about her,
cynical, superior, or plain sentimental.

But they would, wouldn't they?
Standard feelings for a woman doing a dirty job:
after all, earlier,
a woman had washed his feet and got short shrift.
I love her.
God knows,
in his time Jesus had wiped away
tears, sweat, blood, and mucus enough.
Running along the Via Dolorosa
she saw it was his turn now.

Breaking through the embarrassment, the hostility,
the convention, the violence,
she held up everything in the universe
for one small moment,
and wiped the face of God.

It left an impression.
It left an impression lasting a lifetime.
This is what he looks like, she would say,
holding up her precious cloth.

Only if we reach out and touch
the tears, sweat, blood, and mucus of some fallen Jesus
on a twisting, latter-day Via Dolorosa,
only then can we say with Veronica,
This, this is what he looks like.

Seventh Station
Jesus falls for the second time

On the Via Dolorosa Jesus falls for the second time.

So much for Veronica wiping his face,
so much for Simon of Cyrene giving him a hand,
so much for his mother's courage.

Not enough.

We've all been there,
at one time or another.

Aspirin for migraine,
Patience Strong at funerals,
pethidine in childbirth,
tranquillizers in the locked ward,
redundancy pay,
Eventide Homes,
plenty more fish in the sea,
the DHSS,
"Come back tomorrow,"
morphine in the bone.

Not enough.

Two agonies then.
His,
grit between the teeth,
ground down into the muck again.

Theirs,
watching,
knowing nothing,
nothing is enough.

Sometimes –
God knows –
that is what it is to be human.

Eighth Station
Jesus consoles the women of Jerusalem

"Large numbers of women followed him, who mourned and lamented. But Jesus turned to them and said, 'Daughters of Jerusalem, do not weep for me but for yourselves.'"

You have been so silent,
and now you speak – to women.

Women who are crying over a man.

I'm tempted to say, What's new?

This particular man, that's what.

This particular man who in one short lifetime
carved out a tradition of taking women seriously,
listening to them, learning from them, emulating them.

Who taught him to wash feet if not Mary his mother?
And a passionate, flame-filled Magadalene?

On the Via Dolorosa he stops,
expends energy he needs for dying on women in tears.
Don't cry for me, but for yourselves.

Sometimes, sisters,
when you look at his concern, respect, empathy,
friendship, time, deep love, tenderness,
calling for women,
and you realize
what the patriarchs of the churches ask of us –
tea, flowers, and brass polishing –
sometimes, in all honesty,
it is enough to make you weep.

Ninth Station
Jesus falls for the third time

For the third time Jesus falls beneath the weight of the
cross.

We would have interviewed you about this.
Our cameras would have zoomed in
on the terrible detail of your exhaustion.
Some bright whizz-kid reporter would have asked,
But what does it *feel* like to keep falling?

Safe in our parlours
we would have eaten pork chops
to your answer.

From somewhere within the kaleidoscope of
red blood,
black road,
blinding white agony,
you found a new purchase for your feet,
a new position for the cross on your back,
and an old familiar wilderness strength
to get up
and keep on climbing.

Follow me,
you said,
along the lonely road.

Tenth Station
Jesus is stripped of his clothes

Before Jesus was crucified he was stripped of his clothes.
"And the soldiers gambled for his clothing, throwing dice
for each piece."

Women in childbirth,
the terminally ill,
little children in pornographic magazines:
the naked are vulnerable.

Still,
I do not think you were ashamed
of your nakedness.

Only in the jaundiced eyes of
the scribes, the lawyers,
the pharisees, the fickle crowd,
and the latter day Festival of Lighters,
were you rendered objectionable.

As those hardened soldiers
tore off your clothes
for just another execution,
perhaps you remembered Mary,
the sunlight of childhood
etching your prophet's feet,
sawdust between your toes,
while she, laughing gently,
peeled off your tunic for bath-time.

No shame there either,
just the last occasion
someone helped you undress.
That's all.

For the last battle on our behalf,
stripped of everything that might hinder,
you prepare to fight, our splendid, naked warrior,
CHRIST.

Eleventh Station
Jesus is nailed to the cross

"They brought Jesus to the place called Golgotha, and
there they crucified him."

Someone, somewhere,
thought it up, this method of execution.

Was it one man? Or the chairman?
(I choose the word carefully, sisters.)
The chairman of some efficient Roman board?

Oak or ash, sycamore or pine,
beech or elm or lime,
what wood was it, his cross?

Those naturalist's eyes
would have remembered the leaves,
those carpenter's hands felt
the warp and woof of the bark.

He knew the tree –
and the seed from which it grew.

Maybe the very worst thing
at this screaming moment
was not the shuddering physical agony,
but the chilling winter knowledge
that somewhere, at some time,
one of his brothers,
running amok down the dark corridors of imagination
with brilliant, twisted ingenuity,
had thought up this idea of slaughter,
leaving him pinned like a broken butterfly
to a piece of wood, which once,
wind sighing through the filigree of its branches,
had been a living tree.

Twelfth Station
Jesus dies on the cross

"Jesus cried with a loud voice, 'My God, my God, why
have you forsaken me?' "

Three hours of darkness,
and oh, I recognize it,
dwelling deeply, dwelling deeply, in me.

I say, along with millions,
I am his follower.
But sometimes I'd rather kill the Christ
dwelling deeply, dwelling deeply, within me.

Love that wills to this length,
and breadth, and height, and depth
of twisted agony,
still forgiving,
is what I claim to follow.

So don't blame me
if sometimes I'd rather be Barabbas.

Thank God
eyes can become accustomed to the darkness
and catch glimpses of colour.

Blue of his mother's robe,
John, like a slim white sword,
scarlet Magdalene
clinging on to her adoration:
three at the foot of his Cross,
colours in the darkness.

Colours in the darkness saying,
Stand,
at least try and stand
for solidarity with such reckless love...

Thirteenth Station
Jesus is handed to his mother

Joseph of Arimathea, an honoured member of the Jewish
supreme court, gathered his courage and went to Pilate
and asked for the body of Jesus.

Joseph of Arimathea begged for this body.
I think he was caught up
in the 'if only' of bereavement.
If only I had spoken this word,
performed that act of kindness,
listened more seriously to those words,
whistled up more courage while he lived,
walked that extra mile.

Joseph of Arimathea had been a most discreet disciple,
saying not No or Yes to Jesus, but Maybe.
And now he turns up trumps:
after all, someone has to be practical in violent death.
Someone has to climb the ladder of that cross,
and prise Christ down for us.

Anyway, she needed to hold him, his mother.
She had said Yes in spring time,
and given birth to God.
She had said Yes in high summer,
and let him go about his Father's business.
She had said Yes in autumnal festive Cana,
and given birth to joyous sparkling miracles.

Now, as she cradles that gallant head again,
gathers up those limbs
that brought swift peace on the mountains,
now, as Joseph of Arimathea
hands her this Body, this Blood,
I think, just once,
with all of us who have knelt ice cold
before our beloved dead,
she says, Oh, dear God, oh, dear God,
No.

Fourteenth Station
Jesus is laid in the tomb

Joseph brought a long sheet of linen cloth and, taking Jesus's body down from the cross, wound it in the cloth, and laid it in a rock hewn tomb.

> Creation takes him to her heart
> and wraps rock-green darkness
> around his tortured limbs.
>
> The hidden walls
> sweat with anticipation,
> while little animals
> that live beneath the earth
> wait.
>
> Animals had watched
> his lonely cattle-shed birth.
> Now they keep vigil at his wake,
> knowing,
> with the rocks and ferns,
> with underground streams,
> with lichens and tree roots,
> knowing,
> these (dumb?) animals,
> more than
> Peter, James, and John,
> *knowing*,
> waiting,
> these little listening animals,
> for the first tremors
> heralding the earthquake
> of his resurrection...

21

The Silence of the Lamb

Martyn Percy

A dead sheep is not a very promising symbol for a new religious movement. Yet from very early days Christians have proclaimed the Lamb who was slain who has taken away the sin of the world. The image is problematic in today's world for a number of reasons. Very few people have witnessed the slaughter of a lamb, let alone a sacrifice. The image of a dead sheep for modern Britain is more likely to conjure up a sad sight on a moorland ramble, or a cull resulting from foot-and-mouth disease, or even one of Damien Hirst's animals pickled in formaldehyde. How can a dead sheep *do* anything?

Christian tradition and imagery also proclaim Jesus as the great shepherd of the sheep. Stained glass windows and paintings show a Jesus of muscular intensity, with piercing eyes and a kind smile. On his shoulders he carries a sheep: the one who has been lost has been found. It is the parable of the lost sheep, it is the triumph of salvation: I was lost, but now I am found. Jesus is certainly not passive in this picture: he is an active seeker, searching for those in distress or danger.

Yet the stories of his death convert the shepherd into one of the flock. Jesus becomes a victim, one statistic among numberless people butchered by an autocratic state. His is simply a routine execution, something to be started and finished, and then we can go home. He was led like a lamb to the slaughter.

A religion that takes a shepherd and turns him into a sheep makes a deliberate conflation. In portraying Jesus as the Saviour Christianity reaches back to the Jewish tradition of the Passover, of scapegoating, of the paschal lamb. Here, in this death, and by the shedding of this blood, God will redeem his people. To be the victor, you have first to be the victim.

Fittingly, the image of Jesus as a lamb pervades its central act of worship, the Eucharist. The sacrament centres on a meal and give thanks for the Lamb of God who not only takes away the sin of the world, but will one day call us all to a feast.

But there is more to the slain sheep than this. First, the metaphor reflects an unusual kind of passivity. This sheep is sacrificed – it cannot answer back. The silence of the lamb is perhaps more significant than the words that the various versions of the crucifixion have coming from the mouth of Jesus. In the silence he absorbs the pain and the hatred that is visited upon him. The hurt and the violence will not be passed on. And although this may appear passive, such a process is strenuous and costly. In the way that Jesus endures the crucifixion a chain of consequences is broken, and the truth of forgiveness is made real.

Second, early medieval thought came to interpret the blood and the wounds as themselves being of saving power. The blood of Jesus is nourishing, and to feed off it is to participate in the abundant life of God, in which we can truly live for one another. To drink of it, to be covered by it, to be washed in it, symbolized not only purification, but also an intensification of life, in which God was believed to have met and absorbed the pain, violence, and sickness of the world. The blood is central to medieval mysticism, shrines, and devotion.

Third, more than one of those last words from the cross are concerned not with protesting innocence but with forgiveness. Jesus seems to be powerfully aware that his executioners really *do not* know what they are doing. They are ignorant instruments in a system where this kind of death is a familiar event. So, by extension, our sins of ignorance are absolved as well as those conscious sins which, once admitted as did the penitent thief, brings us to paradise.

We are not drawn to the corpses of animals. We pass a dead sheep by on the other side of the footpath. We are repelled rather than fascinated. It is a paradox indeed to place a slain lamb at the heart of the silence and darkness of Good Friday.

Studdert Kennedy captured it well in his poem 'Indifference', written in 1947:

> When Jesus came to Birmingham they simply passed him by,
> They never hurt a hair of him, they simply let him die;
> For men had grown more tender, and they would not give him
>   pain,
> They only just passed down the street, they left him in the rain.
>
> Still Jesus cried, "Forgive them, for they know not what they do,"
> And still it rained the wintry rain that drenched them through
>   and through;
> The crowds went home and left the streets without a soul to see,
> And Jesus crouched against a wall and cried for Calvary.

It was W. H. Auden who observed that "through art we are able to break bread with the dead...and without communion with the dead, a fully human life is impossible." So religion, as well as art, and especially in the Eucharist, invite a particular kind of attentive memory. The image of the slain lamb bids us not forgive and forget, but remember and forgive. This is what we are challenged to do for our neighbours, even those we are at war with. For Christ, first of all, has done that for us.

22

The Shadow of the Crucifix

Rowan Williams

It has taken the post-Freudian suspiciousness of our century to point out the different kinds of ambiguity, the shadows, around the central Christian symbol of the crucifix. We can understand a bit more clearly how such an image of suffering patiently endured can work to produce guilt – "I did this, and yet he loves me" – or passivity – "Jesus endured injustice and pain without complaint: so must I." We might also notice how the crucifix can be a weapon: I identify my (or our) suffering with Christ's, and so endow it with more sanctity and significance than anyone else's: martyrdom can be turned into a not-so-subtle kind of aggression by the spiritually ambitious (something even the early Church noticed). And, most insidious of all, perhaps, there is the scent of something faintly pornographic in some kinds of concentration on this image, a naked man being tortured to death: what does it do to our souls to be confronted by this, day in and day out? We may become desensitized to it, not noticing what it is an image of – which does us no good. Or we may find different ways of doubtful satisfaction in contemplating a suffering body. Either way, what is happening does not speak all that clearly of the absolution and renewal that Good Friday is supposed to be about.

The problem is in the difference between suffering and death. Images of suffering, of pain and terror, are all too completely woven into the fabric of what we are and what our world is like. Our reaction to them in ordinary settings has just the same level of muddled feeling as I have been describing in relation to the crucifix: guilt, despairing resignation, questions as to how an image can be used to good political advantage, and the flicker of prurient fascination. Such images are dreadful but familiar; we have strategies for managing them. But death is something other than this, and true images of death are rare, because it is not easy to find an image of absence, ending, the breaking and dissolution of the world.

Good Friday is importantly about death, not simply about an intense and dramatic suffering. The redemption Christians celebrate is not achieved by the fact that Jesus did or did not suffer more horrifically and deeply than anyone else. How could we know? How could we maintain this in the light of the repeated nightmares of the last hundred years? No, it is achieved by his death. Here, we say, is God's embodiment in a human life, promising welcome for the lost and renewal for humanity; and here are the systems of human meaning and power, religious, social, national, political, combining to destroy him. Good Friday presents us with a stark duality – human power revealed as hostile to meaning and hope, and divine meaning and hope exposed as completely vulnerable to human power. Death: our systems revealed as empty, God revealed as helpless. All images of a unified world go into the dark.

St John of the Cross, in the sixteenth century, wrote that Jesus achieved more in his motionless silence, dead on the cross, than in the whole of his ministry. Before this collision of God's truth and the world's reality, represented by the dead body of the incarnate God, all we can do is keep silent. But, for John of the Cross, as for all Christians, that silence is the beginning of a global renewal. It is the darkness in which God is allowed to be God, in which the world, descending into its inner chaos, returns to the very moment of creation, when God speaks into the darkness. Our silence, our acceptance of the death of the creation in the death of Jesus, makes room for the word that recreates the broken world.

The more we surround this with the fascinating and dangerous emotional freight of suffering considered in itself, the further away goes the silence. Strangely enough, on Good Friday, of all days, the crucifix may be the least adequate sign of what is happening. And what are the images we need? Who is to say?

Confusion is itself an apt response to this. But there is the empty cross, there is the stripped church in which no sacrament is celebrated today, there are the few really persuasive representations of the dead Christ (Holbein, the Gero crucifix in Cologne), and, above all, there is our own stillness, learning to look death in the face.

23

Seven Words

Sylvia Sands

The First Word
The Soldier

Father, forgive them; they do not know what they are
doing.

I'm a soldier.
So I try not to listen when I hammer in the nails.
I try not to listen to what the condemned man may say.
Otherwise you lose your beauty sleep.

"Father, forgive them;
they do not know what they are doing."

I've heard curses and threats and brave defiance,
but never, never, as the hammer swung, concern for me.

At least that's what it seemed
as I was shocked into meeting his eyes,
the hammer heavy and stilled in my hand
for one dreadful, ice-cold moment.

Through the blood and thorns and nails
his eyes met mine with tenderness.
Suddenly I wanted my mother and my wife
and my gentle daughter
to cradle my head in their laps
and hide me, hide me, from this man's gaze.
And here I am, throwing dice,
with his words hammering,
hammering in my head,
hammering, hammering in my heart,
like nails of love and forgiveness, and tenderness,
piercing me, piercing me,
for all eternity.

The Second Word
The Mother

Seeing his mother and the disciple he loved standing near her, Jesus said to her, "Woman, this is your son." Then to the disciple he said, "This is your mother." From that moment the disciple made a place for her in his home.

People are kind.
Come away, they cry.
No need to put yourself through this.
He'll understand.

But I am his mother,
and though nails pierce his body,
and a sword sunders my soul,
I must stand with him,
I must stand by him,
I must stand up in this his hour of dying.

And yet, and yet,
there's more at stake than that.

From somewhere within
this horror of great darkness,
Gabriel-haunted still,
I dream dreams, hear voices, see visions.
I see others.

Mothers, sons, brothers, daughters,
sisters, fathers, friends, lovers,
a vast army who will not turn away;
clad in the armour of fidelity
and hollow-eyed courage,
they will stand by,
stand with,
stand up,
in those slow, dimming,
dove-grey hours of dying...

The Third Word
The Thief

Today you shall be with me in Paradise.

A gibbet is a strange place
to begin to hope,
but this man dying with me,
caring for his executioners,
caring for his mother,
caring for his friend,
this man gives hope.

A gibbet is a strange place
to find faith,
but this man sarcastically labelled
The King of the Jews,
dying regally,
dying purposefully,
dying with me,
this man inspires faith.

A gibbet is a strange place
to feel loved,
but this man dying with me,
promising Paradise,
promising Paradise
from a place of integrity and agony,
this man,
as sure as I'm dying,
will not stop loving even me.

The Fourth Word
The Mother

I thirst.

Always – he was always thirsty.

In the star-filled stable
surrounded by the milk of human kindness
he drank deep.

In the howling, beast-filled wilderness,
finding streams in the desert,
always he was thirsty.

Thirsty for joy and laughter,
and wedding jokes,
tricks of turning water into wine,
throwing his head back, laughing.

Always he was thirsty.

Thirsty for friendship
from fishermen and freedom fighters,
from tax collectors and harlots,
from rich young men and serious young women,
from children,
and from beggars at the roadside.

Always he was thirsty.
And now his thirst fills the whole world,
and waters its broken heart, slowly, slowly,
with nothing but his own red blood.

While I, his mother,
hearing a child's cry in the night,
Mummy, I'm thirsty,
cannot move, cannot reach his lips,
cannot change the wine into water,
but am rooted, rooted helpless to the rock.

The Fifth Word
Mary of Magdala

My God, my God, why have you abandoned me?

I have been waiting
(remembering all the little demons
peeping out from behind my eyes),
I have been waiting
to hear him speak my name,
Mary,
Mary of Magdala.

My God, my God why have you abandoned me?
Now I know he will not,
will not speak my name.
For this God-forsaken cry
is specially for me,
standing God-forsaken
at the foot of his cross.

When did he and I
need things spelt out between us?

So I know this worst cry in all the world,
is for me.

For I am not calm, like his mother,
or comforted, like that thief,
or trembling on the brink of faith,
with that blood-stained centurion,
or purposeful, like John.

Oh no.

I stand
in the utter black-flamed darkness of despair –
but closer, closer than them all,
to his broken, God-forsaken heart.

The Sixth Word
The Disciple

It is accomplished!

What are the words behind the words?

We vied among ourselves
to understand him,
I, John,
and Peter,
and James.

But I cannot lay my head on his breast now,
and ask him gently,
What are the words behind the words?

Here in the darkness,
I grope to see
the mountain he has climbed above Calvary,
the miles walked by his paralyzed feet,
the peace won by his violent wounds,
the wisdom and dignity gained in thorn-filled contempt;
the millions already sheltered in his outstretched arms.

Here in the darkness,
I, John, am praying,
Oh, what are the words behind the words
on Calvary?

The Seventh Word
The Soldier

Father, into your hands I commit my spirit.

I am not easily impressed –
and I *have* seen men die with courage before.

But in these last hours,
it has seemed as if the whole world
has been pivoting around this central cross,
and turned completely upside down.

Thieves have spoken with the voices of children;
the learned have been transformed into mere fools;
women have stood resolutely upright like warriors;
violent men like me have sunk gently to their knees.

He who should be powerless,
pinned to his cross,
has taken control,
has taken heaven by storm,
has taken my breath away
in his final trustful prayer.

And I,
on my knees in the dust,
am forced to say,
rejoice to say,

This man was son of god,
this man was prince of peace.

24

Seven Good Friday Addresses

W. H. Vanstone

I

On this unique occasion of the year, at this Good Friday watch of attention and thought and prayer to which loyalty calls us, I have sometimes heard from the preacher the suggestion that we should imagine ourselves gathered on Calvary at the foot of the Cross: gathered there close at hand and closely attentive while an indifferent world passes by, gathered there receptive of whatever last words may fall from our Saviour's lips, and reflective on the meaning of those words for our own personal lives. Often I have been asked to imagine myself as close to the Cross as I might be to the bedside of a dying friend, and as eager to catch every hint and nuance in our Saviour's words as I should be to understand the last weak whispers of my friend.

But I have never found it easy or even possible to place myself, even in imagination, so close to the Cross or associate myself so intimately with the Crucified. Always, even on Good Friday, I seem to see the Cross a long way off, at such a great distance that is is visible from where I stand only because in itself it is so huge and towers so high. It reaches me not because in imagination or will I can bring myself close to it, but because it is itself so powerful that the sight of what it is, and the sound of what it means, can come even to me. A Passiontide hymn begins with the words, "Lord Jesus, when we stand *afar* and gaze upon thy holy Cross." I think that even on Good Friday, even in this place, it is *from afar* that we gaze upon the holy Cross.

We see the Cross from afar because, in the first place, the actual event – a crucifixion – is so strange to us, so wholly alien to our experience. Once, on the eve of Good Friday, I had to visit the grim prison called Strangeways in Manchester. The area close to it was heavily bombed during the war, and as I walked through it I saw nothing but ash and rubble, dust and waste paper stirred by the bitter March wind, broken beds and window frames, and derelict cars cast aside to rot, and here and there, crouching among them to shield themselves a little from the wind, broken men – grey men, derelict men, down and outs, alcoholics, meths drinkers. It suddenly occurred to me that Calvary must have been like this. Surely it was not a green hill outside the walls of Jerusalem that was used for crucifixion. Surely it was a place more like a rubbish dump, a grim place where unwanted things were cast aside, including unwanted lives. This kind of place is unfamiliar to me, save for a passing glance: it is alien to my experience. Still more alien is what was done in that world's end of a place. I do not know what it would be like to see men crucified alive. I cannot believe that my nerves would stand it. I certainly cannot imagine myself coming close to one of the crucified in quiet and thoughtful receptivity.

The second reason why I can see the Cross only from afar is that the Gospel writers themselves do not really help us to see it from close at hand. We must remember that, before ever they wrote their accounts of the crucifixion, they were deeply aware that one of the crucified three was the Son of God: and this awareness imparts to their accounts an awe-filled reticence. They make no comments of their own: they offer no speculations on the thoughts and feelings of those who were present, least of all on the thoughts and feelings of Jesus. They report with controlled objectivity what was done to Jesus: they mention briefly certain things that He was heard to say. They use no metaphors to make the scene vivid and no emotive words to stir the reader's feelings. It is as if the whole event is too huge for them, and they cope with it only by confining themselves to the basic factuality of certain things that happened. St Mark writes at one point: "They gave Him wine to drink mingled with myrrh: but He did not take it." He does not say by whom the wine was given or for what purpose, and he does not say whether Jesus could not take it or would not take it, or why He could not or would not. He tells just the bare fact. This is how most people write or speak when they are telling of something of awesome significance: they distance themselves from it and write with a kind of clinical objectivity.

So the Gospel writers do not help or encourage us to feel ourselves close to the Cross of Jesus: if anything they bid us keep our distance. Certainly it is from a distance that I shall and must speak this afternoon – a distance created in part by my inability even to imagine myself in that world's end of a place where they crucified him alive, created in part by the bare objectivity of what is told in the Gospels, created most of all, as it must be for all Christians, by a sense of the enormous significance, for all mankind and to the end of time, of the sequence of events which reached its climax on Crucifixion hill.

There is an old Saxon poem, 'The Dream of the Rood', in which the poet tells of a dream in which he was spoken to by the Cross, or rather by the wood which was cut from a tree and made into the Cross. The wood tells its story to the dreamer, and the climax of the story is of course the day when the wood, trembling, bears upon itself and raises from the earth the weight of the Son of God. The final words of the story are these: "So now I tower high and mighty under the skies having power to heal all who will bow before me." "High and mighty under the skies"…"having power"…and requiring of those who would be healed that they should first bow their heads, bow themselves to the ground. This is why the Cross reaches us and affects us, not because we are close to it and intimate with it, but because it towers so very high and is so very powerful.

Let us then think of ourselves today as standing at a distance from the Cross and seeing it across the intervening centuries, and all the change and waste and suffering and sin that those centuries have brought. As the hymn so familiar on Remembrance Sunday puts it, "Still stands the Cross from that dread hour to this, Like some bright star above the dark abyss." It reaches us only because, like the light of a star, it is in itself so very powerful. If we know ourselves to be standing at a distance, and seeing from a distance, we are likely to avoid that dangerous temptation which Good Friday can bring to the faithful – the temptation to feel possessive about the crucified Jesus, to appropriate Him, as it were, to ourselves alone and to think of the inattentive and seemingly indifferent world as excluded from the relevance of the Cross and beyond the range of its meaning. Once on Good Friday I attended this service at a church just off Times Square in New York, and as I walked through the square at noon I passed through the noisy pulsating centre of the vivid and infinitely varied life of the great city. The church itself was quiet and rather dark, and the preacher spoke with a noticeably gentle and gracious voice. The contrast between the inside of the church and what was going on outside was very marked. The sad thing was that nothing that was said inside seemed to have anything whatever to do with what was going on outside. It seemed that the Cross was thought of as the possession of the few rather than the salvation of the many, the salvation of all.

II

The sign of the Cross reaches us and affects us only because it is in itself a very powerful sign. How powerful it has been in the past is familiar to us from history books and literature and legend. One thinks of the Emperor Constantine fortified on the eve of the decisive battle of his life by the dream or vision of a cross blazoned across the night sky and the words around it: "In this sign you shall conquer;" or of Joan of Arc strengthened in the flames by the cross which her chaplain plaited of straw and held before her anguished eyes; of Christian, in *Pilgrim's Progress*, making his way to a cross on a hill top and when he reaches it finding that the burden of his sin is suddenly released from his back and tumbles away to the foot of the hill; of the great Offa who became St Christopher, eager to serve the world's most powerful prince, giving himself for a while to the service of the Devil, until one day he observes that, as the two of them pass a wayside crucifix, the Devil trembles, and then Offa realizes that there is a prince in the world more powerful than the Devil and transfers his allegiance to the Crucified.

In the past, in what we call the ages of faith, the sign of the Cross has been a very powerful sign. But perhaps we are inclined to believe that its power has been lost now or is effective only upon the faithful. I do not think that this is entirely true. Still in our own day, and upon people who neither exhibit nor claim any particular degree of Christian conviction or allegiance, the sign of the Cross may make a very powerful impact, especially when it is encountered unexpectedly or in an unfamiliar form or at a critical time.

I should like to tell two stories from my own experience. One concerns a young soldier, a member of the parachute regiment, Kenneth by name, aged 23, married and with a small daughter. In the autumn of 1970 he fell ill, with much pain, and it was discovered he had developed a cancer which was beyond the range of surgery or any kind of therapy. He was told of his condition and he asked that he might be moved from the army hospital and brought to his home to be nursed for as long as possible by his wife. The Army agreed, and also supplied a trained nurse to stay at his home, to help his wife and in particular to give the three-hourly injections of morphine which by now were necessary.

Kenneth was brought home about Christmas, and his home was in my parish, but so far were he and his family from any connection with any church that it was the beginning of Lent before we heard anything of his illness. By then he was very ill, lying flat on his back and scarcely able to speak. It did not seem right to offer the challenge or even the comfort of religion to someone who literally could not answer back; so my colleague and I used simply to call most days and sit by his bed and smile, and say a few friendly things. We used to notice that half an hour before each injection was due the sweat of agony would appear on his face, and his eyes would turn to the clock on the wall as he watched the minutes pass ever so slowly towards the time of his next relief.

When I called on the evening of Palm Sunday I had a palm cross in my pocket. Kenneth could not speak at all by then, but I still did not want to impose on him any word or action to which he could not of his own will assent. So I simply showed him the cross and told him that we had each received one in church that morning. "This one is mine," I said, "but if by any chance you would like to have it in your house I can easily get another for myself. If you'd like it just nod your head will you, Ken." He did not nod his head, but very slowly and painfully he raised both his hands towards the cross...and took it...and equally slowly and painfully and carefully placed it in his pyjama pocket. Thereafter we noticed that when each half-hour of agony began he would move his right hand slowly across his body and take hold of his cross.

When I called on the night of Good Friday, I happened to go first into the kitchen to have a cup of tea with his wife. "We've had such a strange day," she said. "All this morning he was restless. I couldn't get him to settle. He kept moving his right hand as if he was trying to push something away. I was so worried because I couldn't make out what was troubling him. Then at last I realized that the nurse changed his pyjamas this morning and she had forgotten to put his cross back in the pocket. I fetched it for him, and since then he's been, well, you'll see for yourself how he is." We went into the front room where Kenneth was. He was lying perfectly still and peaceful, with his right hand across his body holding his cross. And so he remained until he died on the morning of Easter Monday.

I do not know exactly what the Cross meant to that young soldier. But we must not say that, because he was not a devout practising Christian, it could mean little or nothing to him. Whatever it did mean to him, it did so powerfully – so powerfully that it was worth holding his cross when other comforts, including the comfort of morphine, failed and fled.

The second story comes from the same parish. The vicarage there stood at the top of a hill and had a blank gable wall which was visible over a wide area of the parish. One year, as Passiontide approached, we decided to fix to that wall a large cross painted a vivid white, and to illuminate it at night with flood-lights. We erected it on the day before Palm Sunday, and when darkness fell and the floodlights were on I walked to the bottom of the hill to see how it looked. It was rather impressive: against the dark background of the wall the cross seemed almost to be suspended in mid air and to glow with its own light. It was still early in the evening, before people were going out for the night's pleasure or business. So the streets were quite quiet, and I stood for several minutes looking at the cross, wondering what people might make of it, wondering if they would give it more than a passing glance.

As I stood there, a man came out of a side street in front of me and turned to go up the hill. He was silhouetted against the light, and I recognized him as a neighbour, a middle-aged labourer with the water board who spent most of his working days in ditches, most of his evenings in the pubs, and no time at all in any church. As he turned towards the cross at the top of the hill, he stopped. In itself that was not surprising: the appearance of the cross, as I say, was rather striking and he could not have seen it before. Anyone might have stopped. But then this man took his cap off and, very slowly, began to walk forward again. He walked right up to the top of the road, stepped on to the grass at the side of the vicarage, walked right across it until he was almost at the foot of the cross, and then knelt down, and I saw his kneeling figure just caught within the aureole of light. A few minutes later, when I followed him up the road and went into the vicarage, he was still kneeling there.

I never told Bert Johnson that I had seen what he did on that night. It would have been unkind to do so. Still less did I ask him why he did it: that would have been impertinence. So I do not know what the Cross meant to this rough, hard-living man when he encountered it so unexpectedly. But we must not say that, be-cause he lived as he did, it can have meant little or nothing to him. Whatever it did mean to him, it did so powerfully, power-fully enough to make him behave for a little while in a most uncharacteristic way, with a kind of ancient piety.

Incidents like these remind us that we must not think of the Cross as our Cross only, the exclusive possession of convinced and committed Christians. We must not suppose that outside the fold of the Church the Cross is just two pieces of wood, vaguely associated perhaps with Jesus but without power and without meaning. Still today, especially when it is encountered unexpectedly at a critical time, it speaks to many people far outside the Church. It speaks even to those who do not tell, perhaps *could* not tell, what it says. Let us remember in our prayers now those many who have stayed far outside the range and ambit of the Church but are still within the range and power of the Cross, those many to whom the Cross still has meaning, those many to whom, as well as to ourselves, the Cross of Jesus still belongs.

III

I was speaking just now of two men, a soldier and a middle-aged labourer, to whom the sign of the Cross meant more than one would have expected. But now an incident of a directly opposite kind. Shortly after the War I helped for a few weeks with a project for the assistance of people who came out from London in the late summer to pick hops in Kent. The conditions in which the hop pickers then had to live were pretty primitive, and a small Christian organization used to set up little centres where certain simple facilities were available, such as fresh milk for babies, and transport for emergency use, and first-aid treatment for small injuries. The first-aid centre where I worked was a bell tent, and to the pole of it someone had attached a small but – to say the truth – rather lurid crucifix. One day three boys aged about thirteen came in for treatment. As they were leaving and I was attending to the next patient, they noticed the crucifix. I remember what they said. The first said, "What's that?" The second said, "I dunno." The third said, "It's what's-'is-name – Jesus." And off they went.

To those three – or at least to two of them – the sign of the Cross meant nothing. It was bound to mean nothing because they did not know who the figure was who hung upon the Cross, or when he hung there or why or anything else. In short, they did not know the story behind the Cross. It is the story that gives power and meaning to the sign of the Cross. To anyone wholly ignorant of the story the sign is just a curious object. The soldier and the labourer of whom I spoke earlier must have had some knowledge and recollection of the story, distant and indistinct perhaps, but enough to give power and meaning to the sign. The boys had never received that knowledge and the possibility of re-membering it.

It was unusual thirty or forty years ago to come across children in this country who knew nothing of Jesus and the story of the Cross. Probably those boys had missed out on all sides of their education as they grew up amid the chaos of the East End of London in war time. Nowadays, one fears, one might meet many more children equally uninformed. And this highlights the importance of that very simple, basic Christian education which can be given to young children at home, in school, in church, in Sunday School, or in some kind of children's organization.

Many Christians who are involved in this kind of Christian education become saddened by what they see as its longterm ineffectiveness. So many children, all attention when they are very young, grow so soon into indifference, drift away, seem to have been taught in vain. No doubt that soldier and that labourer had drifted away when still quite young from wherever they were taught the story behind the Cross, and no doubt someone felt sad, seemingly to have taught in vain. But later, much later, when one was dying in agony and the other living on the edge of squalor, the story was still there, and it gave power and meaning to the sign, so that the one passed into death holding on to the cross of palm and the other brought himself into the light around the cross and knelt on the grass at its foot. What they were taught as children was not taught in vain.

It is the *story* that children need to be taught and to receive into the deep recesses of memory, the story rather than the interpretations of the story or statements of what it means. For adults as well as for children, stories imprint themselves on the memory and on the feelings much more distinctly and lastingly than do interpretations and explanations. When imprinted, they carry their meaning with them. They speak, as we say, for themselves. In our Christian preaching and teaching I think we sometimes make the mistake of not allowing the story of the Cross to speak for itself; we overlay it and obscure it with too many thoughts of our own. The explanation may be perfectly correct, but it tends to be wordy, woolly, abstract; it cocoons the story in a package of long words which both obscures its substance and deadens its impact.

At the centre of the cathedral where I work there is a large, life-size, and very realistic crucifix before which hundreds of thousands of people pass in the course of a year. Many stop and look up at it for a while: one has the impression that it is saying something to them. One does not know what it is saying, and no doubt it is saying different things to different people. But it seems to be saying something. However, it is the custom that on certain days when there are a great many visitors a priest will take a microphone to the pulpit and address the visitors. He will tell them about the meaning and function and purpose of the cathedral, and usually he will centre his remarks on that great crucifix. He tells them what it means, what it implies about God, the world, and ourselves. But as he says it I have so often seen people who are looking up at the crucifix turn away and move elsewhere. It is as if the speaker's explanations have got in the way of what the crucifix itself is saying, have switched off its power, broken its spell. It is sad that his words, so well intentioned, should have this effect: nevertheless they do.

So let us, in the addresses which follow, simply concentrate on the story, simply retell and rehear the story, retell it not precisely in the words of Scripture, for to do that we should have to bring in a great many passages from many different kinds of books of the Bible, far more than there is time for. Let us retell it rather in a kind of summary, the sort of summary, perhaps, that a Christian preacher of the early days might have given one evening to a small group of people gathered in someone's house.

That morning, let us say, that preacher had arrived as a stranger in a city far from his home in Judea. He had come into the market place where the life of the city was centred, and being a stranger he had been noticed, asked where he came from, asked if he had any news. He had replied that he came from the land of the Jews, and that, yes, he did have some news, good news. A little group of people gathered round to hear the news, and the preacher had simply said that in the land of the Jews there had recently lived a man called Jesus of Nazareth. He had gone about doing good, speaking about God and healing many who were sick in body or possessed by evil. But important people in the land had turned against Him, and made accusations against Him to the Roman governor. Jesus of Nazareth had been condemned to death by crucifixion. He had suffered and died. One can imagine some of the hearers murmuring, What a shame, or, I thought He had good news. But then the preacher continued. On the third day Jesus came back from death. He came again to his friends, including me. For a little while He was with us and spoke to us. So we know now that He lives, that He cannot be destroyed even by death. For even now He is our Lord, and He can be your Lord too.

That was all the preacher said. Of course some of his hearers thought he was romancing about Jesus coming back from death, and they drifted away. But one or two were interested. They asked to hear more, and that evening the preacher met them in someone's house and told them a little more fully the story of the Cross.

In the next addresses let us try to hear that story as he might have told it. But before we do, let us remember in our prayers those in our country who have never heard, in childhood or at any other time, the story of the Cross, not because they belong to other faiths but because they have been taught no faith at all. Let us pray for them, and for all who at home, in school, or in church try to tell and teach them that story which is the story of all stories, the story of our salvation, the story which, by the grace of God, all people have the right to hear, and to make and call their own.

IV

It all happened, the preacher begins that evening, among us Jews, people who have been greatly blessed by God. Ages ago God chose our nation, small though it was among the nations of the earth, to be the place where He Himself should first become known. He made our people His intimates, His finest pupils. We were to come to know Him so that, through us, the whole world might come to know Him also. So we came to know God's greatness, that He is the one and only God, without peer or rival, the Creator of all things that are or ever could be. We came to know God's righteousness, that He requires of humankind right living and just dealing. We also came to know His mercy, that though He disciplines and punishes wrong living, He also offers to those who repent a clean slate, a fresh start.

That much we learned. But from learning yet more of God we were inhibited by pride and possessiveness over what we had already come to know. Our knowledge of God became more important to us than God Himself, the privilege of knowing what we did know more important than the duty of imparting it to other nations. We thought of those other nations, and especially those which oppressed or endangered us, as if they were God's enemies, and our expectation of God was not that He would show us yet more of Himself, but that He would vindicate what we already knew by freeing us from our oppressors and destroying His enemies and ours. We expected a God-sent leader, a mighty Messiah, who would prove that we were indeed God's chosen and privileged intimates by making us free and powerful among the nations of the earth.

And then, not long ago, there appeared among us Jesus of Nazareth. He walked from village to village around our quiet countryside, and to some of us who saw and heard Him He seemed to have, as it were, the makings of the Messiah. He seemed to be *very* intimate with God: He spoke in a very natural and confident way about God, as if He knew God better than the most learned scholars of our nation. Certainly we could understand Him more easily than we could understand them: and so His words had great force and authority and power.

There was power in what He did too. He would heal people who were sick or deformed or maddened by evil demons. And sometimes He seemed to have power over natural forces like wind and waves. It was very remarkable, but it was puzzling too. For He never flaunted this power. He used it when it would help people or ease their fears, but He never used it to impress people or prove that He was the Messiah. He seemed to treat His power as if it were only a kind of sideline, much less important than something else. And this something else was His generosity. You see, He was available to everybody: even when people gave Him no rest He never turned them away or kept them at a distance. And though He was so intimate with God He would talk and mix even with the most godless people – Roman soldiers, women off the streets, our corrupt tax collectors – He would even sit at table with them. He talked of the Kingdom of God being near us, all around us, not just around us Jews but around *all* people, as if God was as attractive and generous to all people as Jesus Himself was. I remember Him pointing out that God does not keep His blessings of rain and sunshine for us Jews only or for good people only but sends them on all people alike.

It seemed strange that the mighty Messiah should have this attitude, but all the same we were attracted to Him. More important people, our religious and political leaders, were critical of Jesus – as if He took too much on Himself. But many of our country people in Galilee were as devoted to Him as we were. We thought that in due time, when His following was strong enough, He would go to Jerusalem, our capital city, and show His true colours – unfurl His flag as the nation's leader and call us to rise up against our enemies and oppressors.

One year in the spring He began talking about going to Jerusalem, and going at Passover time when many of His Galilean followers would be there as pilgrims. Now, we thought, the time has come. He is going to rouse the nation and challenge our enemies and lead us on the road to victory. But, strangely, as we set out on the road to Jerusalem, His talk was not of victory but of His own suffering and death. We wondered if He had lost His confidence in God. But as He spoke sadly of His coming death, as one who did not *want* to die, He also told us that, though He should die, all would nevertheless be well, all would come right. We could not understand, and we came to Jerusalem puzzled and anxious.

Looking back now I can see why He led us to Jerusalem at that so well remembered Passover time. It was not to raise a revolt against the nation's enemies, it was to appeal to our nation's leaders. It was to win the nation as a whole to that new knowledge of God which He had already shared with us. He went to Jerusalem when many of His followers would also be there. That was to convince our leaders that His teaching about God was not a wild and foolish idea, that it could win support, that it could be the way for the nation as a whole. The support of His many followers could be an encouragement to our leaders to become followers of Jesus themselves and disciples of the God of whom Jesus taught and spoke.

But Jesus knew that our leaders might take our strong presence with Jesus as a threat to their own position and Himself as a rival for their power. Then, misreading His invitation for threat, they would destroy Him. For this He prepared us as we drew near to the city. His long silences and His sad face showed that He was preparing Himself also. Still He led us on, not wanting or intending to suffer and die, wanting and intending to win our leaders to a new understanding of God, yet knowing the possibility that they would refuse to be won over and would respond to His gracious invitation with the brutality that comes of fear.

So at last we came to the city on the first day of the week, and Jesus made his coming known. He entered the city with gentle ceremonial, riding on a donkey's back. We who were with Him cheered His coming, and our cheers attracted and rallied to His presence other pilgrims to the city who came from Galilee. Many greeted Him enough to show to our leaders that He was no lone eccentric and His teaching no unappealing foolishness. He appeared in the city as one who must be taken seriously, who could not be ignored; and we know now that our leaders, our men of power, began to discuss what they should do. They had just two choices: either they themselves must go along with the simple people who loved and followed Jesus, or they must destroy Him. They must become either His disciples or His executioners...

Before we continue the story of stories, let us remember in our prayers all such people as Jesus came to win in Jerusalem: all people of power, all who hold the wellbeing of nations in their hands, all who are in danger of being corrupted by the power they hold; all who are tempted to maintain their own power at the expense of truth and justice and their people's good. Let us pray for them, knowing that the task of governing any nation is no easy one and that our first duty is to pray for them rather than to blame them.

V

...When we came to Jerusalem with Jesus four days remained before the Passover festival itself began. We had our lodging just outside the city, and each morning when we went in the crowds of pilgrims were larger, and the bustle and excitement in the streets grew greater. Each day Jesus was in or near the Temple, speaking openly and urgently of God, pleading with all who heard that they should not reject the true understanding of God, the true way of God which was also the way of peace. Always among those who listened we recognized representatives of our leaders, the men of power. Sometimes they asked questions; at other times they went away silently, as if to report to their masters what they had heard. We were anxious, not really understanding what was going on, anxious too because in His teaching in those days Jesus spoke often and sadly of the truth of God being rejected by those to whom He would show himself, and the bearers of this truth persecuted by those to whom in God's goodwill they came. It seemed that a crisis was drawing near, that Jesus and the men of power must soon meet each other face to face.

Then came the Thursday evening when, as the custom was, we gathered at a room within the city to eat the festival meal, the Passover. Jesus talked to us as He had never talked before: of the greatness of serving one another and suffering for others' sake, of the glory of that generous, unfailing love which is the love of God Himself, of the path of love and suffering which He Himself must tread as being itself the path of glory. One of us, Judas, slipped away from the meal. It seemed, though we didn't altogether understand, that he was in some way in touch with the men of power, perhaps arranging a meeting between them and Jesus. When he had gone Jesus asked us always to remember Him, as if He were to be taken from us; and He showed us how to remember Him, by sharing a little bread and wine together as we did on that fateful night.

Then He said, Let us go to Gethsemane. It was a garden where we often went. We sensed that He was in great danger and vowed that we would stand by Him. He told us that we wouldn't, yet He didn't blame us. When we came to the garden He asked us to watch. But we scarcely knew what to watch for, and we drowsed and slept. He, we could tell, was watching – watching and waiting – waiting and praying – praying in great earnestness and agony. I think He knew that the men of power were about to come – Judas had arranged that. But how would they come – as disciples or as executioners? I think the hope still breathed in Him that they would come quietly as would-be disciples. So He prayed that the cup of suffering would not be His to drink. But He knew it more than probable that they would come as executioners. So He prepared himself, commending Himself to God and saying that He would take whatever was to come.

They came at last – as executioners with clubs and swords. Their coming roused us, startling us, and in our fear we fled. I fled. I fled and hid. And in the hours that followed only occasionally did I venture out of hiding and come within sight of what they were doing to Jesus. What I glimpsed drove me back into hiding. They bound Him like an animal and interrogated Him like a slave. They beat Him. They dragged Him to the Roman governor and made wild accusations against Him. They said and did what they liked. I kept whispering frantically, Don't let them do it, Master...use your power against them – confound them – strike them dead. But He didn't. You see, He wouldn't use His power for His own sake. He would use it only as the God of whom He had taught us uses His power – always for the sake of others, for our sake, for the world's sake. I've been told that when they arrested Him, one of us struck at the High Priest's slave with a sword, and cut his ear, and that Jesus used His power to heal that poor slave. But He wouldn't use it for Himself. He did nothing against the people who were beating Him, mocking Him, shouting against Him, tearing His head with thorns, and in the end nailing Him up alive on a cross. He didn't even speak against them. In fact I've heard that as they were nailing Him to the wood He actually prayed, Father forgive them. And to the very end He was just as available and just as generous as He had ever been to anyone who needed help. There were two thieves crucified beside Him, and even they turned on Him with mocking and abuse. But one of them showed the other side of his nature and said pathetically, You're different from us, sir: will you remember me? Jesus was as quick as ever to comfort and reassure the poor fellow. You'll be in Paradise this very day, He said, and I will be with you. I've heard too that He was very thoughtful to His mother and the friend who was closest of us all to Him, John. They were standing close to the cross, closer than I would have dared. After a while Jesus asked each to look after the other. He didn't want either of them to be hurt any more by the sight of His suffering.

I was never near. I kept my distance in fear and trembling. It wasn't fear alone that made me tremble. I was aware of an ominous darkness, as if in those hours everything was coming to an end – not Jesus alone, not just the one we trusted and loved and put our hopes in. It was as if all hope was dying at that time, and all the trust and love that the world contains was being mocked, humiliated, and destroyed. Darkness seemed to rule. All the good lights by which men and women live and find their way in life were going out. It seemed that it was more than the death of Jesus that was drawing near. It was our death, and the world's death too. At the end I heard from my distance a loud and despairing cry from the cross where Jesus hung: My God, my God, why have you forsaken me? and I whispered bitterly to myself, There is no God. And it was then that I crept away.

Of the rest of that day, and the day which followed, I remember nothing but despair, despair not only that the Jesus whom I loved had been destroyed, but despair that with His destruction all good things were proved vain. All was folly, all trust misplaced, all hope a broken reed. Look after yourself now, I told myself. Trust nobody, get what you can for yourself and keep it for yourself: it's all you'll ever get. Join the survivors, the men who crucified Jesus. They are still here and He is not: theirs are the ways that really work in the world.

I'll say no more about the days of despair. They're gone for ever. And I'll say very little about the day of wonder which followed. For what happened then was too much to take in all at once. But it was this: I met Jesus again – living. It was all quite quiet. There were rumours early in the day that His dead body was missing from the tomb. Some of us came together to talk about them. And then, quite simply, Jesus was among us – the same Jesus, even down to the nail marks in His hands and feet. The Jesus whom we had known and trusted was still there – crucified but indestructible, killed but living, eliminated from the world but still present in it, deserted by us but coming back to us, taken from us but restoring Himself to us, struck down by men of power but raised above their power. On that day of wonder, the beginning of a season of wonder, we began to ask ourselves, Who is the Jesus whom we know and love? Who is this who outlives death, who is indestructible by earthly power, who, whatever the world does to Him, remains who He is and what He is? Who is this, all-enduring, all surmounting, all-transcending, everlasting, ever-living, ever-loving? Who is this, who can this be, but the eternal One, the divine and holy One, God made known to us, Emmanuel, God among us? In Him God showed and gave this truth to us, the truth of what He is. So now we bring and offer that same truth to you, and not to you only, but to every age and race and nation of humankind...

So our travelling preacher of long ago might have ended his story. Let us pray now, as he might well have done, that the gracious truth of the Cross, the truth of the ever-loving, all-forgiving figure upon the Cross, may be received and recognized by all humankind as the final truth, the truth of the God with whom we have to deal, the truth which saves us all.

VI

In the last two addresses we imagined, not too unrealistically or extravagantly, how a Christian preacher of the early days might have told the story of the Cross. The story ended not with the despair of Good Friday evening but with the wonder of Easter morning. The story could not end before Easter Day, for Easter Day disclosed who it was, who it is, that was suffering and enduring, loving and forgiving, all through Good Friday. Who it was, who it is, was nothing less than God: the Alpha and Omega, the Beginning and the End of all things, the One upon whom all the world depends, the One before whom all human beings stand, from whom all come, to whom all return. The awesome truth of who it was that was raised on the central cross of Calvary came to be known to the followers of Jesus. And this accounts for the reserve, the strict objectivity, with which the Gospel writers tell the story of the Cross. It accounts also for the towering dimensions and the continuing power of the Cross. And it accounts for the distance at which we find ourselves when we set our mind and attention on the Cross. In the Cross of Jesus the mystery of God appears and is disclosed in history.

Some people, though deeply moved by the suffering of Jesus and His patience in bearing it, would nevertheless hesitate to describe this suffering as a disclosure, or an instance, of the suffering of God. That God should suffer, that He should be affected in any way by what the world does, on Calvary or anywhere else, seems to them scarcely possible, seemingly unthinkable. Their vision of God is of one serene, august, apart, of one who calmly orders the world with wisdom and goodwill, who watches over it with care and pity, who achieves in it His own good purposes. This is not an ignoble vision of God. It is, I think, very like the vision of God which prevailed among the Jews in Jesus's own day. This God can no more suffer at the hands of the world of His making than the master of a puppet show can be made to suffer by the toy figures which he himself has made, or by the little drama which they enact, but which he himself has written and whose every move he himself controls. This vision of the high serenity of God is not an ignoble vision: it does justice to the majesty of God. Here is the God in whom Plato and Aristotle and many other great philosophers have believed. Here is the God as the Jews of Jesus's own day had come to understand Him. And here too is the reason why most of the Jews of that time could not accept that the suffering Jesus was or could be the disclosure, or, as we say, the incarnation of the high, serene, and mighty God. The most that our Jewish brothers and sisters down the years have been able to admit about Jesus is that He may have been a great man and a prophet of God who came to a sad and tragic end. This is also of course what our Islamic brothers and sisters believe about Jesus. The possibility that the suffering Jesus might Himself be God has seemed, even to those Jews and Muslims who respect Jesus's goodness, a kind of blasphemy.

But the first Christians were enabled, through Jesus, to recognize a new dimension of the being of God. The old dimension was still there: God in Himself was high and mighty, someone in His own being sufficient in and to Himself, in need of nothing, assailable by nothing. But, they perceived, God of His own will had chosen not only to be but also to love. He had chosen, freely chosen, not to remain alone and complete in Himself, but to make an other – a world, a universe – to be a beloved other, that which He loved.

God had chosen to love: and all human beings who have ever loved know that in doing so they have embarked upon a strange adventure, an adventure which can be either joyful or tragic, but which is always costly. For in loving we always give to that other whom we love a certain power over ourselves. By loving someone we give to him or her a power which was not there before – a power to give us great joy or great pain, a power to delight or worry, a power even to make us angry.

I often think of an incident of many years ago. I knew a wonderful woman who gave a home to, and brought up, five young brothers whose own parents had deserted them. They called her 'Auntie', but in effect she was the best of mothers to them. One day, she told me, the eldest of the brothers went in for a bit of shop-lifting. Auntie had got to know about the offence before the offender came home. "When he came," she said, "I threw him into the garden and said we would have no thieves in this house. When it was bedtime I let him in and kicked him up the stairs. In the morning, Harold was very chastened, very quiet. But after a while he came to me and said shyly, 'Auntie, after what happened last night, do you still love me?' So I said, 'Do I still love you, Harold? But *of course* I still love you. Do you think if I did not love you, you could have made me so angry?'"

I have always thought those words very significant and illuminating. Do you think that if I did not love you, you could have made me angry? By giving this boy her love, Auntie had also given him the power to make her angry – and the power sometimes to cause her great pain, and sometimes great delight. She *gave* him that power by loving him.

God gives that same power to us and the whole world by loving us and the whole world. If God did *not* give that power, He would not be truly loving. His love would be a posture, an affectation, or, at best, a cool and distant condescension or goodwill. Real love is much more than goodwill. It is involvement with an other, self-exposure to an other. It puts us in the hands of an other, so that he or she can affect us, for good or ill, for our weal or woe, to a degree that would otherwise be impossible. We *know* the truth of this in our own experience of loving: we must apply that truth to our understanding of the love of God. When Jesus is put into the hands of men to be treated as men choose and decide, we are to see an image – and more than an image, an instance, a supremely revealing instance – of the everlasting exposure of God to the world which He loved.

High in the roof of our cathedral at Chester there is a thirteenth-century carving of the Crucifixion. On the Cross there hangs the slight and spent figure of the dying Jesus, but behind the Cross, holding it in front of Himself, there is a much larger figure. It is evidently the figure of God the Father. The carving is so high in the roof that it is difficult to discern the detail with the naked eye. But if you focus binoculars on the carving the effect is profoundly moving. For you see that the figure of God the Father is indeed a majestic and powerful figure. The hands are huge. The face is calm, but the calmness is not that of unassailable serenity. It is a kind of *spent* calm, that of someone who knows everything, has felt everything, endured everything, the calmness of one who has absorbed into Himself all that can be endured or suffered. It is the calm that I used to glimpse in the face of a friend who had suffered and endured and survived three years in a prisoner of war camp on the Burma road. When one sees in the carving the spent calm on the face of God the Father, He seems to be saying something about the figure of the crucified Jesus which He holds before Him. He seems to be saying, This is my self-portrait; this is how you are to see me.

The figure of the Crucified is the figure of God. So is the figure of Easter morning, the one who is still there, still Himself, still living and loving in spite of all that has been done to Him. And we must not think of either Good Friday or Easter as what one might call passing incidents in the life and being of God. They happened once in history, but they disclosed then what is permanently and everlastingly true. Here is God who from the beginning of creation loves the whole world and, loving it, bears its weight, is exposed to its flaws and sins, absorbs its cruelty and hatred, shares to the ultimate degree its suffering, and yet is still there, indestructible, ever Himself, ever loving. Here is the truth of God's love, here is the God with whom we have to deal. And it is because we are shown on the Cross the God with whom we have to deal that we receive salvation, that we know ourselves saved. The truth of the Cross is saving truth because it shows to us the all-enduring yet ever-loving God before whom we stand.

VII

The disciples were shown on Easter morning that the Crucified was still there – undestroyed, indestructible, all-enduring, ever-lasting. They told the truth which had been shown to them to their generation. And as succeeding generations went by, there grew up – perhaps understandably – on the fringes of the Church a heresy, a belief that the Crucifixion was not quite real, that there was an element of illusion about the Cross. The holders of this belief accepted that Jesus was divine, was God with us. They reverenced Jesus's teaching as the truth of God and His healing as the work of God. But they could not accept that the suffering of Jesus was the suffering of God. So they imagined that as Jesus was raised on the Cross, His divinity departed from Him and He became, as it were, merely the outward shell of what He had been. Then, they said, on Easter morning God returned to that shell.

This heresy made little headway in the Church. But it was present for a while because its adherents felt that a suffering God could not be a trustworthy God. Faith and confidence in God seemed to them impossible unless God were always and totally *in control*, master of every situation, with limitless resources of power to command, never pressured or under strain. A suffering God *would* be under strain: He would be a struggling God, and a struggling God could not be completely trusted – especially at those times when we ourselves are struggling and under strain and most need the support and help of God.

Some people today feel the same difficulty, unable to trust a suffering, strained, and struggling God. I should like to tell a little parable from my own life which I find helpful in meeting this difficulty. My father was one of those people, not too common many years ago, whose salary was paid directly into the bank. So quite frequently he would have to cash a cheque at the local branch, or, as he would put it, "to get some money from the bank". When I was very small, he would sometimes ask me if I would like to come to the bank with him. I think I always said yes, because the procedure of getting money seemed to me very pleasant and satisfactory. After a friendly chat my father would scribble something on a piece of paper and give it to the teller, who would thereupon give my father what seemed a great deal of money. I think that I must at some time have asked my father if the teller might give me some money, and that my father must have answered something like "not until you are grown up". For a while I had the distinct impression that growing up automatically brought with it the privilege of getting money from the bank, just as it brought the privilege of staying up as long as one liked.

So in my young days I supposed that money was no problem for my father. He had only to scribble something on a piece of paper and the bank would supply him with all that he required. So obviously, through my father, I should always be provided with everything I needed. I could trust my father, and even use my father, at any time that I needed – or wanted – anything. I had a kind of infantile serenity and confidence.

My naivety about how banks work did not last very long. I came to understand that my father did not have limitless re-sources to draw on, far from it. What was provided for me was provided only because my father and my mother were careful and prudent over what money they had. They stinted themselves to provide for me. They provided for me at a cost to themselves, struggled to provide for me, only just managed to provide for me. So my infantile serenity and confidence were lost. But I think they were replaced by something better. Though it was a struggle for my parents to provide for me, I realized that I mattered to them, that they cared about me, that they loved me. I realized that I could not expect to receive from them everything I wanted, but what I did receive came wrapped, as it were, in their care and love. I think that the generous love came to matter more to me than the things that I wanted but did not and could not receive. It gave me confidence too, a confidence in my parents' love which was more worthwhile, and certainly less infantile, than my previous confidence in their limitless resources. I knew that I could trust their care and love, and this trust remained with me even when I no longer needed them to provide me with resources.

Do we not, should we not, grow in a similar way into a more mature trust and confidence in God? Certainly some people do. At first they trust God as the answer to their problems. Their prayer is primarily the prayer of asking, asking that their problems, and the problems of others, may be overcome, asking that their longings, and the longings of others, may be satisfied. Sometimes nothing of what they pray for comes about. And some people are then disillusioned and cease to pray. But others respond quite differently. They have met in prayer, however indistinctly, a God who is with them in their problems, and understands their needs as if He shared them, as if He knew them from the inside, as if He does not need to be told how distressing they are or how heavy they weigh. They have met in prayer a God who already knows how hard things bear, how cruelly they press. To be with such a God in prayer is a blessing which makes the problem, though still unresolved, bearable, and the need, though still unsatisfied, acceptable. The God whom they find is with them in prayer, suffering and struggling yet ever faithful, becomes even more important to them than the great benefit for which they at first prayed. And so, although the benefit does not come, they continue to pray. They continue faithful in prayer to the strained and suffering God who remains ever faithful to them, and not only to them, but to His whole beloved world.

Dietrich Bonhoeffer, one of the noble martyrs of the Second World War, wrote in the concentration camp from which he was taken to his death, "Only a suffering God can help." That he should write such words in such circumstances gives to them a great authority. One might dismiss them if they were spoken by a person in comfortable circumstances. One cannot dismiss them when they are spoken by a suffering man in such a world's end of a place as a Nazi concentration camp. "Only a suffering God can help."

God suffers because He loves, because He chooses to love, because He chooses not to reserve to Himself the power to be, but to expend that power that an other may be, that a world may be, a beloved world. God has committed Himself to loving, and in so doing, as everyone knows who has ever loved, He exposed Himself to suffering, to being affected by joy or pain, by the response of the loved world. And this love, like all authentic love, is not destroyed by the negative and therefore painful response of that which is loved. This love, like all authentic love, is not destroyed when it is rebuffed. It is faithful love, and therefore indestructible, and therefore to be trusted. The rebuffed, the strained, the struggling love of God is to be trusted, as the disciples discovered when, on Easter Day, the one in whom the suffering love of God was disclosed to them was found to be still there, still just the same, indestructible and everlasting. To the one whose love they had known and whose suffering they had seen, the disciples found themselves committed for all the future. Dietrich Bonhoeffer expressed the nature of their commitment, of all Christian commitment, in a poem he wrote in those grim circumstances of his prison. The poem is called 'Christians and Unbelievers' and here are two stanzas of it:

> Men come to God when they are sore bestead,
> Pray to Him for succour, for his peace, for bread,
> For mercy for their sick, sinning, or dead –
>   All men do so, Christian and unbelieving.

> Christians comes to God when He is sore bestead,
> Find Him poor and scorned, without shelter or bread,
> Whelmed under weight of the wicked, the weak, the dead –
>   Christians stand by God in His hour of grieving.

25

Darkness at Noon

The Crucifixion and Death of Jesus Christ

The afternoon of Good Friday
12 noon – 3 pm

Compiled by Jim Cotter

A three-hour devotional service on Good Friday has become customary in many churches. It takes a variety of forms, not least a series of addresses and prayers on 'the seven last words from the Cross'. This commemoration is based on the ancient liturgies for Good Friday, supplemented with hymns and recorded music, poetry, and comment. Allowing up to a minute for each of the silences, the whole can be taken at a measured pace and lasts approximately three hours.

Music: String Quintet by Schubert: The slow movement

Prayer

Eternal and most loving God,
yearning with compassion for the peoples of the world,
draw us to yourself with the magnet of the cross of Jesus Christ.
Beloved by you, springing from your very heart,
he embraced the way of suffering
in the marvel of a steadfast will and love,
betrayed and deserted by his friends,
given up into the hands of the powers that be,
enduring pain and death upon the cross,
trusting in you beyond all sense of your presence,
that the whole creation might be restored
and that we might come to know a bliss beyond our imagining.

In the power of the Holy Spirit we give you praise and glory,
this Friday which we now deem Good.

**Reading: *The Fourth Poem concerning the Servant of
God, from the Book of the Prophet Isaiah, chapter 52,
verse 13 to chapter 53, verse 12***

Silence

Poem: *'Buna' by Primo Levi*

Torn feet and cursed earth,
The long line in the gray morning.
The Buna smokes from a thousand chimneys,
A day like every other day awaits us.
The whistles terrible at dawn:
"You multitudes with dead faces,
On the monotonous horror of the mud
Another day of suffering is born."
Tired companion, I see you in my heart.
I read your eyes, sad friend,
In your breast you carry cold, hunger, nothing.
You have broken what's left of the courage within you.
Colourless one, you were a strong man,
A woman walked at your side.
Empty companion who no longer has a name,
Forsaken man who can no longer weep,
So poor you no longer grieve,
So tired you no longer fear.
Spent once-strong man.
If we were to meet again
Up there in the world, sweet beneath the sun,
With what kind of face would we confront each other?

Silence

Psalm 22: Part One

My God, my God,
why have you forsaken me?
Why are you so far from helping me?
O my God, I howl in the daytime
but you do not hear me.
I groan in the watches of the night,
but I find no rest.

Why, silent God, why?

Yet still you are the holy God
whom Israel long has worshipped.
Our ancestors hoped in you,
and you rescued them.
They trusted in you,
and you delivered them.
They called upon you:
you were faithful to your covenant.
They put their trust in you
and were not disappointed.

Pause

But as for me, I crawl the earth like a worm,
despised by others, an outcast of the people.
All those who see me laugh me to scorn:
they make mouths at me,
shaking their heads and saying,
"He threw himself on God for deliverance:
let God rescue him then,
if God so delights in him."

Why, silent God, why?

You were my midwife, O God,
drawing me out of the womb.

I was weak and unknowing,
yet you were my hope –
even as I lay close to the breast,
cast upon you from the days of my birth.
From the womb of my mother
to the dread of these days,
you have been my God, never letting me go.

Pause

Do not desert me, for trouble is hard at hand,
and there is no-one to help me.
Wild beasts close in on me,
narrow-eyed, greedy and sleek.
They open their mouths and snarl at me,
like a ravening and roaring lion.

Why, silent God, why?

My strength drains away like water,
my bones are out of joint.
My heart also in the midst of my body
is even like melting wax.
My mouth is dried up like a potsherd,
my tongue cleaves to my gums.
My hands and my feet are withered,
you lay me down in the dust of death.

Why, silent God, why?

The huntsmen are all about me:
a circle of wicked men hem me in on every side,
their dogs unleashed to tear me apart.
They have pierced my hands and my feet –
I can count all my bones –
they stand glaring and gloating over me.
They divide my garments among them
they cast lots for my clothes.

Why, silent God, why?

The tanks of the mighty encircle me,
barbed wire and machine guns surround me.
They have marked my arm with a number,
and never call me by name.
They have stripped me of clothes and of shoes,
and showered me with gas
in the chamber of death.

Why, silent God, why?

I cry out for morphine but no-one hears me.
Pinned down by straitjacket
I scream the night through.
I suffocate through panic in the oxygen tent.
Sweating with fear, I await news of my doom.

Why, silent God, why?

No-one comes near with an unmasked face,
no skin touches mine in a gesture of love.
They draw back in terror, speaking only
in whispers behind doors that are sealed.

Why, silent God, why?

Be not far from me, O God:
you are my helper, hasten to my aid.
Deliver my very self from the sword,
my life from the falling of the axe.
Save me from the mouth of the lion,
poor body that I am, from the horns of the bull.

Silence

Silent God,
we bring the cries of our battered hearts,
the cries of those burdened by illness,
the cries of those bowed down with the weight of
    oppression.
We bring them so that we may not be silent...
Hear us in the name of Jesus, forsaken on the Cross.

Silence

Reading from The Drowned and the Saved
by Primo Levi

And there is another, vaster shame, the shame of the world.

It was memorably pronounced by John Donne, and quoted innumerable times, pertinently or not, that "no man is an island", and that every bell tolls for everyone. And yet there are those who, faced by the crime of others or their own, turn their backs so as not to see it and not feel touched by it: this is what the majority of Germans did during the twelve Hitlerian years, deluding themselves that not seeing was a way of not knowing, and that not knowing relieved them of their share of complicity or connivance.

But we were denied the screen of willed ignorance, T. S. Eliot's "partial shelter": we were not able not to see. The ocean of pain, past and present, surrounded us, and its level rose from year to year until it almost submerged us. It was useless to close one's eyes or turn one's back to it, because it was all around, in every direction, all the way to the horizon. It was not possible for us, nor did we want, to become islands; the just among us, neither more nor less numerous than in any other human group, felt remorse, shame and pain for the misdeeds that others, and not they, had committed, and in which they felt involved, because they sensed that what had happened around them in their presence, and in them, was irrevocable. It would never again be able to be cleansed; it would prove that man, the human species – we, in short – were potentially able to construct an infinite enormity of pain; and that pain is the only force that is created from nothing, without cost and without effort. It is enough not to see, not to listen, not to act.

Silence

Psalm 22: Part Two

I will declare your Name to my friends:
in the midst of the congregation I will praise you.
In wonder and awe I stand in your Presence:
I remember, and glorify your Name.
For you have not shrunk in loathing
from the suffering in their affliction.
You have not hid your face from them,
but when they called to you, you heard them.

I recall your mercies of old:
why have you hidden yourself now?
Doubts and tremblings overwhelm me:
nevertheless I will deepen my trust.

My praise is of you in the great congregation,
my vows I will perform in their sight.
We shall praise you
with thanksgiving and wonder.
We shall share what we have with the poor:
they shall eat and be satisfied,
a new people, yet to be born.
Those who seek you shall be found by you:
they will be in good heart for ever.

I recall your mercies of old:
why have you hidden yourself now?
Doubts and tremblings overwhelm me:
nevertheless I will deepen my trust.

So shall my life be preserved in your sight,
and my children shall worship you:
they shall tell of you to generations yet to come:
to a people yet to be born
they shall declare your righteousness,
that you have brought these things to fulfilment.

I recall your mercies of old:
why have you hidden yourself now?
Doubts and tremblings overwhelm me:
nevertheless I will deepen my trust.

So let all the ends of the world remember
and turn again to their God.
Let all the families of the nations
worship their Creator.
For all dominion belongs to you,
and you are the ruler of the peoples.

Silence

O God of enduring love, whom the clouds obscure,
may our eye of faith turn steadily towards you,
patiently waiting in hope for the fulness of your
    salvation,
bearing the pain of evil days, in Jesus of the Cross,
who loved his own even to the end, and who kept
    on trusting,
even when there was no answer to his cry.

Silence

Poem: 'For Adolf Eichmann' by Primo Levi

> The wind runs free across our plains,
> The live sea beats for ever at our beaches.
> Man makes earth fertile,
> Earth gives him flowers and fruits.
> He lives in toil and joy;
> He hopes, fears, begets sweet offspring.

...And you have come, our precious enemy,
Forsaken creature, man ringed by death.
What can you say now, before our assembly?
Will you swear by a god? What god?
Will you leap happily into the grave?
Or will you at the end, like the industrious man
Whose life was too brief for his long art,
Lament your sorry work unfinished,
The thirteen million still alive?

Oh son of death, we do not wish you death.
May you live longer than anyone ever lived.
May you live sleepless five million nights,
And may you be visited each night
By the suffering of everyone who saw,
Shutting behind him,
The door that blocked the way back,
Saw it grow dark around him,
The air filled with death.

Silence

Psalm 22: Part Three

Can we now hold on to such faith?
Has the name of God become an offence to our ears?
Is God deaf to the cry of the child,
offering no relief to the burning of pain,
letting the horror of life run wild,
sitting lofty and high, refusing to act?

Pause

So do we argue and wrestle in faith,
fiercely refusing to loosen our hold.
We demand that you listen to whisper and howl,
that your deeds may fulfil your nature and name.

Pause

This is our story from Jeremiah and Job,
from all who find you obscure and perplexing.
Who are you? Who do you say that you are?
Why must we be buffeted by malice and chance?

Pause

Is our cry no more than our pride?
Is our mind too small? Is our eye too dim?
Do not quiet our pain with dazzling display.
The open wound of the child accuses you still.

Pause

Is there a cry in the depths of your being,
in the heart and soul of your chosen Christ-Self?
Stretched between earth and the heavens,
we see a striving so awesome,
a strange and harrowing love,
a bearing of pain between father and son,
a loving right through to the end,
through the worst of devil and death.

We trust in the folly of the Cross.

Truly you are an offence, O God,
and scandalous too are the outcries of faith.
They bite deep into the lines of our faces,
as we strive to be faithful and true.

Keep us from the scandal of hypocrisy,
selfish and faithless, prayers merely mouthed,
so far from the Place of the Skull,
too indifferent to be in conflict with you,
too icily cold for your friendship.

We trust in the folly of the Cross.

Today if you hear the voice of *this* God,
your heart need no longer be hardened.

Silence

O God of the Cross,
**keep us passionate through our wrestling with
 your ways,
and keep us humble before the mystery of your great
 love, known to us in the face of Jesus Christ.**

Silence

Psalm 22: Part Four

And can those who are buried give you worship,
those ground to the dust give you praise?
Will nothing be left but the wind and the silence,
a dead earth, abandoned, forgotten?

Pause

But you are a God who creates out of nothing,
you are a God who raises the dead,
you are a God who redeems what is lost,
you are a God who fashions new beauty,
striving with the weight of your glory,
bearing the infinite pain.

In the depths of our darkness
you are rising, O Christ.

The footfalls of faith may drag through our days,
God's gift of a costly and infinite enduring.
We remember your deliverance of your people of old,
we remember the abundance of the earth you have given us,
we remember the care and compassion of folk,
we remember your victory of long-suffering love.

In the depths of our darkness
you are rising, O Christ.

The power of the powers is but a feather in the wind!
Death is transfigured to glory for ever!

Silence

Dying and rising Christ, breaking the bonds of death,
shine on us with eyes of compassion and glory.
Let light flood the dungeons of our downtrodden selves.
So may the oppressed go free, the weak rise up in
    strength, and the hungry be fed, now in these our
    days.

Silence

Reading from the First Letter of Paul to the Corinthians,
chapter 1, verses 18 to 31

Silence

Hymn by Brian Wren, to the tune Kocher *by J. H. Knecht (1752–1817)*

Here hangs a man discarded,
a scarecrow hoisted high,
a nonsense pointing nowhere
to all who hurry by.

Can such a clown of sorrows
still bring a useful word
when faith and love seem phantoms
and every hope absurd?

Can he give help or comfort
to lives by comfort bound
when drums of dazzling progress
give strangely hollow sound?

Life emptied of all meaning,
drained out in bleak distress,
can share in broken silence
our deepest emptiness.

And love that freely entered
the pit of life's despair
can name our hidden darkness
and suffer with us there.

Lord, if you now are risen,
help all who long for light
to hold the hand of promise
and walk into the night.

Introduction to the Reading of the Passion

The Passion of Jesus Christ according to John

*Each and every member of the congregation is invited to say aloud the part of
Jesus.*

Narrator	When Jesus had spoken these words, he went forth with his disciples across the Kidron Valley, where there was a garden which he and his disciples entered. Now Judas, who betrayed him, also knew the place; for Jesus often met there with his disciples. So Judas, procuring a band of soldiers and some officers from the chief priests and the Pharisees, went there with lanterns and torches and weapons. Then Jesus, knowing all that was to befall him, came forward and said to them,
Jesus	**Whom do you seek?**
Soldiers	Jesus of Nazareth.
Jesus	**I am he.**
Narrator	Judas, who betrayed him, was standing with them. When he said to them, "I am he," they drew back and fell to the ground. Again he asked them,
Jesus	**Whom do you seek?**
Soldiers	Jesus of Nazareth.
Jesus	**I told you that I am he. So, if you seek me, let these men go.**
Narrator	This was to fulfil the word which he had spoken. "Of those whom you gave me I lost not one." Then Simon Peter, having a sword, drew it and struck the high priest's slave and cut off his right ear. The slave's name was Malchus. Jesus said to Peter:

Jesus **Put your sword into its sheath; shall I not drink the cup which the Father has given me?**

Narrator So the band of soldiers and their captain and the officers of the Jews seized Jesus and bound him. First they led him to Annas; for he was the father-in-law of Caiaphas, who was high priest that year. It was Caiaphas who had given counsel to the Jews that it was expedient that one man should die for the people. Simon Peter followed Jesus, and so did another disciple. As this disciple was known to the high priest, he entered the court of the high priest along with Jesus, while Peter stood outside at the door. So the other disciple went out and spoke to the maid who kept the door, and brought Peter in. The maid said to Peter,

Maid Are you not also one of this man's disciples?

Peter I am not.

Narrator Now the servants and officers had made a charcoal fire, because it was cold, and they were standing and warming themselves; Peter also was with them, standing and warming himself. The high priest then questioned Jesus about his disciples and his teaching. Jesus answered,

Jesus **I have spoken openly to the world; I have always taught in synagogues and in the temple, where all Jews come together. I have said nothing secretly. Why do you ask me? Ask those who heard me, what I said to them; they know what I said.**

Narrator When he had said this, one of the officers standing by struck Jesus with his hand, saying,

Officer   Is that how you answer the high priest?

Jesus   **If I have spoken wrongly, bear witness to the
               wrong; but if I have spoken rightly, why do you
               strike me?**

Narrator   Annas then sent him bound to Caiaphas the high
               priest. Now Simon Peter was standing and warming
               himself. They said to him,

Bystanders   Are you not also one of his disciples?

Peter   I am not.

Narrator   One of the servants of the high priest, a kinsman of
               the man whose ear Peter had cut off, said,

Servant   Did I not see you in the garden with him?

Narrator   Peter again denied it; and at once the cock crowed.
                   Then they led Jesus from the house of Caiaphas to
               the praetorium. It was early. They themselves did not
               enter the praetorium, so that they might not be defiled
               but might eat the Passover. So Pilate went out to them
               and said,

Pilate   What accusation do you bring against this man?

Priests   If this man were not an evildoer, we would not have
               handed him over to you.

Pilate   Take him yourselves and judge him by your own law.

Priests   It is not lawful for us to put any man to death.

Narrator   This was to fulfil the word which Jesus had spoken to show by what death he was to die. Pilate entered the praetorium again and called Jesus to him and said,

Pilate   Are you the King of the Jews?

Jesus   **Do you say this of your own accord, or did others say it to you about me?**

Pilate   Am I a Jew? Your own people and the chief priests have handed you over to me: what have you done?

Jesus   **My kingship is not of this world. If my kingship were of this world, my servants would fight, that I might not be handed over to the Jews; but my kingship is not of this world.**

Pilate   So you are a king?

Jesus   **You say that I am a king. For this I was born, and for this I have come into the world, to bear witness to the truth. Everyone who is of the truth hears my voice.**

Pilate   What is truth?

Narrator   After he had said this, he went out to the Jews again and told them,

Pilate   I find no crime in him. But you have a custom that I should release one man for you at the Passover; will you have me release for you the King of the Jews?

Priests   Not this man, but Barabbas!

Narrator   Now Barabbas was a robber. Then Pilate took Jesus and scourged him. And the soldiers plaited a crown of

thorns, and put it on his head, and arrayed him in a
purple robe; they came up to him, saying,

Soldiers   Hail, King of the Jews!

Narrator   Pilate went out again, and said to the Jews,

Pilate   See, I am bringing him out to you, that you may know
that I find no crime in him.

Narrator   So Jesus came out, wearing the crown of thorns and
the purple robe.

Pilate   Here is the man.

Narrator   When the chief priests and the officers saw him, they
cried out,

Priests   Crucify him! Crucify him!

Pilate   Take him yourselves and crucify him, for I find no
crime in him.

Priests   We have a law, and by that law he ought to die, because he has made himself the Son of God.

Narrator   When Pilate heard these words, he was the more
afraid; he entered the praetorium again and said to
Jesus,

Pilate   Where are you from?

Narrator   But Jesus gave no answer.

Pilate   You will not speak to me? Do you not know that I have
power to release you, and power to crucify you?

Jesus	**You would have no power over me unless it had been given you from above; therefore he who delivered me to you has the greater sin.**
Narrator	Upon this Pilate sought to release him, but the Jews cried out,
Priests	If you release this man, you are not Caesar's friend. Every one who makes himself a king sets himself against Caesar.
Narrator	When Pilate heard these words, he brought Jesus out and sat down on the judgment seat at a place called The Pavement, and in Hebrew, Gabbatha. Now it was the day of Preparation for the Passover; it was about the sixth hour. He said to the Jews,
Pilate	Here is your King!
Priests	Away with him, away with him, crucify him!
Pilate	Shall I crucify your King?
Priests	We have no king but Caesar.
Narrator	Then he handed Jesus over to them to be crucified. So they took Jesus, and he went out, bearing his own cross, to the place called The Skull, which is called in Hebrew Golgotha. There they crucified him, and with him two others, one on either side, and Jesus between them. Pilate also wrote a title and put it on the cross; it read, Jesus of Nazareth, the King of the Jews. Many of the Jews read this title, for the place where Jesus was crucified was near the city; and it was written in Hebrew, Latin, and Greek. The chief priests of the Jews then said to Pilate,

Priests	Do not write, The King of the Jews, but, This man said, I am the King of the Jews.
Pilate	What I have written I have written.
Narrator	When the soldiers crucified Jesus they took his garments and made four parts, one for each soldier. But his tunic was without seam, woven from top to bottom; so they said to one another,
Soldiers	Let us not tear it, but cast lots for it to see whose it shall be.
Narrator	This was to fulfil the scripture, They parted my garments among them, and for my clothing they cast lots. So the soldiers did this. Standing by the cross of Jesus were his mother, and his mother's sister, Mary the wife of Clopas, and Mary Magdalene. When Jesus saw his mother, and the disciple whom he loved standing near, he said to his mother,
Jesus	**Woman, behold your son.**
Narrator	Then he said to the disciple,
Jesus	**Behold your mother.**
Narrator	And from that hour the disciple took her to his own home. After this, Jesus, knowing that all was now finished, said (to fulfil the scripture),
Jesus	**I thirst.**
Narrator	A bowl full of vinegar stood there; so they put a sponge full of vinegar on hyssop and held it to his mouth. When Jesus had received the vinegar, he said,

Jesus   **It is finished!**

Narrator   And he bowed his head and gave up his spirit.

Silence

Narrator   Since it was the day of Preparation, in order to pre-
               vent the bodies from remaining on the cross on the
               sabbath (for that sabbath was a high day), the Jews
               asked Pilate that their legs might be broken, and that
               they might be taken away. So the soldiers came and
               broke the legs of the first, and of the other who had
               been crucified with him; but when they came to Jesus
               and saw that he was already dead, they did not break
               his legs. But one of the soldiers pierced his side with
               his spear, and at once there came out blood and water.
               He who saw it has borne witness – his testimony is true
               – that you also may believe. For these things took place
               that the scripture might be fulfilled, Not a bone of him
               shall be broken. And again another scripture says,
               They shall look on him whom they have pierced.

               After this Joseph of Arimathea, who was a disciple
               of Jesus, but secretly, for fear of the Jews, asked Pilate
               that he might take away the body of Jesus, and Pilate
               gave him leave. So he came and took away his body.
               Nicodemus also, who had first come to Jesus by night,
               came bringing a mixture of myrrh and aloes, about a
               hundred pounds' weight. They took the body of Jesus,
               and bound it in linen clothes with the spices, as is the
               burial custom of the Jews. Now in the place where he
               was crucified there was a garden, and in the garden a
               new tomb where no-one had ever been laid. So be-
               cause of the Jewish day of Preparation, as the tomb
               was close at hand, they laid Jesus there.

Silence

Hymn: 'When I Survey the Wondrous Cross'
by Isaac Watts (1674-1748) to the tune **Rockingham,**
adapted by Edward Miller (1731-1907)

Poem: 'The Coming' by R. S. Thomas

> And God held in his hand
> A small globe. Look, he said.
> The son looked. Far off,
> As though through water, he saw
> A scorched land of fierce
> Colour. The light burned
> There; crusted buildings
> Cast their shadows; a bright
> Serpent, a river
> Uncoiled itself, radiant
> With slime.
>   On a bare
> Hill, a bare tree saddened
> The sky. Many people
> Held out their thin arms
> To it, as though waiting
> For a vanished April
> To return to its crossed
> Boughs. The son watched
> Them. Let me go there, he said.

Silence

Music: *The Prelude to* Parsifal *by Wagner*

Silence

Hymn: 'Love's Endeavour, Love's Expense',
by W. H. Vanstone (1923–99), to the tune **Savannah** *c. 1740*

Penitence

We shall have to confront
what we did not do
because we did not dare...

Poem

> God may reduce you
> on Judgment Day
> to tears of shame
> reciting by heart
> the poems you would
> have written, had
> your life been good.

The Reproaches: a version by Janet Morley

**Mysterious God, dark and strange,
holy and intimate, have mercy on us.**

I brooded over the abyss,
with my words I called forth creation:
but you have brooded on destruction,
and laid waste the earth and seas...

Silence

O my people, what have I done to you?
How have I offended you? Answer me.

**Mysterious God, dark and strange,
holy and intimate, have mercy on us.**

I breathed life into your bodies,
and carried you tenderly in my arms:
but you have armed yourselves for war,
breathing out threats of violence…

Silence

O my people, what have I done to you?
How have I offended you? Answer me.

**Mysterious God, dark and strange,
holy and intimate, have mercy on us.**

I made the desert blossom before you,
I fed you with an open hand:
but you have grasped the children's food,
and eroded fertile lands…

Silence

O my people, what have I done to you?
How have I offended you? Answer me.

**Mysterious God, dark and strange,
holy and intimate, have mercy on us.**

I abandoned my power like a garment,
choosing your unprotected flesh:
but you have robed yourselves in privilege,
and chosen to despise the abandoned…

Silence

O my people, what have I done to you?
How have I offended you? Answer me.

**Mysterious God, dark and strange,
holy and intimate, have mercy on us.**

I would have gathered you to me as a lover,
and shown you the ways of peace:
but you have desired security,
and you would not surrender yourself...

Silence

O my people, what have I done to you?
How have I offended you? Answer me.

**Mysterious God, dark and strange,
holy and intimate, have mercy on us.**

I have torn the veil of my glory,
transfiguring the earth;
but you have disfigured my beauty,
and turned away your face...

Silence

O my people, what have I done to you?
How have I offended you? Answer me.

**Mysterious God, dark and strange,
holy and intimate, have mercy on us.**

I have laboured to deliver you,
as a woman delights to give birth;
but you have delighted in bloodshed,
and laboured to bereave the world...

Silence

O my people, what have I done to you?
How have I offended you? Answer me.

**Mysterious God, dark and strange,
holy and intimate, have mercy on us.**

I have followed you
with the power of my spirit,
to seek truth and heal the oppressed:
but you have been following a lie,
and returned to your own comfort...

Silence

O my people, what have I done to you?
How have I offended you? Answer me.

**Mysterious God, dark and strange,
holy and intimate, have mercy on us.**

Turn again, my people, listen to me.

Silence

Let your bearing towards one another
arise out of your life in Christ Jesus.
He humbled himself
and in obedience accepted the death of the cross.
But I have bestowed on him
the name that is above every name,
that at the name of Jesus every knee should bow
and every tongue confess
that Jesus Christ is Lord.

Turn again, my people, and listen to me...

Silence

The Nails of the Cross

As an act of penitence, and of acknowledgment that we too are among the crucifiers, we may wish to take a nail from the bowl and press it into the wood of the cross.

Music: Aria, 'He was despised', from Handel's Messiah

Silence

Poem: 'The Place of Prayer' by May Crowther

> This is the place of prayer,
> where the inward-pointing nails converge,
> the ever-narrowing gate
> when the world of time and space
> yields up its measured form.
>
> Here in the needle's eye,
> dark upon dark,
> the aching, echoing void
> of the hollowed heart
> suspended
> at the point of change.
>
> Unknowing
> (and that is the agony)
> bearing the unknown
> to the mystery
> at the place of prayer.

Silence

Prayer of Recognition

O Christ, in whose body was named all the violence of the world, and in whose memory is contained our profoundest grief,

we lay open to you the violence done to us in time beyond memory; the unremembered wounds that have misshaped our lives; the injuries we cannot forget and have not forgiven...

Silence

The remembrance of them is grievous to us:
The burden of them is intolerable.

We lay open to you the violence done in our name in time before memory; the unremembered wounds we have inflicted; the injuries we cannot forget for which we have not been forgiven...

Silence

The remembrance of them is grievous to us:
The burden of them is intolerable.

We lay open to you those who have pursued a violent knowledge the world cannot forget; those caught up in violence they have refused to name; those who have enacted violence which they have not repented...

Silence

The remembrance of them is grievous to us:
The burden of them is intolerable.

We lay open to you the victims of violence whose only memorial is our anger; those whose suffering was sustained on our behalf; those whose continued oppression provides the ground we stand on...

Silence

The remembrance of them is grievous to us:
The burden of them is intolerable.

We wholeheartedly repent of the evil we have done,
and of the evil done on your behalf.
We look for grace to offer forgiveness,
and to know ourselves forgiven.
Wounded God, bear the burden of our prayer
    deep into your heart.
Unstop our ears that we may receive the gospel
    of the Cross.
Give light to our eyes that we may see your glory
    in the face of Jesus Crucified.
Sharpen our minds that your truth may make us whole.
Warm our hearts with the radiance of your love
    that we may love one another,
        forgiving to seventy times seven.
Wounded God, may the scars of this day shine
    with light.
Amen.

Silence

Hymn: 'A Body, Broken on a Cross' by Brian Wren,
to the tune Melita, *by J. B. Dykes (1823–76)*

> **A body, broken on a cross,**
> **with watching women's helpless grief,**
> **and men in heedless, headlong flight,**
> **through fear, despair, or disbelief –**
>   **in this, though still we find it strange,**
>   **are life, and hope, and power to change.**

A people weaponless and weak,
not many wealthy, great or wise,
but women, labourers, and slaves,
absurd to Greek and Roman eyes,
    their Caesar's rages could forgive,
    out-die, out-suffer, and out-live.

And still today, abroad, at home,
from suburb or from shanty-town,
the Spirit's new, surprising word,
in ours or other faiths, or none,
    our sad routines will disarrange
    with gospel-hope of power to change.

When disillusion chains our feet
and might and money turn to dust,
when exile, desert, or defeat
have left us nothing else to trust,
    at last our spirit understands
    the strength of peaceful, nail-scarred hands.

A nation drifting in decline
can turn to just and loving ways,
and people empty, bruised, ashamed,
can find rebirth to joy and praise,
    and churches, wakened, can exchange
    a huddled death for power to change.

Prayer of Intercession

Eternal God,
loving us and all the world,
creating us, sustaining us, and giving us new life,
in the Spirit of Jesus,
crucified for the liberation of humankind,

we come in prayer to align our wills with yours,
to bring into mind's eye and heart's presence
  the needs of this our earth and all her peoples:

Bless the catholic communion of churches throughout
  the world.
Give unity in faith, in witness, and in service.
Bless those who lead and guide your people.

[In particular, bless...]

Bless those preparing to be baptized and confirmed this Easter.
Bless those who are mocked and persecuted for their faith.
Confirm us all in faith, increase our love, deepen our joy.

God of the churches, your will be done:
Your love be shown.

Eternal and loving God,
**by whose Spirit the whole Body of the Church
  is guided and sanctified,
receive the desires of our hearts
  for all your faithful people,
that in our varied vocations and ministries
  we may serve you in holiness and truth,
to the glory of your name.
We pray this in the Spirit of the Crucified. Amen.**

Bless the peoples of the world and their leaders.
Bless the Parliament of this land.
Bless the countries of the European Union.
Bless the United Nations Organisation.
Bless the peacemakers and the peacekeepers.
Bless those who administer the law
  and those who work to reform it.

[In particular, bless...]

Bless all who strive for justice for the oppressed
    and reconciliation for the estranged.
By your help may the world live in peace and freedom.

God of the world's kingdoms, your will be done:
Your love be shown.

Gracious God,
whose will is our peace,
turn our hearts to yourself,
that by the power of your Spirit at work within us,
the peace which is founded on justice
    may spread throughout the world.
We pray this in the Spirit of the Crucified. Amen.

Bless your ancient people the Jews,
called in faith and love to be a light to the nations of the world.
Give all Christian people the spirit of repentance
    for the ill we have done to our Jewish brothers and sisters.
Bless the Muslim peoples and all who live in the Middle East.
Increase understanding among all who inherit their faith
    from the same ancestors.
Remove our common blindness and hardness of heart.
Enable us to be faithful to your covenants
    and to grow in love for your name.

God beyond our conceiving, your will be done,
Your love be shown.

God of Abraham and of Sarah,
bless all their descendants in faith.
Take from us all fear of the stranger
and hasten the gathering of the nations
    to the city of peace,
the dwelling-place of all who love you.

**We pray this in the Spirit of the One
who was crucified outside Jerusalem. Amen.**

Bless those who do not believe that the fulness of your Love
    dwelt bodily in Jesus Christ.
Bless those who follow other faiths and creeds.
Bless those who have never heard a message of salvation.
Bless those who have lost their faith.
Soften the hearts of the contemptuous and the scornful,
those who hate Christ and persecute the followers of the Way,
and those who in the name of Christ persecute others.
Open our hearts to the truth,
and lead us all in ways of faith and obedience.

God of overflowing generosity, your will be done,
Your love be shown.

Merciful God,
**Creator of all the peoples of the earth,
have compassion on those who do not know you
and on those who have hardened their hearts against
    your love.
May the grace and power of that love gather us
    together in your Presence.
We pray this in the Spirit of the One who forgave them
    for they knew not what they did. Amen.**

Bless those who care for this planet earth.
Bless those who repair the ravages of war.
Bless all the creatures of land and sea and air.
Give us the will to replenish the earth
    and a new spirit of reverence for all living things.

God of abundant blessing, your will be done,
Your love be shown.

Creator God,
**ceaselessly at work through the groaning of the
     universe,**
**transform the body of this earth that it might shine
     with your glory,**
reflected in the wounds of the Crucified,
in whose Spirit we pray. Amen.

Bless those who suffer.
Bless those deprived of nurture for body or mind,
     emotions or spirit.
Bless those oppressed by others' lusts and fears.
Bless the doubting and despairing, the lonely
     and the imprisoned.
Bless those falsely accused and those who have been violated.
Bless those who are ill and those who are at the point of death.

[In particular, bless...]

Bless those who watch and care and pray
that, through them, all who suffer may be assured
     of your presence and your love.

God of suffering, your will be done,
Your love be shown.

Living, loving God,
**the comfort of the sorrowful and the strength
     of the weak,**
**pour out your compassion on those who cry in
     their distress.**
And to all who are troubled give mercy and relief,
your springs of living water in their desert place.
We pray this in the Spirit of the Crucified,
the Bearer of our pain. Amen.

We commend ourselves and all people to your unfailing love.
We pray for the grace of a holy life.
Bless all who have died in the overarching Peace of Christ,
both those who have confessed faith in you and those whose
    faith is known to you alone;

[In particular, bless…]

that with them we may come to the fulness of eternal life and
    the joy of the resurrection.

God of new and unexpected life,
your will be done,
Your love be shown.

God of the living,
in whose embrace all creatures live,
in whatever world or condition they may be,
we remember in your presence those whom we have
    known and loved,
whose names and needs and dwelling place are known
    to you.
We give you thanks for our memories of them.
In you, O God, we love them.
May this our prayer minister to their needs and
    to their peace.
We ask this in the Spirit of the Crucified,
who broke the barrier of death and lives for evermore.
    Amen.

Abba, Amma, Beloved,
your name be hallowed,
your reign spread among us,
your will be done well,
at all times, in all places,
on earth as in heaven.

**Give us the bread
we need for today.
Forgive us our trespass
as we forgive those
who trespass against us.
Let us not fail
in time of our testing.
Spare us from trials
too sharp to endure.
Free us from the grip
of all evil powers.
For yours is the reign,
the power and the glory,
the victory of love,
for now and eternity,
world without end,
Amen and Amen.**

Silence

The Cosmic Christ

As memory and imagination, experience and meaning, worked
their way into the stories surrounding the horror of the crucifixion, the wailers of the Great Laments, and the writers of the
Gospels of the Passion, looked long into that terrible event, and
believed that it echoed throughout the creation. They reported
that at the time of the Crucifixion the earth quaked and split
open, and the veil of the Temple was torn in two. They said that
after his death Jesus descended to the place of the departed. They
came to understand his death as cosmic in scope, reaching to the
ends of the universe, to the heart of God, and to the boundaries
of the lost.

Music: The 'Agnus Dei' from Missa Gaia (Earth Mass) by Paul Winter

The voices in the distant background during the introduction and in the middle of the piece are harp seals, recorded on the ice near the Magdalen Islands in the Gulf of St Lawrence. Dr Wilfred Grenfell, medical missionary to Labrador in 1909 wrote: 'It has not been easy to convey to the Eskimo mind the meaning of the Oriental similes of the Bible. Thus the Lamb of God had to be translated "Kotik" or "young seal". This animal, with its perfect whiteness as it lies in its cradle of ice, its gentle, helpless nature, and its pathetic, innocent eyes, is probably as apt a substitute, however, as nature offers.

> *O Lamb, O Seal, of God,*
> *taking away the sin of the world,*
> *have mercy on us,*
> *give us your peace.*

Poem: 'I see his Blood upon the Rose' by Joseph Plunkett

I see his blood upon the rose
And in the stars the glory of his eyes,
His body gleams amid eternal snows,
His tears fall from the skies.

I see his face in every flower;
The thunder and the singing of the birds
Are but his voice – and carven by his power
Rocks are his written word.

All pathways by his feet are worn,
His strong heart stirs the ever-beating sea,
His crown of thorns is twined with every thorn,
His cross is every tree.

Silence

Poem: 'For Martin' by David Scott

Strange how gorse
has thorn and rich flower
both – all along
the hills and roadsides
from Carrowkeel to Portsalon
and on the slopes of Murren.

My Saviour caught his coat
on gorse. Fingering
the torn cloth and trammelled thread
he spoke of death being
thorn and rich flower,
both.

Silence

Canticle of Praise

God, be gracious to us and bless us,
show us the light of your countenance
and be merciful to us.

We glory in your Cross, O Christ,
and praise you for your mighty resurrection.
For by virtue of the Cross joy has come into the world.

Let your ways be made known upon earth,
your liberating power among all peoples.

We glory in your Cross, O Christ,
and praise you for your mighty resurrection.
For by virtue of the Cross joy has come into the world.

Let the peoples praise you, O God,
let all the peoples praise you.

We glory in your Cross, O Christ,
and praise you for your mighty resurrection.
For by virtue of the Cross joy has come into the world.

Hymn: 'Sing, my Tongue, the Glorious Battle'
by Fortunatus (530–609), to the tune **Grafton,**
based on the tune **Tantum Ergo**

An act of remembrance of the participants in the Passion

It was at the ninth hour, at three in the afternoon, that Jesus died.

At such an hour a passing bell might toll.

John Donne wrote:
Who bends not his ear to any bell, which upon any occasion
rings? But who can remove it from that bell which is passing a
piece of himself out of this world? No man is an island, entire of
itself: every man is a piece of the main; if a clod be washed away
by the sea, Europe is the less, as well as if a promontory were, as
well as if a manor of thy friends or of thine own were; any man's
death diminishes me, because I am involved in mankind; and
therefore never send to know for whom the bell tolls: it tolls for
thee.

So let us bring to mind those whose stories have been woven into
the drama of the Passion of Jesus, along with countless human
beings before and since who have played similar parts in the un-
folding of this world's story:

Simon the leper,
who was hospitable to Jesus at Bethany,
and all those who have been rejected,
and yet sheltered the persecuted and outcast...

The unnamed woman
who anointed Jesus with expensive ointment,
and all who have given of themselves with reckless generosity...

Judas Iscariot,
who betrayed Jesus,
and all who have sold their friends out of fear or greed
or from mistaken loyalties...

Peter the Rock,
who denied Jesus yet whose heart was true,
and all who have let others down through cowardice,
yet have repented and been forgiven...

The disciple whom Jesus loved,
who lay close to him at the Last Supper,
and all who have found through their love for each other
something of the love of God...

The young man
who followed Jesus to Gethsemane,
and all who have been attracted to Jesus and his Way...

The disciples
who slept in the garden and then ran away,
and all who have fled through weakness from a test of courage...

Caiaphas,
who acted out of loyalty to his tradition,
and all who have refused the deeper challenges of their
    ancestors' faith...

Herod,
bewitched by a desire for dazzling displays of magic,
and all who have yearned for knowledge and power alone,
without the way of faith and love at heart...

The soldiers,
who did their job, but with cruelty,
and all who have misused the law with excess of force...

Simon of Cyrene,
who was compelled to carry the cross,
and all who have been forced to obey an oppressor's whim...

The thief who repented and the thief who did not,
and all who have been faced with their past life at their last hour
    on earth...

The bystanders and crowd,
who mocked and bayed and gaped,
and all those who have been swept along by rhetoric
    to do harm...

The centurion,
who was impressed by the way in which Jesus died,
and all who have been moved to a moment of faith by the
    example of others...

Mary Magdalene, Mary the mother of James and Joses,
    Salome, and the other women,
who had ministered to Jesus, and now looked on from
    a distance,
and all who have been forced to serve within the limits set
    them by those in power...

Mary the mother of Jesus,
whose heart was pierced, but who bore him there still,

and all who have been sore wounded by the unjust death of
    those they loved…

Joseph of Arimathea,
who was bold to ask Pilate for the corpse of Jesus,
and all who have found within themselves unexpected reserves
    of courage…

Nicodemus,
who had come to Jesus by night,
and all who have listened to the wind and done good,
    even if by stealth…

And at the ninth hour Jesus cried out with a loud voice,
Eloi, Eloi, lama sabachthani? which means,
My God, my God, why have you forsaken me?
And some of the bystanders hearing it said,
He is calling Elijah.
And one ran, and filled a sponge full of vinegar
and put it on a reed and gave it to him to drink.
Wait, let us see whether Elijah will come to take him down.
And Jesus uttered a loud cry, and breathed his last.

Music: **Kol Nidrei,** *the Jewish evening hymn,*
by Max Bruch

Notes

For 'The Nails of the Cross' the following equipment is needed:
    large cross from dead wood secured in bucket of sand or soil,
    green twine to secure the two pieces of wood together,
    a strip of balsa wood, thick enough to press a nail into without its falling
        out, attached to the upright of the cross with green twine,
    broad-headed masonry nails,

suitable bowl to contain nails,
small table for bowl.

I gladly acknowledge May Crowther as the author of 'The place of prayer'.
I have no further information about whether or not it has been published.
Apologies for an incomplete acknowledgment.

Brian Wren's 'A Body Broken on a Cross' can be found in his book, Piece
Together Praise © *1989 Stainer and Bell Ltd., London, quoted with*
permission.

The Prayer of Intercession is adapted from that found in Lent, Holy
Week, and Easter, *op. cit. pp. 212-216. The last prayer, 'O God of the*
living' was inspired by some work of J. V. Taylor and is acknowledged with
thanks.

Joseph Plunkett's poem 'I see his Blood upon the Rose' is printed on p. 95
of Susan Dwyer's anthology of religious poetry, Playing with Fire, *pub-*
lished by Villa Books, Dublin, in 1980. The poet lived from 1887–1916.

'For Martin' is an early poem by David Scott and is used with the
permission of the poet, and with my thanks. It is to be found in his Selected
Poems, *published by Bloodaxe Books in 1998.*

For the 'Act of Remembrance' a church bell can be tolled. A substitute is
a gong and something to sound it.

A Sample Introduction to the Reading of the Passion
with gratitude to the work of John Dominic Crossan

We are about to participate again – or perhaps for the first time
– in a half-dramatized presentation of the story of the crucifixion
and death of Jesus as told through the eyes and mind and heart
of the anonymous poet who wrote the Gospel we now call that
according to John. It is a story which mingles history with lament,
argument, prayer, and imagination. It was written for a Christian
community at the turn of the first and second centuries, as distant
from the actual events as we are from the abdication of Edward
VIII. It was a story for its own day, and it can become a story for
ours only with a spiritual health warning.

Piety is false when honour draws a veil over horror.

Remember those sixty years or more between the death of Jesus and the crafting of this story. The first generations of the followers of Jesus have had time to deepen their faith in this man as truly the Anointed One of God. By the year 100, the moment of greatest suffering has been perceived, in faith, as the moment of greatest glory, the moment of defeat as the moment of triumph, the moment of death as the moment of life. Uniquely among the Gospels, in this interpretation of history Jesus is in control throughout. God is working a great deed of deliverance. Death is swallowed up in life.

All of which may be true, in faith, but the honour draws a veil over the horror.

You become especially aware of this when you pay attention to the account of the burial. It is a *royal* burial of honour: only this Gospel tells of spices being brought to embalm the corpse of a king. With a flourish of exaggeration, with due honour indeed, we are told there was a *hundredweight*. No wonder we have a Nicodemus as well as a Joseph of Arimathea to carry them.

Now I do not suppose that the horror had been forgotten. After all, crucifixions were a daily event in the Roman Empire. They were so familiar to people that there was no need for a storyteller to give a detailed description. The trouble for us is that piety looks at the one cross and tells of The Crucifixion, capital T, capital C. And we are glad to move away from Mark to John. John ends on a note of triumph: It is accomplished! Mark ends on a note of despair: Why have you forsaken me?

And we so easily forget the whole point of *crucifixion* for the Roman Empire. Roman executions were brutal, yes, whether by fire or by beasts or by crucifixion. What was most horrible was that afterwards there was nothing left to bury: ashes blown on the wind, a corpse devoured and digested by wild beasts, a corpse on a cross whose flesh was pecked by the carrion of the air and whose bones were gnawed by wild dogs. That there was nothing left for families and friends to *bury* was the ultimate shame, disgrace, *dis-honour*, in ancient societies of the Mediterranean world.

With the hundreds of archaeological digs in and around Jerusalem, there has been only one skeleton ever discovered of a crucified man, and he clearly came from a wealthy family. For if you have money you can bribe the powers that be to release a corpse before sunset and so fulfil the law of your people. Even so, to approach the authorities was in itself a risk: you might easily be dishonoured by association.

A few may well have been buried by their enemies, especially if there was unrest and the authorities wished to avoid too much trouble. But the burial would have been in a shallow grave, hurried and casual. And darkness would soon fall, and the dogs would be there to scrape away the surface soil.

That is history. That is horror.

Faith, sometimes clearing to conviction, sometimes shadowed by doubt, may whisper, Even in this horror, God was *not* absent. God is never absent from any horror. But it is very much a matter of faith to interpret history in this way.

Piety so easily draws a veil over horror, too quickly calls this Friday Good, jumps smoothly from a so-called triumphant entry into Jerusalem on Palm Sunday to a cry of victory on Easter Day, Good Friday being a minor blip, better forgotten or even ignored altogether in a welter of work, lawn-mowing, and hot cross buns. But we do no favours to faith or to the hellish experiences of humankind to play down the horror. And faith still brings its haunting question, Can this our Great Story of history and of faith hold and transform the very worst of devil and death?

In a time of war, kings and governments, emperors and politicians, dictators and generals always seek to draw a veil of honour over the horrors. After all, the populace might get too restless if they knew what was really going on – not least for the poor, for the elderly, for the children, who always suffer most.

It may just be that we are beginning to learn from the horrors of this century. At least we talk now of grim necessities and no longer of glory and honour: they perished for ever in the mud of the Somme. Auschwitz and Hiroshima cast their shadows and their warnings. Television brings us the immediate, and courageous reporters reveal at least some of the worst – from Vietnam to Cambodia, from Sierra Leone to Rwanda, from Bosnia to Kosovo. And it has been estimated that as many American soldiers committed suicide in the years after their return from Vietnam as died in combat there. And how many more, in both countries, languish to this day in perpetual shock?

And yet, slowly and painfully, we are beginning to recognize that only international law and peacekeeping forces can contain the genocidal brutality of the bullies, both leaders and, alas, so many ordinary people who are swept up by ancient emotions and clever rhetoric.

But those who cry out, victims of the horror, as we cry out from the places of our own desolation, want to know that a faith that claims that death is defeated does not dodge the worst. Here is a poem about the worst. It is called 'Tortured Till Dead' and is written for the crucified victims of repression. The writer is Thomas Greenan, in a book of poems, *Give Sorrow Words*, published in 1995 by SCIAF and reproduced in the Holy Week edition of *The Tablet* in 1999:

> Mocked king clown,
> stag thorn-crowned,
> carpenter's nails impale wrists and feet.
> Stripped peasant,
> powerless slave sold
> for thirty silver pesos.
>
> Back bled, skin flayed,
> failed prophet
> forgotten for all time,
> writhes displayed.
> Man's creation
> bitter fruit on tree of damnation.
>
> Heat, sweat, thirst,
> shroud of darkness curse.

Yeshoua screams,
lungs burst
in deep, sea-deep
despair.

Head bows,
heart tears,
corpse slumps limp
into night's silent vault.

Remember these things as we participate in the reading of the Passion. Remember the vultures and the wild dogs. Darkness at noon indeed.

And as a coda, remember this also. That first generation of the followers of Jesus were Jews, as Jesus was. And, as Jews always do, they argued with their fellow Jews, Pharisee Jews, Saduccee Jews, Essene Jews, Zealot Jews, trying to convince them that Jesus was indeed God's Anointed. But by the time the Gospels of Matthew and of John came to be written, the Temple in Jerusalem had been destroyed, Judaism was dispersed among the synagogues, and Christianity had become a new religion. Church now argued with Synagogue, and the Jews as a whole were blamed for the death of Jesus – that terrible cry of 'His blood be upon us and upon our children.' It was no longer the religious and political powers that be that always act in defence of their securities, comfort, and traditions, as do we when we, as we usually do, collude. Humanity is in the dock for all its crimes of terror and of horror.

The argument between Christian and Jew was not of course particularly dangerous as long as neither had political power. But that changed in the fourth century with Constantine. As soon as Christianity became the state religion, argument became lethal weapon, and the horror began of persecution, pogrom, and holocaust. Darkness at noon indeed.

There may be much in this reading for faith. But there is the danger, *as always*, that bland piety and the desire for honour forget the horror and the desolation and the cries of the children...

26

The Groaning of Creation

Sylvia Sands

I
The Song of the Bird

He loved us,
birds of the air.
Listen to his stories
of ravens and eagles --
and even sparrows:
two sold for a farthing,
and not one falls to the ground
without the Father knowing.

Here I am,
perched on his cross,
eyeing those thorns
burrowing blackly and blindly,
burrowing secretly, searingly,
into his brow.

Tell me,
where is that damned dreamy
dove of peace now?
His beak is longer and stronger than mine.

Look, I've tried.
I've flown into,
under his sweat-soaked,
blood-drenched,
once-beautiful hair.

I've tried to wrench out
one, just one, of those thorns.
I've beaten – nearly broken – my wings,
against his face;
and all I've done
is to draw more blood.
Fierce are those thorns,
force-driven into his head.

With what strength I have left
I'm flying,
flying away from my failure,
flying away lest I forget
the music trapped in my breast
for sunset and dawn:
flight and music –
his gifts.

As I fly
a hoard of young sparrows
come twittering and taunting,
laughing and crying after me:
Red breast! Red breast!
Whoever saw a red breast before?

I glance down as I fly
and see my breast flame crimson
against the gathering dusk.

The fellowship of his sufferings:
in my heart, as if to break it,
creep sunset and dawnbreak,
and in my soul a new song is born
with which to greet them.

II
The Lament of the Trees

Have you ever considered the longing of the trees?
Our branches outstretched in silhouetted prayer,
yearning, yearning, towards the sky?
Our branches stooping with aching desire,
like washerwomen over water?
Have you ever considered the language of the trees?

In the spring we whisper to one another.
Oh, to be honoured,
part of a temple;
to be useful,
a boat curving through water,
the door of a loved home,
the plough of a farmer,
the yoke of an ox,
the toy of a child.

On the breeze come the rumours:
A master carpenter in Nazareth,
whose carved birds fly away,
whose sculptured horses ride the wind,
whose tables seat twelve.
Oh, to end up in his hands!

Hear then our shame,
take note of our lament,
to have those same creative hands
crucified on our branches,
and to soak up the lifeblood
of a man who loved trees.
Across the world in autumn,
across the world in fall,
we shed our tears.
And the willows have been weeping,
the willows have been weeping,
ever since this bitter, twisted Friday.

III
The Cross of the Donkey

I've always been laughed at:
Silly ass,
just a donkey,
two a penny,
a beast of burden.

So when I hit the heights that Sunday,
palm branches beneath my hooves,
easing the pain of the Jerusalem hills,
carrying the Carpenter of Nazareth
on my back like a king,
I thought:

Never,
never again,
will they break sticks across my back,
or leave me starving in fields,
untrimmed feet grown ridiculous,
obscene and crippling.
Oh, no, the world will know
a donkey, *a donkey*,
carried the Prince of Peace into Jerusalem.
The laugh's on *them* now.

That's what I thought.
I should have known better.
With hindsight they blame me.
I should have *known*
I was carrying him to his death,
that's what they say.
Of all creatures I should know
how fickle humans are.
Why didn't I bolt?
Why didn't I stop dead in my tracks?
Dig my hooves in?

So I have stood
broken, despairing,
all through this unending night,
remembering his gentle hands on the reins,
his thoughts finding a place in my heart.
We have a battle of love to win, little donkey,
he said.
And just when I thought my darkness would never end,
at dawn,
a little bird with a blooded breast
flew over.

Hold your head up, noble creature,
she cried,
your back is marked with the sign of his cross!

Donkeys all over the world
are beaten, starved, tortured,
worked till we drop.
But sometimes,
sometimes,
a man or woman is humble enough
to trace with reverent hands across our backs,
the imprint of his cross,
and kneel,
kneel before a donkey.

IV
The Nocturne of the Night

Twelve o'clock in the afternoon,
and one of the stars in the universe
began screaming,
while down the hill of Golgotha
pounded a young lad,
scattering five loaves and two fishes
as he ran,
crying,
Turn out the sun,
turn out the sun!
Words – it so happened –
that found a place in a mother's heart,
who, in her anguish,
had been groping wretchedly and in vain
for a prayer – any prayer – to cry.
Yes, turn out the sun, she echoed.

In answer to the screaming star,
in answer to the boy's cry,
in answer to the distracted mother,
I the Night,
already fearful and brooding,
descended.

Tenderly I came,
wrapping my cloak of darkness
round his twisted limbs,
as his mother once wrapped him
in swaddling clothes.

Slowly I came,
sending arms of darkness
round the shaking shoulders
of his disciples,
hiding in the fields.

Gently I came,
dropping a jet blanket
over the trembling form
of a beautiful woman in scarlet
prostrate in the dust of Calvary.

Relentlessly I came,
stopping the heartless rattle of dice,
dulling the brazen glint of swords,
and spears,
and armour.

At twelve o'clock,
earlier than ever before or since,
I, the Night, came to Calvary,
ushering in black shadows
in which humanity could hide its face like a child,
ushering in at twelve o'clock in the afternoon,
ushering in the dark night of the soul.

V
The Anger of the Earth

Saint Francis, they say,
that intuitive dreamer, went too far,
believing that the ravines and caves
hollowed out on Mount Alverna,
were created by an earthquake when Jesus died.

But lovers of the Earth know Saint Francis was right.

I, the Earth, declare it.
Every falling drop of his blood
shook my depths;
every groan from his lips
shifted the subsoil;
stalactites shivered like crystals,
falling like chandeliers.

Enraged,
I could hear the anger stirring in my bowels;
enraged,
I shook my mountainous shoulders
in preparation for a great explosion against humanity
for its callous cruelty,
its exploitation of trees and metals, wood and nails.

Seven words stopped me,
seven words spoken from his cross.

Ever since,
every Friday,
I, the Earth, remember,
remember the final whisper from his dying lips,
releasing through the world
an earthquake of love
that broke in two my mighty heart.

All lovers of the Earth know Saint Francis was right.

27

Buried Truth

Rowan Williams

The verdict in the David Irving case is rightly being seen as something of a landmark. George Steiner drew attention several years ago to the 'irresponsibility' of language. The danger and exhilaration of words is that, in the simplest possible sense, you can say what you like. And for Steiner, as for others, Holocaust denial is the most frightening example of this sinister freedom. But this is not the whole story. What we can in the abstract say, we must in the concrete defend. We can say what we like, but we cannot expect what we say to be left unchallenged, unanswered. And although the Irving verdict does not change the character of the moral world, a world that is increasingly careless and relativistic about what can be said unchallenged, it serves as a sharp reminder that sooner or later the balloons filled with ideology and fantasy, self-justification, impregnable system-making, and all the rest, are going to drift towards the thorn bushes.

Neat and comforting fictions, historical, philosophical, or religious, are in the long run vulnerable to another sort of language. In the Irving trial, what settled the verdict was a mixture of personal testimony, documentation in word and picture, the relentless building up of a whole world of detail, sometimes confused and confusing, but clear enough both to pin down specific distortions of fact and to display an enormous context within which the denials of Irving and those like him could not be sustained. Say what you like: some utterances die in the air. There are things that words cannot change, the things that are contained in the stumbling and blurred recollection of an old woman, or in the tattered remains of an official invoice, or a parenthesis in a letter. All this is the language that ideology and fantasy should fear.

You can say what you like, but words cannot be relied on to

bury truth. Even where the winners have rewritten the history, where a language and a civilization have been destroyed, what is suppressed and buried still so often returns. You think you have silenced the dissenting voice, but your own words carry the tell-tale trace of what you have tried to deny. The buried truth finds its way in from the margins, laps against the shore of the winner's version.

Good Friday, at the very least, has something to do with this. Biblical commentators often remind us of the utterly routine nature of the crucifixion of a peasant in an occupied country. It is almost a commonplace to recognize that Pilate is unlikely to have remembered one more agitator dealt with in the usual way. The story told today is about a suppression, a silencing; those who organized the killing of Jesus of Nazareth would not even have bothered to deny what had happened because they were confident that the systems of the day would ensure that their version was the only one that counted. So the very fact that nearly two thousand years later the victim has not been silenced should make us think about all systems that assume it is ultimately possible for words to bury truth, to obliterate the traces of pain or outrage. The crucified says to all of us, believer or unbeliever, something about what, after all, we can and cannot say.

To the Church, the crucified says more. After two thousand years of putting the cross to our own uses, two thousand years of using it, again and again, to silence and suppress others (Jews above all, but also all those who died at the hands of crusaders and conquistadors bearing the cross), what we have to make sure is that this naked suffering and murder is not obliterated by our theologies or our holy wars. It is there to judge us still.

It is there, we believe, because of who it is who hangs there. God's word to the world is the body of a victim. When God speaks to us, the language used is the language of those that the systems of the world would like to forget, and we are sharply told that if we want to hear God speaking, we had better start listening to that language. And because this dead body is the body in which God lives, it cannot remain a dead body. If God speaks in the language of the forgotten, anonymous sufferers, their reality is somehow caught up in his life, broken open to his future. When Christians look at the cross, they see not only a reminder of how words cannot bury the truth of injustice and oppression; they see that truth itself transformed. It is no longer just an intolerable memory from the past (though it is at least that), but also something waiting for God's future.

But that waiting becomes an empty optimism if it does not start in truthfulness, in the journey beyond ideology and system to stand before the crucified body and before whatever bodies, whatever wounds, we are most encouraged to forget or ignore. There is no short cut to Easter. It would be a bitter paradox if the effect of Easter hymns and Easter preaching were to bury the reality of the crucified. Good Friday is a day for remembering that words do not change memory, words do not transform the world. If they did, the liar and the ideologue would have things their own way. But the Good of this Friday for the Christian is in knowing that there is another and a true transformation, if this death, this silent body, is also the word and act of the world's creator.

28

The Sound of Silence

Martyn Percy

Like many people, our family probably watches too much television. At the end of a long day, and sometimes before a long evening, the shoes are kicked off and the gin and tonic pressed into the hand. Television requires little mental effort; it soothes; we watch to forget, to relax. The set may be switched on but we switch off. When we listen we have to watch differently and start visualizing with our minds. Our imaginations stretch us. Our senses work harder.

To go into a church on Good Friday is to find no flowers, no decoration, no celebration, only stark simplicity and the figure of a man hanging on a cross. He slumps, he dies. To return on Easter Day is to be presented with a riot of colour, golds and whites and yellows, flowers and festivity.

The Saturday stands between, an atmosphere subdued but expectant.

But there is nothing to see. So the imagination has to get to work. There is no wondrous cross to be surveyed, and as yet no empty tomb to look into. The time of vigil has come, and we wait in silence, in stillness, and as evening draws on, in darkness. The visual images of Good Friday have gone, over-familiar to us from paintings, films, and television. But it is not easy to capture pain and dying in a portrait. In the very act of committing them to canvas or screen something of the reality is lost.

Suppose though that on the Saturday we no longer try and *look*. Suppose we shut our eyes and *listen*. What would you hear?

A friend of mine won a competition to write a short play for radio. It had to be three minutes long, witty and wry, and use sound effects. He chose to write on the first three chapters of Genesis, and his play featured two lowly 'angels' who were back-room boys. They were in God's workshop and their task was to 'dub' sound on to creation. The story tells us that God created fish, birds, animals, seas, rivers – but not a thing about the sounds they make.

The two angels set about their task grumbling, "It's all right for 'im upstairs to say 'Let there be birds,' but who's gotta put the soundtrack on a flock of bleedin' seagulls – muggins 'ere. And it must be different from the parrot, the sparrow, and the cormorant..." As they talk about their work and why waves on pebbles must make a different sound to the 'plop' of a pebble in still water, attention focuses on a box in the corner of the sound workshop. "What's that box for?" asks the junior, apprentice angel. "Ah, you don't want to touch that," replies the senior angel. "That box is full of sounds you don't want to hear – a child crying, a mother dying, the sound of war, screams, the rattle of death. Once you open the box, you'll release the noises of chaos, and you'll never get them back in."

When the senior angel leaves for a coffee break, the apprentice goes to the box and inspects it more closely. It looks such a nice box. How can one small box contain so many sounds? He prises open the lid and lifts it slightly. He hears no scream, nor the sound of war, only the crunch of teeth into a delicious, crisp, green apple.

Lent is about acknowledging all those sounds that were let out long ago, sounds we have so little control over. Good Friday and Easter Day are about hearing them contract and redeemed in the events of crucifixion and resurrection. The sounds of fury on Good Friday cancel out the sound of the Fall, and bring the peace of Easter on a bright spring day. Listening in silence, and imagining, stops us being seduced by the anodyne portraits that fix the crucifixion in a frame, a moment of sacred but very safe contemplation. So Holy Saturday is a prelude to a mystery, one that defies sight. The philosopher Wittgenstein reminds us that "whereof we cannot speak we must be silent." So, from now on, silence is what must be, listening and waiting. [You might like to turn to Sylvia Sands' poem on page 147.]

Good Friday and Easter Day are linked by a fierce but tender sound, that of ground breaking and earth quaking. But they carry different messages. This Saturday night, all over the world, people will sit in the dark silence between those sounds. In the vigil they keep they will remember the story of their creation and redemption as it unfolds in the pages of the Scriptures. They will wait and watch for a spark, the first flame of the Light of Easter. At its appearance there will be a new sound – shouts of acclamation and celebration. And once again the Silenced Word will speak.

29

At the Beginning of the Night

In Preparation for Easter

The early evening of Easter Eve
8 pm onwards

Compiled by Jim Cotter

This celebration of Easter is in two parts – a Vigil of Preparation as light fades on Easter Eve and the great ceremonies of Easter Dawn. As on Maundy Thursday, there are differences of mood and place to be kept in mind.

Easter Eve itself is a day of preparation – every feast depends on one. And for this celebration, there is scope for many talents – building a bonfire, making decorations, arranging floral displays, rehearsing music, preparing food and drink.

The Vigil works well informally, indoors, around a fire. Treat the readings and psalms as a quarry. They can of course be used as they are, much as on Maundy Thursday: they can be said in church during the night and lead straight into the dawn celebration. Allow two hours for the whole sequence.

However, there is much to be said for separating the Vigil from the main celebration, not least to avoid exhaustion. And if there are no more than thirty people present, an informal gathering is practicable. Not all twelve readings need be used. If those who wish are asked beforehand to choose one of the readings, they can introduce their choice by saying why they have been drawn to that particular passage. Readings could also be taken from books other than the Bible, and, informally, people can be invited to reflect on what Easter means to them and how they have celebrated the feast in times past, their memories, stories, fears, and hopes.

Given that the dawn celebration begins very early, not everyone may wish to stay for the whole of the Vigil, while others may be drawn to keep the whole night in prayerful watch.

Kettles should be kept handy...

Introduction

We have gathered to prepare ourselves for the Great Festival of Easter, for our celebration, at tomorrow's dawn, of the Resurrection and the Living Presence of Jesus Christ.

We have come to renew our participation in the same process of dying and rising, the movement of transfiguration of all that is of the earth into unimagined glory.

We meet as the darkness of night deepens; we look forward to the light of the new day.

We shall then remember the buried Jesus; we shall kindle and gather round a new fire; we shall process with torches from that fire; and we shall light a single candle flame to proclaim Christ penetrating the darkness in resurrection and eternal life.

We shall recall the drowning waters through which we were baptized into that new and risen life, and we shall share the bread and wine, bearers to us of the life-giving Body and Blood of the crucified and risen One.

But first, in this time of vigil, we shall read from the Book of the Older Covenant, and look forward to the initiation of the Newer Covenant, sealed in the Spirit of the Lifeblood of Christ, poured out and spent for us, enriching and fulfilling the promises of God made to our ancestors of faith so very long ago.

So we pray:

Eternal God, whose power is love,
**ceaselessly at work for the glorifying of the universe
and for the flourishing of each and every one,
rescue us and all peoples from everything that
enslaves us,
as you rescued our ancestors from slavery in Egypt,
and free us from the grip of evil and death,
making us heirs of a new transformed creation,
in the realm of Jesus Christ, our dying and rising
Redeemer.**

The Vigil

One

A Reading from the Book Genesis chapter 1, verse 1 to chapter 2, verse 3

Psalm 33.1–9

Let those who serve you praise you, O God,
let the true of heart give you thanks.
Let the harmonies of the universe sound,
accompanying our words in your praise.

The earth is full of your lovingkindness.

Dear God, you are the God of creation,
by your word was the universe made,
the numberless stars by the breath of your mouth.
You held the waters of the sea in the hollow of your hand,
you gathered to yourself the waters of the deep.

The earth is full of your lovingkindness.

Let the whole earth be joyful in you,
all the inhabitants of the world greet you with joy.
For you spoke, and the wonderful deed was done,
you commanded, and it came to pass.

The earth is full of your lovingkindness.

For your Word is true,
your deeds are faithful to your covenant.
You love the justice of relationships made right,
the world is full of your steadfast love.

The earth is full of your lovingkindness.

Silence

Father God, Mother God,
by the energy of creative love
   you have brought all things into being,
continually creating and restoring us,
making us in your image,
sharing in our humanity
   that we might come to share in your divinity.
We contemplate your creation:
the darkness of this night,
the light of the dawn,
our birth in the waters,
our life sustained and transformed by you.
Mother God, Father God,
we rest in the silence of your presence.

Pause

Two

A Reading from the Book Genesis, chapter 3

Psalm 130

Empty, exhausted, and ravaged,
in the depths of despair I writhe.
Anguished and afflicted, terribly alone,
I trudge a bleak wasteland, devoid of all love.

I wait in the darkness for your mercy.

In the echoing abyss I call out:
no God of Compassion hears my voice.
Yet still do I pray, Open your heart,
for my tears well up within me.

I wait in the darkness for your mercy.

If you keep account of all that drags me down,
there is no way I can ever stand firm.
Paralyzed and powerless, I topple over,
bound by the evil I hate.

I wait in the darkness for your mercy.

But with you is forgiveness and grace,
there is nothing I can give – it seems like a death.
The power of your love is so awesome:
I am terrified by your freeing embrace.

I wait in the darkness for your mercy.

Drawn from the murky depths by a fish hook,
I shout to the air that will kill me:
Must I leave behind all that I cherish
before I can truly breathe free?

I wait in the darkness for your mercy.

Suspended between one world and the next,
I waited for you, my God.
Apprehension and hope struggled within me,
I waited, I longed for your word.

I wait in the darkness for your mercy.

As a watchman waits for the morning,
through the darkest and coldest of nights,
more even than the watchman who peers through the gloom
I hope for the dawn, I yearn for the light.

I wait in the darkness for your mercy.

You will fulfil your promise to bring me alive,
overflowing with generous love.
You will free me from the grip of evil,
O God of mercy and compassion.

I wait in the darkness for your mercy.

Touching and healing the whole of my being,
you are a God whose reach has no limit.
All that has been lost will one day be found:
the communion of the rescued will rejoice in your name.

Silence

Through the dark despairing depths
and the drought of the desert,
through the abyss opened up by our failings and folly,
we dare to risk our cry to the living God.
For you will not let us escape from our greatest good.
In our struggle with you, fierce, fiery Lover,
let some new glory be wrought,
and new and unexpected life come to birth.

Pause

Three

*A Reading from the Book Genesis, chapter 7, verses 1 to 5
and 10 to 18; chapter 8, verses 6 to 18; and chapter 9,
verses 8 to 13*

A Psalm based on Psalm 105

You sustain your covenant with Noah,
with the living creatures of the earth,
that never again will you destroy them,
with a flood laying waste to the world.

You keep faith with the earth for ever.

Your love is for the whole of our planet,
a vow of restraint and protection for ever.
Again and again you renew your promise,

putting a new heart and spirit within us,
through a covenant sealed with your blood,
your last will and testament for us.

You keep faith with the earth for ever.

You demand no unthinking obedience,
a loyalty blind and correct.
You do not try to control us,
you seek the pledge of our wills and our hearts.

You keep faith with the earth for ever.

You are the One who endures our betrayals,
with a precarious and vulnerable love.
You keep faith with us and humble us,
and so renew us in hope.
You laid down the power of coercion,
and gave of yourself with generous love.

You keep faith with the earth for ever.

Our hearts burst out with gratitude,
in awe at the wonder of your goodness.
You have bound us to yourself – we belong to you,
and to one another – there is no way to escape.

You keep faith with the earth for ever.

Keep us responding in friendship and service,
giving and receiving your presence among us,
protecting those who are weak and in need,
trust deepening in sacraments of love.

Silence

In the mystery of Divine Love,
we become gifts to one another,
bound together in the covenants of God.

In the paradox of our free will and destiny,
let us embrace one another and all humankind,
choosing in friendship to share our being and
    becoming.
And with that divine love, and in the spirit of that love,
let us promise
to be steady and reliable in our loving,
to work for our mutual well-being
    and for the cherishing of the earth,
to honour one another as God's dwelling place,
and to keep loyal and full of faith, our life-day long.

Pause

Four

***A Reading from the Book Genesis, chapter 22,
verses 1 to 18***

Psalm 16. 7–11

We give you thanks for the wisdom of your counsel,
even at night you have instructed our hearts.
In the silence of the darkest of hours
we open our ears to the whisper of your voice.

In your countenance is the fulness of joy.

We have set your face always before us,
in every cell of our being you are there.
As we tremble on the narrowest of paths,
the steadying of your hand gives us courage.
Fleet of foot, with our eyes on the goal,
headlong in the chasm we shall not fall.

In your countenance is the fulness of joy.

Therefore our hearts rejoice and our spirits are glad,
our whole being shall rest secure.
For you will not give us over to the power of death,
nor let your faithful ones see the pit.

In your countenance is the fulness of joy.

You will show us the path of life:
in your countenance is the fulness of joy.
From the spring of your heart flow rivers of delight,
a fountain of water that shall never run dry.

In your countenance is the fulness of joy.

Silence

God of the living,
**of the mountain peaks and the fire and the burning
    stars,**
hold us true to the goal of our journey,
that we may be fleet of heart,
**and in all our dying leap to the embrace of the One
    who lures us with love,**
the pioneer of our salvation,
Jesus, our elder brother and our faithful friend.

Pause

Five

A Reading from the Book Exodus, chapter 14, zverses 15 to 31

A Psalm based on part of Psalm 105

You brought Israel out with silver and gold,
and not one of our tribes was seen to stumble.

Egypt was glad at our going,
for dread of Israel had fallen upon them.

Glory to God who has delivered us.

You spread out a cloud for our covering,
and fire to lighten the night.
The people asked and you brought us quails,
and satisfied us with manna from your hand.
You opened a rock so that the waters gushed,
and ran in the parched land like a river.

Glory to God who has delivered us.

For you had remembered your holy word,
the promise to Abraham your servant.
So you led out your people with thanksgiving,
your chosen ones with shouts of joy.

Glory to God who has delivered us.

You gave us the land you had promised,
and we inherited the toil of others,
so that we might keep the gift of your law,
and faithfully fulfil your covenant.

Glory to God who has delivered us.

Silence

Merciful and compassionate God,
save all who drown,
the oppressed and those who oppress them.
Wash away all iniquity in the torrent of your justice,
yet save also the Egyptians,
and bathe them in your tears of mercy,
wider and deeper than all the oceans of the earth.

Pause

Six

A Reading from the Book Deuteronomy, chapter 31, verses 22 to 29

Psalm 19

The law of God is perfect,
refreshing the soul.
The words of God are sure,
and give wisdom to the simple.

Write your Wisdom in our hearts.

The justice of God is righteous,
and rejoices the heart.
The commandment of God is pure,
and gives light to the eyes.

Write your Wisdom in our hearts.

The fear of God is clean,
and endures for ever.
The judgments of God are true,
and just in every way.

Write your Wisdom in our hearts.

They dance as the stars of the universe,
perfect as the parabolas of comets,
like satellites and planets in their orbits,
reliable and constant in their courses.

Write your Wisdom in our hearts.

Silence

God of law and wisdom,
of justice and truth,
keep us true to your commandments of love,
that we may desire them more than gold
and find them sweeter than honey from the comb.

Pause

Seven

A Reading from the Book of the Prophet Isaiah, chapter
54, verses 5 to 14

Psalm 30

From the depths of despair I cried out,
seared with pain and with grief.
Where are you, O God?
How long must I suffer?

God of healing, you are making us whole.

You drew me up from the deeps,
like a prisoner out of a dungeon,
a flesh-body touched by your hand,
flickering and trembling with life.

God of healing, you are making us whole.

You brought me out of a land full of gloom,
a place of hollow silence and cold.
You melted my paralyzed fear:
the warmth of your Sun coursed through my veins.

God of healing, you are making us whole.

The wrath of your Love lasts but a moment,
for a lifetime your mercy and healing.
Heaviness and weeping last through the night,
yet day breaks into singing and joy.

God of healing, you are making us whole.

I will praise you, O God,
for you are making me whole.
I will give you great thanks
in the midst of your people.

God of healing, you are making us whole.

Silence

Living God,
look upon us with eyes of compassion,
call us with the words of healing and forgiveness,
again and again, to seventy times seven,
that we may at last hear and see,
and turn our stricken and wounded faces,
and know ourselves accepted and embraced,
loved into a healing and a joy
beyond measure and without reserve.

Pause

Eight

A Reading from the Book of the Prophet Isaiah,
chapter 55, verses 1 to 11

Canticle based on Isaiah 12

I will praise you, O God:
though in your love you were angry with me,

your anger has melted away,
and you have comforted me.
Surely you are my saviour:
I will trust you and not be afraid.

Praise to the God whose love has triumphed.

You are my strength and my song,
you have become my salvation.
I give you thanks and praise you,
and rejoice in your holy name.
I will make known the wonders you have done,
and I will proclaim your name and nature.

Praise to the God whose love has triumphed.

I will sings hymns to you,
for your way of love has triumphed.
Let this be known to the whole world.
Shout aloud and sing for joy, people of God:
great in our midst is the Holy One of Israel.

Praise to the God whose love has triumphed.

Silence

Come, Living Christ,
with burning coals and purge our lips;
come with the judgment that saves,
and give us back our sense of worth
because it matters what we do;
come with passionate desire
and sweep us into your arms;
come with the love that will not let us go.

Pause

Nine

A Reading from the Book of Job, chapter 14, verses 1 to 14

Psalm 23

Dear God, you sustain me and feed me:
like a shepherd you guide me.
You lead me to an oasis of green,
to lie down by restful waters.

Dwell in me that I may dwell in you.

Quenching my thirst, you restore my life:
renewed and refreshed, I follow you,
a journey on the narrowest of paths.
You keep me true to your name.

Dwell in me that I may dwell in you.

Even when cliffs loom out of the mist,
my step is steady because of my trust.
Even when I go through the deepest valley,
with the shadow of darkness and death,
I will fear no evil or harm.
For you are with me to give me strength,
your crook, your staff, at my side.

Dwell in me that I may dwell in you.

Even in the midst of my troubles,
with the murmurs of those who disturb me,
I know I can feast in your presence.
You spread a banquet before me,
you anoint my head with oil,
you stoop to wash my feet,
you fill my cup to the brim.

Dwell in me that I may dwell in you.

Your lovingkindness and mercy
will meet me very day of my life.
By your Spirit you dwell within me,
and in the whole world around me,
and I shall abide in your house,
content in your presence for ever.

Dwell in me that I may dwell in you.

Silence

Wise and loving Shepherd,
guiding your people in the ways of your truth,
leading us through the waters of baptism,
and nourishing us with the food of eternal life,
keep us in your mercy,
and so guide us through the perils of evil and death,
that we may know your joy at the heart of all things,
both now and for ever.

Pause

Ten

***A Reading from the Book of Baruch, chapter 3, verses 9
to 15 and 32 to 37, and chapter 4, verses 1 to 4***

Psalm 1

Woe to us when we walk
in the way of wickedness,
when we bend our ear to the counsel of deceit,
and scoff at what is holy from the seat of pride.

Keep us true to your Way.

Blessings upon us
when we delight in the truth of God,
and ponder God's Law by day and by night,
when we stand up for truth in face of the lie,
when we mouth no slogans and betray no friends.

Keep us true to your Way.

Then we shall grow like trees
planted by streams of water,
that yield their fruit in due season,
whose leaves do not wither.

Keep us true to your Way.

We struggle with evil in our hearts,
tossed to and fro like chaff in the wind,
a rootless people whose lives have no meaning,
unable to stand when judgment comes,
desolate, outside the house of our God.

Keep us true to your Way.

May ways of wickedness perish among us:
forgive us, O God, and renew us,
lead us in paths of justice and truth,
obedient to your Wisdom and Will,
trusting in the hope of your promise.

Keep us true to your Way.

Silence

Giver of life,
save us from the desert of faithlessness,
and nourish us with the living water of your Word,
that we may bring forth fruit that will last,
in the name of Jesus Christ our Saviour.

Pause

Eleven

**A Reading from the Book of the Prophet Ezekiel,
chapter 36, verses 25 to 28**

Psalm 42–3

As a deer longs for streams of water,
so longs my soul for you, O God.
My soul is thirsty for the living God:
when shall I draw near to see your face?
My tears have been my food in the night:
all day long they ask me,
Where now is your God?
As I pour out my soul in distress,
I remember how I went to the temple of God,
with shouts and songs of thanksgiving,
a multitude keeping high festival.

**Why are you so full of heaviness, O my soul,
and why so rebellious within me?
Put your trust in God,
patiently wait for the dawn,
and you will then praise
your deliverer and your God.**

My soul is heavy within me:
therefore I remember you from the land of Jordan
and from the hills of Hermon.
Deep calls to deep in the roar of the waterfalls,
all your waves and your torrents have gone over me.
Surely, O God, you will show me mercy in the daytime,
and at night I will sing your praise, O God my God.
I will say to God, my rock,
Why have you forgotten me?
Why must I go like a mourner because the enemy oppresses me?
Like a sword piercing my bones,

my enemies have mocked me,
asking me all day long, Where now is your God?

**Why are you so full of heaviness, O my soul,
and why so rebellious within me?
Put your trust in God,
patiently wait for the dawn,
and you will then praise
your deliverer and your God.**

O God, take up my cause and strive for me
with a godless people that knows no mercy.
Save me from the grip of cunning and lies,
for you are my God and my strength.
Why must you cast me away from your presence?
Why must I be clothed in rags, humiliated by my enemy?
O send out your light and your truth and let them lead me,
let them guide me to your holy hill and to your dwelling.
Then I shall go to the altar of God,
the God of my joy and delight,
and to the harp I shall sing your praises, O God, my God.

**Why are you so full of heaviness, O my soul,
and why so rebellious within me?
Put your trust in God,
patiently wait for the dawn,
and you will then praise
your deliverer and your God.**

Silence

Loving God,
**as we join our cries with those who are depressed
    and in despair,
renew in us the spirit of hope,
the yearning for life in you alone,
and the expectancy that even when every door is closed,
yet you will surprise us with joy.**

Pause

Twelve

**A Reading from the Book of the Prophet Ezekiel,
chapter 37, verses 1 to 14**

Psalm 126

When God takes us home from our exile,
we shall wake from this nightmare and live again.

Home at last, contented and grateful.

Bars of iron will be shattered: we shall walk free
from gulag and ghetto, from dungeon and tower.

Home at last, contented and grateful.

We shall sing and laugh for joy,
echoed by birdsong and breeze of the spring.

Home at last, contented and grateful.

The land itself will rejoice in God,
the whole world give praise for the wonders we have seen.

Home at last, contented and grateful.

Lead us home, renew our hope, bring us to life,
like impossible rivers in the cursed and barren desert.

Home at last, contented and grateful.

We go on our way sadly, with tears sowing seeds that will die,
we shall return with joy, with gladness bearing our sheaves.

Home at last, contented and grateful.

Silence

Restore the years, O God, that we have lost,
that the locusts have eaten.
Give to us the future that we thought we should
    never see.
Make of the present moment a firstfruit of true
    liberation.
Even when we feel exiled, locked in, despairing,
move secretly within us and among us,
and without our realizing it,
keep us moving on our journey to your city.

Pause

Psalm 90

God of eternity, God beyond time,
our refuge and hope from one generation to another:
before the mountains rose from the sea,
before the rivers carved the valleys,
before time itself began, you are God, eternal.
From dust we came, to dust we return.
"Be shaped from the clay, be crumbled to earth."
Creator of life, of death, so did you order our ways.
A thousand years in your sight are as yesterday.
As a watch in the night comes quickly to an end,
so the years pass before you, in a flicker of the eye.

Amidst the confusions of time,
may we hear eternity's heartbeat.

The years are like the grass,
which in the morning is green,
and by evening is dried up and withered.
As the grass shrivels in the smoke,
so is our pride consumed in your fire:
we are afraid of the burning of the dross.

All our misdeeds and deceits are brought to light before
  your eyes,
all our secret sins made clear in the light of your truth.
When you are angry, our days are as nothing:
our years come to an end, vanishing with a sigh.

Amidst the confusions of time,
may we hear eternity's heartbeat.

The decades soon pass, no more than a handful.
Some show vigour in age, yet even they are soon gone.
So much of our span is wearisome, full of labour and sorrow.
O the speed of it all, and the vanity of the years:
all I have done is like straw, and most of it forgotten already.
Success crumbles into dust: there is nothing to pay love's
  account.

Amidst the confusions of time,
may we hear eternity's heartbeat.

Who is even aware of the purging of your wrath?
Who pays a moment's attention to the fierceness of your love?
Teach us to number our days, and apply our hearts to wisdom.
Turn again, O God, do not delay: give grace to your servants.
Satisfy us in the morning with your lovingkindness.
So we shall rejoice and be glad all the days of our life.
Give us days of gladness to make up for those of affliction,
  for the years of adversity.
Show your servants your deeds, and your glory to our children.
May your grace be upon us: fill us with the Spirit of love.
For in the evening of our days when we come to be judged,
we shall be known only by love, delivered only by love.

Amidst the confusions of time,
may we hear eternity's heartbeat.

Silence

Eternal God,
thank you for your gift of time
and the measure death gives to our days.
They pass so quickly as to dent our pride.
May we neither rely on our achievements
nor be downcast at our failures.
Keep us but faithful to your love,
and dependent on your grace alone.
We ask this in the Spirit
of the One who died a human failure,
and died so young.

Pause

A Psalm out of Psalm 22

And can those who are buried give you worship,
those ground to the dust give you praise?
Will nothing be left but the wind and the silence,
a dead earth, abandoned, forgotten?

In the depth of our darkness
you are rising, O Christ.

But you are a God who creates out of nothing,
you are a God who raises the dead,
you are a God who redeems what is lost,
you are a God who fashions new beauty,
striving with the weight of your glory,
bearing the infinite pain.

In the depth of our darkness
you are rising, O Christ.

The footfalls of faith may drag through our days,
God's gift of a costly and infinite enduring.
We remember your deliverance of your people of old,
we remember the abundance of the earth you have given us,
we remember the care and compassion of folk,
we remember your victory of long-suffering love.
The power of the powers is but a feather in the wind!
Death is transfigured to glory for ever!

**In the depth of our darkness
you are rising, O Christ.**

Silence

30

As Darkness Yields

The Resurrection of Jesus Christ
The Dawn of Easter Day

Starting an hour before first light

Compiled by Jim Cotter

The Dark Night

We gather in a churchyard or an open space where we have already placed the crosses of wood that we have made. It is an hour or so before first light.

The day after Good Friday has been the day of burial, and it has been followed by the dark night. In heart and mind and presence, we watch and pray at the tomb of Jesus of Nazareth, remembering his suffering and death, and bearing witness to the strange mystery of his descent into the place of the departed.

For Christ faced all that evil could do, in and beyond death, outside the familiar limits of space and time. Those who have endured a crushing affliction of mind or spirit know something of the endlessness of terrible pain. Those who have really loved know that to love is a kind of death.

And this is the faith that we have been given: we see God face to face in the Jesus who lived, suffered, died, and descended to the depths, confronting all hell let loose upon him. We see the divine love incarnate enduring pain and dread, the seeming harsh defeat by death and hell. And we see that love, unbounded and eternal, rising on the further side of emptiness and loss.

So it is that, however low we sink, God is beneath us, gloriously able to sustain us and raise us up. Christ is with us even when all sense of love has gone. And we may wait in trust that the new light will dawn, transforming even the wastes of despair into a new world of glory.

We gather by this dead wood. We remember the funeral pyres and the burial grounds, the churchyards, cemeteries, and crematoria. We know that we are in many ways entombed. And we know that one day we shall die.

We stand in the darkness, in the silence, waiting in trust, however faint or sorely tried...

Pause

We remember the generations that have passed before us, ancestors of flesh and faith, the wise and the foolish, grandmothers, grandfathers, mothers, fathers, sons, daughters, sisters, brothers, lovers, friends...

Pause

Let us pray for one another, and for all humankind, that we may be delivered from the tombs of terror and despair, and from the power of evil and death...

Pause

Let us pray for the redeeming of God's whole creation, that all that is of life and love may not be lost but be restored, through the light of the gospel of the glory of God in the face of Jesus Christ.

We take our crosses of wood out of the ground and walk with them to the place where the bonfire has been prepared.

The New Fire

The new fire is lit, we add our crosses and further wood to it, and, gathered round, we watch it grow to illuminate the night. And then this prayer:

Creator God, holy is your name among us,
and blessed is Jesus Christ, our hope of glory.

We offer ourselves to you as a living sacrifice,
to you, Flame of Love, our consuming fire.

Come with the baptism of Spirit and of fire,
illuminate the darkness of our night,
and inflame us with your love.

You came to bring fire to the earth
and wished it were blazing already.

You challenged us to be salted with fire,
for those who are near you are near the fire,
and those who are far from you are far from the Kingdom.

Come among us now, purify us, refine us,
that our faith may be proved and sharpened,
and that we may leap into life
as pure flames of unquenchable love.

Come, Holy Spirit of love and fire,
bearing witness to Christ in warmth and light,
breaking the dread chains of hell,
shattering all our tombs of fear.

Go before us now,
transform our darkness into light,
and illuminate our hearts and minds,
that we may go forward into exodus,
freed from oppression and slavery,
this night and for ever.

An appropriate extract of poetry here is 'The Dove Descending', two stanzas from T. S. Eliot's Four Quartets, *towards the end of the fourth, 'Little Gidding'.*

The New Light

From the fire we light several flares, and move with them to the entrance of church or house. where a taper will be lit from one of the torches, and it in turn will light the Easter Candle.

Eternal God,
who made this most holy night to shine with the brightness
   of your one true light,
set us aflame with the fire of your love,
and let it spread until the whole universe is alive to your glory,
through the cosmic Christ, our Saviour.
Amen.

The outline of the Cross is made on the Paschal Candle, also the letters of the beginning and end of the Greek alphabet (Alpha and Omega), and the numerals of this Anno Domini; and five nails are inserted, to the accompaniment of these words:

Christ yesterday, today and for ever,
Alpha and Omega, the beginning and the end.

All time belongs to Chris:t, and all the ages.
To Christ be all love and glory, now and for ever.

By your holy and glorious wounds,
O Christ our Saviour, heal and guard us.

May the light of Christ, rising in glory,
banish all dread, despair, and death
from our bodies, hearts, and minds.

We enter the church or house in procession behind the bearer of the Candle, singing Alleluias softly as we go. When the Cantor stops to intone the words, The Light of Christ, we respond on the same notes, Thanks be to God.

The Exultet

The Candle is held in the middle of the church or at the entrance to the room
of celebration, and we light our own candles from it before proceeding to pew
or chair, or simply gathering round the Candle if there is room. The Cantor
then sings the Exultet, the Easter Proclamation of Praise, a medieval prose
poem in celebrâation of the night of the Risen Christ.

Rejoice, heavenly powers; sing, choirs of angels.
Exult, all creation, around God's throne.
Jesus Christ, our king, is risen.
Sound the trumpet of salvation.

Rejoice, O earth, in shining splendour,
radiant in the brightness of your king.
Christ has conquered, glory fills you,
darkness has vanished for ever.

Rejoice, People of God, exult in glory.
The risen Saviour shines upon you.
Let this place resound with joy,
echoing the mighty song of the Church universal.

My dearest friends, standing with me in this holy light,
join me in asking God for mercy,
that I an unworthy servant may have grace
to sing God's Easter praises.

It is truly right
that with full hearts and minds and voices
we should praise the unseen God,
the all-powerful Father,
and his only Son, our Lord Jesus Christ.
For Christ has rescued us with his life's blood,
and paid for us the cost of Adam's sin.

This is our passover feast,
when Christ the true Lamb is slain,
whose blood consecrates the homes of all believers.

This is the night
when first you saved our ancestors:
you freed the people of Israel from their slavery
and led them dry shod through the sea.

This is the night
when the pillar of fire destroyed the darkness of sin.

This is the night
when Christians everywhere,
washed clean of sin and free from all corruption,
are restored to grace and grow together in holiness.

This is the night
when Jesus Christ broke the chains of death
and rose triumphant from the grave.

What good would life have been to us
had not Christ come as our Redeemer?
Father, how wonderful your care for us,
how boundless your merciful love.
To rescue a slave you gave away your Son.

O happy fault! O necessary sin of Adam!
which gained for us so great a redeemer.

Most blessed of all nights,
chosen by God to see Christ rising from the dead.
Of this night the Scriptures say:
The night will be as clear as the day:
it will become my light, my joy.

The power of this night dispels all evil,
washes guilt away,
restores lost innocence,
brings mourners joy.
It casts out hatred,
brings us peace,
and humbles earthly pride.

Night truly blessed
when heaven is wedded to earth
and human beings are reconciled to God.

Therefore, heavenly Father,
in the joy of this night,
receive our sacrifice of praise,
your Church's solemn offering.
Accept this Easter Candle,
a flame undivided but undimmed,
a pillar of fire that glows to the honour of God.
Let it mingle with the light of heaven,
and continue bravely burning
to dispel the darkness of this night.
May the Morning Star which never sets
find this flame still burning:
Christ, that Morning Star,
who came back from the dead
and shed his peaceful light on humankind,
your Son who lives and reigns for ever and ever.
Amen.

The Water of Baptism

The Easter Candle is carried to the font, while a drumbeat sounds the rhythm of the human heart. We turn to face the Candle and when it reaches the font, the heartbeat stops. It is the moment of death, and the reading follows from Paul's Letter to the Romans:

A Reading from the Letter of Paul to the Romans, chapter 6, verses 3 to 11

The Profession of Faith

In times of belief and in times of doubt, in times of assurance and in times of perplexity, in times of presence and in times of absence, human beings in all their variety have come to recognize the divine mystery, and desired to grow in the ways of love, to embody that love in intimacy and justice.

We whisper our trust:

that we and all human beings, and all that is being created, are dearly loved by God for ever;

that in Christ we are freed from the powers of oppression and fear, of evil, pain, and death;

that we are called to follow the Way of Jesus, embracing the outcast in friendship and renouncing the ways of worldly power, at whatever cost and wherever it may lead;

that the Holy Spirit empowers us and guides us on that Way;

that we must resist evil, all that tempts us to deceit and falsehood, all that isolates us from one another, and that day by day we need to turn continually to the truth and love that shines through the face of Christ.

So let us reflect:

Are we willing to turn again to Christ,
to turn to the deep things of God,
to the Spirit of God moving within and among us,
to God the Source and Goal of all that is,
to the Mysterious Companion who is the Other within us,
    Christ, truly divine and truly human,
living the way of unconditional love?

Are we willing day by day
to turn our hearts and minds in repentance
    towards the God of Love,
confessing our failures to love,
forgiving ourselves and others, and being forgiven,
absorbing hurts and not passing them on
    in a spirit of retaliation?

Are we willing to refuse the way of evil,
of self-hatred and the hating of others,
to keep steadfastly to the true path,
the Way, the Truth, and the Life of Jesus,
to refuse the easy and comfortable way,
to have the courage to become aware
    of all that is pressing upon us,
to embrace the Way of the Cross
and participate in the Way of Compassion?

Silence

Let us renew our commitment to this faith and to this Way.

I answer the call of the God who is creating us.
I follow the Way of Jesus who is beckoning us.
I trust in the Holy Spirit who is guiding us.

We inherit a faith that has been expressed in various ways at various times, in the myriad languages and cultures of the world.

Join with me now in solidarity with our ancestors of faith, our voices resonating with theirs.

or

Listen with me now in solidarity with our ancestors of faith, in a musical setting by *N* of an ancient Creed.

I believe in God, the Father almighty,
creator of heaven and earth.
I believe in Jesus Christ, his only Son, our Lord,
who was conceived by the Holy Spirit,
born of the Virgin Mary,
suffered under Pontius Pilate,
was crucified, died, and was buried;
he descended to the dead.
On the third day he rose again;
he ascended into heaven,
he is seated at the right hand of the Father,
and he will come to judge the living and the dead.
I believe in the Holy Spirit,
the holy catholic Church,
the communion of saints,
the forgiveness of sins,
the resurrection of the body,
and the life everlasting. Amen.

And/or a credal hymn is sung, for example:

Yes – I trust in AbbaAmma,
Source of all that comes to be,
Goodness, Truth, and marvellous Beauty,
Surging Life – Love's Mystery.

And I trust in Love embodied,
Jesus born in Galilee,
Healing outcasts, eating with them,
Crucified upon the Tree:

Bearing pain with all creation,
Willing love to victory,
Loosening evil's grip for ever,
Death no more the enemy.

Foe and friend, in Love's acceptance,
Each and all alike are formed,
Freed by touch and word and water,
Fed by bread and wine transformed.

And I trust the Hidden Spirit
In and through our common life
Weaving threads all torn and broken,
Shaping justice out of strife.

So I trust in Love's Communion,
Lover, Loved, and Mutual Friend,
Seated at the welcoming table,
Gently bidding us attend.

The Declaring of Names

We remember our names:

the name we have inherited from the past, from our ancestors in time immemorial;

the name we were given by those who first nurtured us and gave us a glimpse of intimate, generous, and enduring love;

the name we came to choose as we embraced the Christian Way, reminding us that we belong to a communion of saints.

Let each and all of us tell our names to this company now gathered / to those around us.

Names are said aloud.

The Blessing of Water

Water is poured into font or bowl, and the Easter Candle is lowered into the water.

Living Creator God,
**bless this water
and bless us who are touched by it in baptism
    and renewal.
We ask a blessing in the name of the Giver of Life.
We ask a blessing in the name of the Bearer of Pain.
We ask a blessing in the name of the Maker of Love.**

Here is the water of our survival day by day, drawn up as from a well.

Here are the waters that were broken to give us birth.

Here is the water of life that flows so often hidden underground.

Here is the water that purifies, scours, and cleanses us of all that is toxic.

Here is the water of refreshment and pleasure, of fountain, fall, and pool.

Here is the water of raging power, of tidal wave and destroying flood.

Here is the water that draws back and allows us to pass dryshod.

Here is the water of the Jordan river, rite of passage from slavery and oppression to the freedom of a promised land.

Here is the water of eternal life, bubbling cheerfully as an ever-flowing spring.

Here is the water of buoyancy, of the ocean of divine love.

Here is the water of chaos and the creatures of the profound unknown, the roaring wind and fearful silence challenging us to deepen our trust.

Here is the water of drowning, of the death of grasping self, of the decay of flesh and blood.

Here is the water of dying, bearing us across the ancient river.

Here is the water that is the simplest gift to the thirsty, and that washes the weary traveller's feet.

Here is the water that springs up in barren ground to our unexpected joy.

Here is the water that flows for the healing of the nations.

Let us take to ourselves again our baptism in water,
in the name of the Creator, the Life-Giver,
**   Father-Mother of us all;**
in the name of the Redeemer, the Pain-Bearer, the Son;
in the name of the Sanctifier, the Love-Maker,
**   the Holy Spirit.**

Friends of God,
drawn close in passion and tenderness –
Citizens of God's Domain,
called to embody love in justice –
Newborn of the Holy Spirit to abundant life –
through these waters our life is hidden for ever in Christ,
at one with his way and mission,
at one in his death and resurrection.

The Mark of the Cross

Let us receive on our foreheads the mark of Christ, the Cross, where evil, pain, and death strive with goodness, joy, and life, the place that will again and again test our trust in the power of Love to redeem tragedy and loss.

Let us keep faith in Christ throughout our days, wrestling with all that would drag us down, convinced of our dignity and worth as daughters and sons of the Living God.

Each person present is marked in water with the sign of the cross. Small bowls with water taken from the font may be passed from person to person, each marking the forehead of his or her neighbour with the sign of the cross, saying,

Receive on your forehead the mark of Christ.

While this is done, candles may be given to those nearby to hold. Alternatively, one or more people may carry the bowls and mark the foreheads of those who stay still and receive.

The Anointing with Oil

Eternal and loving God,
bless this oil and bless those who receive its anointing,
that it may be for our strengthening, our consecration,
    and our joy,

in the name of Jesus, whose word and touch gave healing,
who pioneered the narrow pilgrim way,
who gave the laughter of abundant life.

By this oil
may we be warmed and soothed:
may the healing Spirit penetrate the cells and fibres of our being,
that we may become whole,
give thanks to God,
and venture further on the way of faith.

By this oil
may we renew the consecration of our lives in the service and
     friendship of God,
being not afraid of dying to live,
nor of bearing the burdens of those with whom we have to do.

By this oil
may lamps be lit and feasting begin,
may gladness and rejoicing surge in our hearts.

Through faith in the power and will of the Healing One
     to make us whole and holy,
to consecrate us with joy for ever deeper service and friendship,
to give us courage to go through the narrow gates of our journey,
let us anoint one another with oil
in the name of God who gives us life, bears our pain,
     and makes us whole.
Amen.

*Small bowls of oil may be passed from person to person, each marking the
palms of his or her neighbour's hands with the letters CHR, and saying,*

     I anoint you for your wellbeing in God.

*While this is done, candles may be given to those near by to hold. Again, an
alternative is for a few people to anoint the many as they stay still and receive.*

The Recognition of One Another

We have taken these lights from the Candle of the Risen Christ,
that God may illuminate our flesh and minds,
our hearts and our imagination.
May the Light of Christ shine in dark places,
the deep places of our own being,
the darknesses wherever we may meet them,
that the Way may be followed
until we all greet the Great Dawn with joy.

Let us look around us.
Here are our sisters and brothers,
our friends in Christ for time and for eternity.
We belong to a Living Communion,
the Organism that is the Body of Christ.
We are joined together
    in the Unfolding of the Word,
    in the Breaking of the Bread,
    in the Fellowship,
    and in the Prayers.
Here we belong.
Here is our place.
Here we help one another to discover
    how we may, each and all,
bring our unique gifts to the building up of the community,
and in the service of the common good of all humankind
    and all creation.

The Rededication

Let us continue to live faithfully
as members of the Body of Christ.
With God's help we will.

Let us persevere in resisting evil,
in holding back the lie,
in enduring the unresolved,
in puncturing solemn pride with laughter.
With God's help we will.

Let us seek in prayer and presence
to embody the love of Christ.
With God's help we will.

Let us seek discernment and courage
in speaking words of truth and consolation
to those who are confused or full of grief.
With God's help we will.

Let us strive for justice and peace among all peoples,
seeking to overcome oppression
and respecting the dignity of every human being.
With God's help we will.

The Prayer for the Holy Spirit

Holy Spirit, Strengthener, Counsellor, Wisdom,
give to us, friends and servants of God, all the gifts we need.
Confirm us in the faith that we have professed.
May we continue in the way of Christ all the days of our life,
until as a pilgrim people we come to dwell in the City of God
     for ever.

*The host lays hands on the heads of those at the end of each row (or on the
head of the person to left or right if the company is in a horseshoe), and the
action is passed from neighbour to neighbour, with the words:*

Be strengthened in the Holy Spirit.

The last to receive comes to lay hands on the head of the host.

Living God,
Make us ready for the Great Day
when the whole cosmos shall be united
in the Christ of the new creation,
and all shall shout Glory to you, our God,
our Beginning and our End. Amen.

The Alleluias

Beginning softly and rising to a crescendo, as many as wish in turn give the
Easter greeting, in as many languages as are known to those present, and we
all respond, sounding bells etc. on the Alleluias.

Christ is risen:
Christ is risen: Alleluia! Alleluia!

Candles are extinguished as the main lights are switched on, and the Alleluias
from Mozart's Exultate Jubilate *are sung, during which flowers and other*
decorations are brought into the place of celebration. And any who wish may
use any available space to turn cartwheels! The music is followed by these
Acclamations, again with bells etc. sounding on the Alleluias:

You are risen, O Christ.
Let the gospel trumpets speak,
and the news, as of holy fire,
burning and flaming and inextinguishable,
run to the ends of the earth.
Christ is risen! Alleluia!

You are risen, O Christ.
Let all creation greet the good news with jubilant shout,
for its redemption has come,
the long night is past,
the ancient trap is sprung.
Christ is risen! Alleluia!

Death and life have engaged each other
in a wondrous struggle:
Death is swallowed up in victory.
Christ is risen! Alleluia!

Death yield strange gifts to life,
its colours deep and radiant,
life more solid and more real.
Christ is risen! Alleluia!

All you that sleep, awake, rise from the dead,
the Light of Dawn will shine upon you.
Christ is risen! Alleluia!

We bless you, God of love and glory,
utterly giving of your very self in Jesus.
Christ is risen! Alleluia!

In your great mercy we have been born anew to a living hope
by the resurrection of Jesus Christ from the dead.
Christ is risen! Alleluia!

*Trumpet fanfares and/or organ and/or other musical instruments lead us into
singing the Easter hymn, bells ringing out on the Alleluias:*

Jesus Christ is risen today, Alleluia!
Our most glorious holy day, Alleluia!
Who did once in life and death, Alleluia!
Fill the earth with Love's true breath: Alleluia!

Hymns of praise then let us sing, Alleluia!
Unto Christ, our Servant-King, Alleluia!
Who endured the cross and grave, Alleluia!
Sprang to life from out the cave: Alleluia!

So the pains that he endured, Alleluia!
Love's release have now secured, Alleluia!
Death's dread sting itself now dies, Alleluia!
Christ in glory fills the skies: Alleluia!

The Peace

The glory of the risen Christ shrivels up our pride!
The power of the risen Christ sets us free from evil's grip!
The touch of the risen Christ heals our deepest wounds
     and sorrow!
The life of the risen Christ swallows up our fear of death!

We are indeed healed, forgiven, embraced in love,
set free to live in the Spirit of the Risen Christ.

The Peace of the Risen Christ spread among us.
Alleluia!

Let us share with one another a greeting of Peace.

Hymn: 'The Day of Resurrection'

Gloria

Sung by a choir, or from a recording of, for example, Mozart's Coronation
Mass.

The Word

Prayer

Living Christ,
bringing with the dawn the joyful news
that every tomb is always empty,
raise us from disintegration and death
to new life and unbounded joy.
Amen.

The Gospel: A reading from the Gospel according to John, chapter 20, verses 1 to 18

Response to the Gospel

The One who walked among us,
in the Spirit obedient to the One who called,
in the sight of all created powers:
Risen Christ, we greet you: Alleluia!

You have been proclaimed among the nations,
believed in throughout the world,
transfigured into glory.
Risen Christ, we greet you: Alleluia!

We have set our hope on you,
the human face of God,
the Saviour of all the world.
Risen Christ, we greet you: Alleluia!

To the Ruler of all the ages,
unseen and eternal, the only true God,
be honour and glory, now and for ever.
Risen Christ, we greet you: Alleluia!

Sermon

Hymn, to the tune **Maccabaeus**

> *pp* **Disintegrating,**
> **Human flesh shall fade,**
> **Shadow on a pavement –**
> **Seemingly unmade;**
> **Earth to earth returning,**
> **Ashes on the breeze,**
> **Drowned in depth of ocean:**
> **Truths that faith must seize.**

[No refrain]

Corpse never buried,
Crucified and gone,
Vultures flesh devouring,
Dogs that strip the bone.
p   Faith yet knows a presence:
In the darkest night,
See a wounded body,
Shining now with light.

mf   Pain, death, and evil:
Every sting is drawn:
Love is not defeated:
Glorious is this dawn!

Love recreates us:
Bodylines redrawn,
Matter tuned more finely,
Spirit takes new form,
Human eyes now seeing
What is always so:
Life at cost of dying!
Wellspring's endless flow!

Pain, death, and evil:
Every sting is drawn:
Life eternal blossoms:
Glorious is this dawn!

f   Stories of angels
Rolling back the stone
Celebrate faith's triumph:
From the tomb he's gone!
Graveclothes cannot hold us!
God is very near!
Every tomb is empty!
Nothing left to fear!

Pain, death, and evil:
Every sting is drawn:
Alleluia!
Glorious is this dawn!

"Touch one another,
Tremble with new life,
Passion joined with kindness
Overcomes your strife.
Loosen all the bindings
That constrict and maim,
Claim my Risen Presence,
Dare to live Love's Name!"

ff   Pain, death, and evil:
Every sting is drawn:
Jesus lives for ever:
Glorious is this dawn!

The Prayers

O Christ, radiant Light, shining in our darkness,
most glorious of the children of earth,
Holy One, setting captives free:
Christ of the living God,
give freedom to the peoples of the world.

O Christ, stooping low in great humility,
obedient to death, walking the way of the cross,
calling us to follow to death and to resurrection:
Christ of the living God,
keep your people faithful to your way.

O Christ, burning in us
all that is not kindled by your presence,

melting in us all that freezes and keeps us cold:
Christ of the living God,
give us the gifts of friendship.

O Christ, saving us in our poverty,
reconciling us to the Source of all that is,
making us a holy people, a commonwealth,
and priests to our God:
Christ of the living God,
bring new life and hope in the midst of human pain.

O Christ, granting us the fulness of your grace,
saving us from the fear of death,
giving us a share in your life:
Christ of the living God,
**cause us to walk with confidence the waters
    of our dying.**

O Christ, the new and living way,
the dawn of the new creation,
we bring into our presence and into yours
those whom we would especially remember
this Easter morning.

A time for the naming of names, silently or aloud.

Christ of the living God,
make us one with all those whom we love.

Praying in Christ

**Abba, Amma, Beloved,
your name be hallowed,
your reign spread among us,
your will be well done,
at all times, in all places,
in heaven and on earth.**

Give us the bread
we need for today.
Forgive us our trespass
as we forgive those
who trespass against us.
Let us not fail
in time of our testing.
Spare us from trials
too sharp to endure.
Free us from the grip
of all evil powers.
For yours is the reign,
the power and the glory,
the victory of love,
for now and eternity,
world without end,
Amen and Amen.

Hymn: 'Christ is Risen' by Brian Wren, tune Lux Eoi

Christ is risen! Shout Hosanna!
Celebrate this day of days!
Christ is risen! Hush in wonder:
all creation is amazed.
In the desert all-surrounding,
see, a spreading tree has grown.
Healing leaves of grace abounding
bring a taste of love unknown.

Christ is risen! Raise your spirits
from the caverns of despair.
Walk with gladness in the morning,
see what love can do and dare.
Drink the wine of resurrection,
not a servant, but a friend.
Jesus is our strong companion.
Joy and peace shall never end.

Christ is risen! Earth and heaven
nevermore shall be the same.
Break the bread of new creation
where the world is still in pain.
Tell its grim, demonic chorus:
"Christ is risen! Get you gone!"
God the First and Last is with us.
Sing Hosanna everyone!

At the Taking of the Bread and Wine

God of our ancestors,
blessed be your name for ever.
Yours is the greatness, the power, the glory,
the splendour, and the majesty.
For everything in the heavens
and on the earth is yours.

From your hand come all the blessings of life,
open gifts of goods and honour,
secret gifts in pain and dying.
Even in the midst of change and decay,
O God, you reign for ever and ever,
pouring out your life in love for us,
even to weakness, to emptiness and dread,
yearning for us to respond,
drawing us closer to your presence.

And so we give you thanks, O God,
and praise your glorious name,
for all things come from you,
and of your own do we give you.

Blessed are you, eternal God, Source of all creation:
through your goodness we have this bread to offer,
which earth has given and human hands have made;
it will become for us the Bread of Life.
Blessed be God for ever.

Blessed are you, eternal God, Source of all creation:
through your goodness we have this wine to offer,
fruit of the earth and work of human hands;
it will become for us the Lifeblood of the World.
Blessed be God for ever.

Blessed are you, eternal God, Source of all creation:
through your goodness we have ourselves to offer,
gift of the womb and shaped by human hands;
we will become for you a Living Body.
Blessed be God for ever.

The Prayer of Thanksgiving

The God of Love is in the midst of us:
The Holy Spirit dwells among us.

We surrender our hearts to our faithful Creator:
We open them to God and to one another.

Let us give thanks for the wonder of God's glory,
for the gift of this our planet,
beautiful and fragile in the heavens,
for our responsibility as guardians of all that is being created,
for the vision of one human commonwealth
with peace known on earth
and goodwill shared among all people.

Drawn by the magnet of the living God
ever closer in the Presence of the Mystery,
we adore the God who gives us life.

Let us give thanks for Jesus of Nazareth,
living the truth of us and the truth of God,
glad to be born of Mary to dwell with us,
a man most wonderfully alive,
yet enduring to the end and dying
as the means of our reconciliation and our healing,
who is most gloriously risen,
the pioneer of our salvation.

Drawn by the magnet of the suffering God
ever closer in the Presence of the Mystery,
**we praise the Christ who bears our pain
and makes us whole.**

Let us give thanks for the Holy Spirit,
moving invisibly deep within us,
spinning the thread of attention among us,
bringing to life in us the Way and Wisdom of Jesus,
nurturing us with the food of the living God,
and with the fountain of water that wells up to eternal life,
sending us into the heart of the conflicts of the world,
to speak the words and live the lives
of justice and of peace, of truth and of healing,
and so become transformed by the yearning love of God.

Drawn by the magnet of the loving God,
ever closer in the Presence of the Mystery,
**we give thanks for the Spirit who makes love with us
in the dance of the new creation.**

So let us give thanks to God
for accepting us in the Beloved,
who in the night of loneliness and desolation,
of agony and betrayal,
took the bread that sustains us all,
gave thanks, and broke it,
and gave it to his disciples and said,

**Take, eat, this is my Body, my Living Presence,
given for you: do this to re-member me,
to bring us together in the world.**

In the same way he took the cup of wine,
the wine of our sorrow and our solace,
gave thanks, and gave it to them and said,

**Drink of this, all of you, this is my Blood,
my Very Life, spent for you: do this to re-member me,
to bring us alive in the world.**

Silence

Creator Spirit,
as we celebrate the one great sacrifice of love,
hover now over your people,
over this bread and wine,
that they may be to us the Body and Blood of Christ,
for in the mystery of faith:

**Christ has died,
Christ is risen,
Christ is here,
Christ will come.**

Come, Holy and Mysterious Spirit of the Risen Christ.
Come, Love Divine, Heartbeat of the Universe.

Come, True Vine and Living Bread,
  Resurrection and Eternal Life.
Come, Paschal Lamb, Slaughtered Victim,
  Helpless and Vulnerable Lover, Living Sacrifice,
  Lifeblood of the Universe.
Come, Christ of Pain, dying, descending to the depths
  to face all hell let loose,
  and meeting there the Joy
  that redeems all tragedy and all loss.
Come, Risen Christ, with glorious wounds
  to touch and heal and forgive.
Come, Life-giving Spirit,
  Bearer of the Risen Christ to us in this bread and wine.
Come, Spirit of Easter Fire,
  transfigure this thanksgiving meal
  into the food of the pilgrim people,
  sustaining us with Christ's Body and Christ's Blood.
Come, now and at the end of time,
  and spread the Easter Banquet of our salvation.

Dying, you destroyed our death!,
Rising you restored our life!
Living Christ, come in glory!
Alleluia! Alleluia!

And now, with all who have ever lived,
with saints and martyrs
and forgotten faithful people,
with angels and archangels
and all the heavenly company,
with all who are alive
and all who are yet to be born,
with all creation in all time,
with joy we give praise:

Holy, holy, holy,
eternal God of Power and Love,
all space and all time show forth your glory:
Alleluia! Amen!

Hymn, to the tune Woodlands

Sing, choirs of God, let saints and angels sing,
The universe exult in harmony.
We greet you, Christ, now risen from the grave,
And join our voices to the symphony.

Sing, choirs of God, behold your light has come;
The glorious wounds of Christ shine full and clear.
We lift our hearts for love has conquered pain,
The night is gone, the dawn at last is here.

Sing, choirs of God, exult in joy outpoured,
The gospel trumpet tell of victory won.
Dear Christ, you live, and love us to the end,
We shout with all the world the long Amen.

The Breaking of the Bread

The bread which we break
is a sharing in the Body of Christ.

The wine which we bless
is a sharing in the Blood of Christ.

Body and Blood of one humanity,
we shall be transfigured to glory.

Agnus Dei

Lamb of God,
taking away the sin of the world,
having compassion upon us –

Beloved of God,
affirming the worth of the world,
accepting us in love for ever –

Healing God,
bearing the pain of the world,
making us and all creation whole –

Pour mercy upon us,
whisper your love for us,
give us peace.

The Communion

Let us open our hands,
open our hearts,
open the hidden places of our being,
and into our deep soul-self
let there enter the heartbeat of those we love,
the lifeblood of our villages, towns, and cities,
the lifestream of the tides and currents and seasons,
the pulsing of our planet and of the stars;
let there enter all the joys and pains our cup can bear,
let us be nourished by the new life
   that comes through what is broken;
and in and through it all,
to transform it to glory,
let us receive the Body, the Living Presence,
the Blood, the Very Self, of Jesus,
and let us feed and live and love,
in faith, with gratitude.

Beloved, we draw near to be loved by you,
in deep yet trembling trust,
through this matter of your creation,
this material stuff of bread and body,
this fluid of wine and blood,
that your desire for us and ours for you
may be blended in deep joy and ecstasy,
that we may be enriched and doubly blessed.

We draw near to receive this offering of yourself,
your intimate, vulnerable, and naked body,
imparted to us, incorporated in us,
that we may dwell and love and create,
you in us and we in you.

We pass the elements to our neighbour. To the words, The Body of Christ, it
might be thought appropriate to respond, I Am; to the words, The Blood of
Christ, Amen.

Proceeding

The Easter Anthems

We praise you, O Christ,
risen from the dead,
breaking death's dominion,
rising from the grave.

Absorbing in yourself
the force of evil's ways,
you destroyed death's age-old sting
and now you are alive for evermore.

Let us find our life in you
breaking through our fear of everlasting void.
For you are risen from the dead,
the firstfruits of those who sleep.

From the days of first awareness
we betrayed the call of life,
yet yearned for the communion
which still we dimly sense.

Pain and evil, malice and cruel greed,
these deepened the sorrow of our hearts.
Yet they are done away
in light of glorious dawn,
the victory of resurrection day.

At one with all who've lived,
so all of us have died,
at one with your humanity,
all shall be made alive.

Hymn by Brian Wren to the tune Offertorium

> To Christ our hearts now given,
> we join in joyful praise,
> and pray, in all our living,
> to grow in loving ways.
> The freeing grace that found us,
> God's healing, winning call,
> in freedom now has bound us
> to love, and give our all.
>
> From many tribes and places,
> with thankful songs we come
> to blend our gifts and graces,
> and pray and work as one.

We vow, whate'er betide us,
in love and truth to stay,
Christ moves on beside us,
and guides us on our way.

Wherever we may venture
to witness, heal, and care,
the spirit of our Saviour
has long been lodging there.
Then let us give with gladness,
not claiming to deserve
the wisdom, strength, and kindness
of those we kneel to serve.

The freeing grace that found us,
the love that makes us one,
is ranging far beyond us,
and bids us travel on
to share God's great salvation,
defend our neighbour's worth,
dismantle domination,
and heal our aching earth.

The Blessing

The Blessing of God be with us,
Father and Mother, Sustainer of our earth,
Source of all that is and that shall be.

**The Blessing of God be with us,
our Messiah, our Christ,
our Risen and Glorious Loved One and our Friend.**

The Blessing of God be with us,
Spirit spreading love and joy in our hearts,
giving hope to the battered ones,
inspiring justice and peace for the little ones.

May this rich blessing be with us,
with all humankind living and departed,
and with all the creatures
of land and sea and air.
May our days be long on this good earth.

For we have been nourished by the Bread of Life,
we have been quickened by the Lifeblood of the Universe.

With courage and in hope
let us continue on the journey.
Amen. Thanks be to God.

Hymn to the tune Easter Hymn

Christ once crucified now lives, Alleluia!
Blessedness to all he gives, Alleluia!
Laughter echoes round the earth, Alleluia!
Grief gives way to joy and mirth, Alleluia!

Hell no longer holds us fast, Alleluia!
Fate has loosed its grip at last, Alleluia!
Love has melted every fear, Alleluia!
Death proves kindly, Christ is near, Alleluia!

Celebrate this joyful feast, Alleluia!
People all, the greatest least, Alleluia!
Drop your masks of pomp and pride, Alleluia!
Greet the Clown with wounded side, Alleluia!

Notes

Here is a summary of what needs to be done, along with a check
list of equipment:

Collecting of paper, cardboard, wood
Making of bonfire
Decorating of Easter Candle
Night lights on saucers
Personal candles and holders –
    suggest large circular card covered with festal paper
Preparation of floral and other decorations
Preparation of Easter Garden
Rehearsal with
    cross-carrier,
    fire-lighters,
    flare-carriers,
    candle-bearer,
    nails-bearer,
    matches and taper-holder,
    incense-swinger,
    Exultet singer,
    drum-beater,
    readers,
    operator of tape recorder/CD player

Checklist of equipment needed:

Crosses from Good Friday
Electric torches
Dead wood
Cardboard
Newspaper
Firelighters
Matches
Night lights to mark hazards en route –
    or to mark the whole route

Flares
Easter Candle
Tapers
Nails on saucer
Incense, charcoal, censer
Small chocolate eggs
Large splendid bowl (if no font)
Large beautiful jug full of water
Ikon light containers
Drum
Oil
Small bowls for oil
Small bowls for water
Bread
Wine
Plate
Cup
Cloths
Musical instruments, rattles etc
Gong
Bells
Easter Garden
Flowers

The Dark Night

Begin an hour before first light, even if there are sodium lights within range. Gather in a churchyard, among the graves and tombs, or in a garden. On Easter Eve place there the large cross used in the Good Friday commemoration. Also, encourage people to make their own small crosses, using dead branches and green twine, and place them around the large cross.

Take the *night* seriously, well before the darkness begins to yield to the dawn. Take seriously *death* and *burial*, the disintegration of corpses, the earthly fading of all that is recognizable as a human being. Easter Eve is rarely kept by acts of corporate prayer, but to start the Easter celebration in this way both compensates for that lack and gives a vivid contrast to the exuberance of the morning to come.

Do not hurry. Allow time to absorb the atmosphere. Pause for reflection. Then, after the prayers, take up the crosses, including the large one, and move slowly and silently to the place where the bonfire has been prepared.

The New Fire

Make the bonfire as large as time, energy, and safety allow. To skimp is not to feast. Again, there is no hurry. Let the fire really get going, enjoy it, warm yourselves by it. Only then throw on to it your crosses of wood and move into the prayers.

Here are some hints on making a bonfire guaranteed to light without hitches (well, almost).

Prepare a long straight branch. Lay it on the ground, one end where the middle of the fire will be. As the wood is piled, make sure that the branch can move freely in and out of the centre.

At the centre pile paper and wood shavings and hold them in place with flat sheets of cardboard. Include a few fire lighters if you're not feeling confident!

Build outwards with branches of dead wood, starting small. You may want to include some long thick branches to provide a 'wigwam' frame to hold the structure firm.

Keep some of the wood back, making a couple of piles near-by, so that as the fire gets going, people can feed it (along with the crosses that have been brought from the graveyard).

Remove the long straight branch, bind a taper to the end with twine. Check that it still moves freely in and out of the centre.

Give the branch plus taper, and a box of matches, to the person who will light the fire.

Place plastic sheeting over the wood and weigh it down with stones. This should be sufficient protection from wet weather, and the bonfire should blaze into life even if it is raining at the time.

The New Light and the Exultet

You will need half a dozen flares; the kind you stick in the soil for parties on summer evenings work well. Let six people carry the torches in procession from the bonfire to the entrance porch of church or house. Even a stiff breeze shouldn't extinguish them – but any wind at all is likely to snuff the Easter Candle if it is lit without protection.

The porch is a good place to light the Candle, and it can be carried into the entrance hall or into the church. The more space there is the better, so that people can gather round it for the singing of the Exultet. In a traditional church, don't go near the font and don't go as far as the chancel.

The Exultet is best thought of as similar to the ancient creeds. Here are profound expressions of Christian faith as understood by our ancestors, poems rather than dogmas, better sung than said. We might want to put things differently (see some of the hymns and prayers later), but we use some of our ancestors' scripts so as to remind ourselves that we belong together with them in a communion that stretches through time and space.

The Water of Baptism

This takes place around the font or in a room specially prepared for the rest of the celebration. Usually, this part happens after the Easter Alleluias, but dramatically, it works well if the explosion of lights and the extinguishing of candles takes place after and not before this section that focuses on Baptism.

The script as laid out in this book assumes that people will be renewing their own baptismal promises, but if there are those who, at this dawning of the light, are to be baptized and confirmed, the necessary adaptations are easy enough to make.

This section is the only part of this book that has not been well tried in practice. Previously, material from the *Alternative Service Book* of 1980 has been used. The suggestions here come partly from dissatisfaction with that rite, and even more dissatisfaction with the new services prepared for *Common Worship* in the Church of England. They seem pastorally almost unworkable, as well as having too much a flavour of examinations ('candidates') and duty ('Do you submit to Christ as Lord?'). In any case, all the churches still seem to be in a muddle about these things. So, what you have here is an offering from the wings.

At this particular celebration, because of its unreasonable time of day, and because it lasts a long time, to include Baptism and Confirmation can hardly be the norm in practice, however much it proclaims everything together at Easter. My own sense is that we need, on the whole, to make separate occasions for Baptism, Confirmation, and First Communion. There is more than enough to absorb in one of these, let alone all three.

(Incidentally, the naming and welcoming of a baby into the human community, along with the thanksgiving and dedication of parents and families, surely needs its own rite, to parallel the other rites of passage of marriage and death. And babies could even be sprinkled with blessed water without there being a confusion with Baptism. But all that is for another occasion.)

Back to the Easter Dawn. There may well be two or three teenagers or adults who are drawn into this particular way of celebrating their Christian initiation, as long as they are not expecting all their families and friends to turn up at 4.30 am.

One last remark. The drumbeat (or hands on books or wood), in the rhythm of the human heart, with its sudden stop, as in a heart attack, is perhaps as good a symbol as we can get in our generation of a dramatic moment of death. (Not that it is foolproof. One six-year-old was once heard to ask, When are they coming to scalp him?)

The Alleluias and the rest of the celebration

As the Easter Greeting is given, in as many languages as possible, candles are extinguished, the main lights switched on, bells are rung, and, if timed well, the dawn chorus is in full voice. As soon as the Alleluias begin to flag, switch on a recording of the

Alleluias from Mozart's *Exultate Jubilate*. As the music plays, bring in the floral displays, so allowing the arrangers to have their moment of delight (and, one may hope, with the usual spirit of competition having been thrown on to the bonfire earlier).

The acclamation in the two sections that begin, "You are risen, O Christ", is adapted from a prayer by Eric Milner-White.

From now to the end of the celebration, let the bells be rung every time Alleluia is sung.

A sermon is almost superfluous on this occasion, but keep it short! A time for silent mulling may be more appropriate.

As to the hymns:

'Jesus Christ is Risen Today' is an adaptation of the version in *Hymns Ancient and Modern New Standard*, which itself is *Lyra Davidica* (1708) and others. It preserves, I hope, the note of triumph without being triumphalist. The usual tune is *Easter Hymn*.

'The Day of Resurrection' can be sung to the tune *Ellacombe*. The words are J. M. Neale's nineteenth-century translation from the Latin of St John of Damascus who died *c.* 754.

'Disintegrating' is by Jim Cotter and can be sung to the tune *Maccabaeus*. The fifth and sixth lines in the last verse come from a poem by Elizabeth Jennings.

'This Joyful Eastertide' is adapted from the original by G. R. Woodward (1848–1934), to the tune of the same name.

'Christ is risen! Shout Hosanna!' is by Brian Wren, no. 5 in his collection, *Praising a Mystery*, Hope Publishing Company, Chicago, 1986. The tune *Lux Eoi* is reasonably well known, though the one set in Brian Wren's collection is a new one by William P. Rowan, *Jackson New*, also copyrighted by Hope Publishing Company in 1986. In the UK, copyright permission should be obtained from Stainer and Bell Ltd. The words can also be found in his book *Piece Together Praise*. Permission has been given for the purposes of this book. © 1986.

Where 'Sing, Choirs of God, let saints and angels sing' is concerned, I have lost track of the original, but it has been considerably adapted, and mine is the responsibility for its current form. I apologize that I am unable to acknowledge the source which has inspired it. The hymn can be sung to *Woodlands*.

'To Christ our heart now given is' also by Brian Wren, written in 1995, copyright as above. The metre is 7.6.7.6.D Iambic, e.g. *Wolvercote, Offertorium*.

'Christ once Crucified now Lives' is original. *Easter Hymn* is the obvious tune.

Fasting and Feasting

Some suggestions and menus

Maundy Thursday
A large cooked breakfast
Vegetable soup and salad for lunch
Tea and plain biscuits in the afternoon
No supper, but fruit juices available

Good Friday
No breakfast or lunch, but fruit juices available
Tea and hot cross buns at 3.30pm
Fish pie supper with fruit salad as dessert

Easter Eve
Juices, cereal, toast, tea and coffee for breakfast
A simple lunch
A simple meal in the early evening before dusk

Easter Day
To end the Easter Celebration in the early morning: Gran
Marnier and Pascha, the Russian Orthodox Easter sweetmeat:

Recipe for Pascha:
1   Stir the following ingredients into a saucepan:
       4lbs of curd cheese, sieved if possible
       half pound unsalted butter
       half pint sour cream
       10 eggs beaten together with
       1lb caster sugar
       1 teaspoon vanilla essence

315

      2 ounces chopped almonds

      4 ounces chopped peal and glacé fruits

2 Gently heat the ingredients, stirring all the time.

3 When it steams, turn off the heat: do not allow to boil or it will curdle.

4 Line a deep-domed colander, or a clean flower pot, with a fresh tea towel or muslin, and pour in the cooked mixture. (It's the holes in the colander that are important.) Don't worry if it seems a little liquid.

5 Set the colander over a basin, and weight the top, to press it down.

6 Put the colander and basin in the fridge for 24 hours, and the Pascha will firm up as the sugary liquid drips away.

7 Turn it out carefully on a plate.

Breakfast: Include boiled eggs, decorated of course beforehand.

Mid-morning: Tea and coffee with Danish pastries.

Mid-day or early afternoon: An Easter Feast, with roast lamb for the main course and a splendid nut roast for vegetarians. Use your imagination for starters and dessert. My choice would be smoked salmon for starter and either creme brulée or lemon meringue pie for dessert!

References and Acknowledgments

In Deepest Night – Christmas Eve and Morning

The poem, 'The Coming of the Cold' by Theodore Roethke, is to be found in the *Collected Poems of Theodore Roethke*, Faber and Faber, 1968, and used with permission.

The poem, 'Advent 1955' by John Betjeman, is to be found in his *Uncollected Poems*, John Murray, 1982; used with permission.

The meditation, 'Cries of Advent' is by Jim Cotter, and is published separately as a desk calendar or as separate cards by Cairns Publications.

The poem, 'The Innkeeper's Wife' by Clive Sansom can be found in his collection, *The Witnesses*, Methuen, 1956. Permission requested.

The carol, 'The Sheep Stood Stunned in Sudden Light' by Thomas Troeger can be found in his collection of hymns, *Borrowed Light*, Oxford University Press, 1994; used with permission.

The painting, 'Adoration of the Shepherds' by Rembrandt, a reproduction of which, with commentary, can be found in the book *Immanuel* by Hans-Ruedi Weber, World Council of Churches, 1984.

The carol, 'On Rembrandt's Adoration of the Shepherds' by Kenneth Cragg, *Poetry of the Word at Christmas*, Churchman Publishing, 1984. It can be sung to the tune *Kocher*. The second verse has been altered in consultation with the author. The whole is quoted with his permission.

The reading from 'On the Incarnation' by Rubem Alves, the reference unfortunately incomplete.

The reading, 'On Christmas' by Thomas Merton, reference unfortunately incomplete.

The carol 'For an Up-Over Christmas' is by Jim Cotter and was written in Melbourne, Australia, on Christmas Eve, 1996.

The extract from Richard Holloway's Christmas sermon is quoted with permission.

John V. Taylor's poem, 'Christmas Venite' can be found in *A Christmas Sequence and Other Poems*, The Amate Press, Oxford, 1989, and is used with permission.

'Carol for the Last Christmas Eve' by Norman Nicholson is to be found in *Five Rivers*, Faber, and is used with permission.

'John Bunyan at Christmas' is by Kenneth Cragg, again slightly altered in consultation, and used with permission.

The carol, 'Along the Roads the People Throng', by Kenneth Cragg, is to be found in *Poetry of the Word at Christmas*, Churchman Publishing 1987. It can be sung to *O Waly, Waly*, used with permission.

The first verse of 'O Little Town of Bethlehem' is by Phillips Brooks, the second by Kenneth Cragg, op. cit., and used with permission.

The version of the Lord's Prayer is based on the work of Louis Evely in his book *Our Father*, the reference unfortunately incomplete.

The Thanksgiving Prayer is by Janet Morley, to be found in *All Desires Known*, SPCK, 1992, and adapted slightly by Jim Cotter. Permission requested.

Maundy Thursday

Brian Wren's hymn, 'Great God your love has called us here', was originally published in his collection, *Faith Looking Forward*, Oxford University Press, 1983, no. 6. It can be sung to *Sagina*, *Melita*, or *Surrey*. This hymn can also be found in some recently published hymn books. His current collected hymns are gathered in his book *Piece Together Praise*.

The prayer after the Gospel reading comes from Janet Morley, *All Desires Known*, op. cit., p. 13, with the first line altered.

Brian Wren's hymn, 'When love is found' is no. 28 in the same collection as the first hymn, also in *Piece Together Praise*, and can be sung to *O Waly, Waly*.

The prayers that begin 'On this night' and the proclamation after the Peace which begins 'At the Eucharist we are one' come from *Lent, Holy Week, and Easter*, Church House Publishing, 1982,1984, pp. 188–9 and pp. 190–91 respectively, the second slightly adapted.

Gregory Dix's *The Shape of the Liturgy* was published in 1945 by the Dacre Press. The quotation is from pp. 743–4.

Most of the Thanksgiving Prayer is by Janet Morley, with some additions by Jim Cotter. Janet Morley's original version is in *All Desires Known*, op. cit. Permission requested.

Good Friday – see also page 229

The pieces of recorded music:

the slow movement from Schubert's String Quintet acting as a kind of 'overture', hinting at the themes to come;

the Prelude to Wagner's great last opera, *Parsifal*;

the aria 'He was despised' from Handel's oratorio, *Messiah*;

the 'Agnus Dei' from Paul Winter's *Missa Gaia*;

and *Kol Nidrei*, Max Bruch's haunting music of the Jewish evening hymn;

are but suggestions. The possibilities are legion, but these have been of help in the overall structure of the commemoration, as well as being prayerful in themselves.

These are the references for the quotations from the work of Primo Levi, the Italian chemist who was imprisoned in Auschwitz and survived to write one of the classic accounts of the concentrations camps, *If this is a man*:

the poem 'Buna' is to be found in his *Collected Poems*, published in Brian Swann's translation by Faber and Faber in 1988, 1992, p. 5, and used with permission;

the next reading is from *The Drowned and the Saved*, published in Raymond Rosenthal's translation by Michael Joseph in 1988, pp. 65–6. Permission requested;

the second poem 'For Adolf Eichmann' comes from the same collection as the first, p. 24, also used with permission.

Brian Wren's hymn 'Here hangs a man discarded' comes from *Faith Looking Forward*, op. cit. p. 19 and is also to be found in his book *Piece Together Praise*. The latter is the definitive version. The first line of verse 3 now reads, "Yet there is help and comfort," followd by the word "For". In the last verse the first line reads, "Christ, in our darkness risen," and the last line, "Till faith receives its sight." The author prefers that this version be used but does not insist. The more questioning original seems more appropriate on Good Friday and is used in this book. © 1975, 1995 Stainer and Bell Ltd., London, quoted with permission.

The Introduction to the Passion can take the form of an address, an example of which is given at the end of the commemoration.

The Passion according to John can be said by a solo voice or chanted to plainsong, fully dramatized or, as here, semi-dramatized. Six voices can take the solo parts, all joining together as the soldiers, the priests, and the crowd. It is dramatic licence to suggest that the whole congregation say the lines attributed to Jesus himself. But it can have a powerful devotional effect.

'The Coming' first appeared in R. S. Thomas's collection, *H'm*, p. 35, published by Macmillan in 1972. Permission has been requested from the Estate of R. S. Thomas.

W. H. Vanstone's hymn 'Love's Endeavour, Love's Expense' was originally a coda to his book of the same title, published by Darton, Longman and Todd in 1977. It can also be found as no. 496 in *Hymns Ancient and Modern New Standard*.

Janet Morley's version of The Reproaches can be found in *All Desires Known*, op. cit. pp. 43–5, and the Prayer of Recognition as the Confession in the same book, pp. 41–2. Permission requested.

I have been unable to trace the origin of the two short pieces, 'Penitence', and 'A Poem'. I think the latter is by W. H. Auden but I cannot find it in the *Collected Poems*. My apologies for an incomplete acknowledgment.

Easter Dawn

The acknowledgments of Brian Wren's hymns for Easter Dawn are in the notes attached to that celebration.

Copyright

It is becoming more and more difficult and complicated to track down copyright holders. Some have come to light as this book is going to press. Permission has been requested, acknowledgment has been made, and of course a fair fee will be paid.

As to Jim Cotter's own material in this book, he gives permission for copies to be made for purposes of education and worship. A donation is requested to further the ministry of prayer and hospitality in small pilgrim places.